W9-BJB-001

HOW TO NOT DIE ALONE

The Surprising Science That Will Help You Find Love

LOGAN URY

Simon & Schuster
New York   London   Toronto   Syndey   New Delhi

Simon & Schuster
1230 Avenue of the Americas
New York, NY 10020

First Simon & Schuster hardcover edition February 2021

SIMON & SCHUSTER and colophon are registered trademarks of Simon & Schuster, Inc.

For information about special discounts for bulk purchases, please contact Simon & Schuster Special Sales at 1-866-506-1949 or business@simonandschuster.com.

The Simon & Schuster Speakers Bureau can bring authors to your live event. For more information or to book an event, contact the Simon & Schuster Speakers Bureau at 1-866-248-3049 or visit our website at www.simonspeakers.com.

Interior design by Carly Loman

Manufactured in the United States of America

10 9 8 7 6 5 4 3 2 1

Library of Congress Cataloging-in-Publication Data has been applied for.

ISBN 978-1-9821-2062-7
ISBN 978-1-9821-2064-1 (ebook)

To Scott, the best decision I ever made.

*And to my parents, whose love and
support made everything possible.*

CONTENTS

AUTHOR'S NOTE

When it comes to academic research, here's the bad news: Most studies to date focused primarily on cis heterosexual couples. Fortunately, when researchers *have* studied LGBTQ+ relationships, they've found they share many of the same problems—and benefit from much of the same advice—covered in the existing research.

In writing this book, I interviewed people across the range of sexual orientations and identities. I wanted to share LGBTQ+ love stories and dating experiences. All of the stories in this book are true, although some of the characters are composites of several individuals. Names and identifying characteristics have been changed and dialogue has been re-created.

After completing this manuscript I took a job as the Director of Relationship Science at the dating app Hinge. This role allows me to help millions of people learn how to date more effectively. All of the research and opinions in this book are completely my own.

INTRODUCTION

You might think you shouldn't have to buy a book on love. Love is something effortless, natural, organic. You *fall* in love, you don't *think* your way into it. It's a spontaneous chemical reaction, not a calculated decision.

And yet here you are. Holding this book because you want to find love, and so far it hasn't worked out for you. Here's the truth: While love may be a natural instinct, dating isn't. We're not born knowing how to choose the right partner.

And if we were, I wouldn't have a job. I'm a dating coach and matchmaker. I studied psychology at Harvard and have spent years researching human behavior and relationships. This work has led me to **Intentional Love,** my philosophy for creating healthy relationships. Intentional Love asks you to view your love life as a series of choices rather than accidents. This book is about being informed and purposeful—in acknowledging your bad habits, adjusting your dating techniques, and approaching crucial relationship conversations.

Great relationships are *built,* not discovered. A lasting relationship doesn't just happen. It is the culmination of a series of decisions, including when to get out there, whom to date, how to end it with the wrong person, when to settle down with the right one, and everything in between. Make good decisions, and you propel yourself toward a great love story. Make bad ones, and you veer off course, doomed to repeat the same harmful patterns over and over.

SPOILER ALERT: WE'RE IRRATIONAL

But often we don't understand why we make certain decisions, and that leads to mistakes. And those mistakes thwart our quest to find love. Behavioral science can help.

Behavioral science is the study of how we make decisions. It offers a way to peel back the layers of our mind, peek inside, and see why we tend to make certain choices. Spoiler alert: We're irrational. We often make decisions that are not in our own best interest.

This happens in all realms of life. It's why we say we want to save for retirement and then max out our credit cards on decorating our apartments. Or tell ourselves we'll exercise more, then use our treadmill as a clothing rack. No matter how often and or how earnestly we set goals, we get in our own way.

Fortunately, this irrationality isn't random. Our brains lead us astray in predictable ways. Behavioral scientists use that knowledge to help people change their behavior, with the goal of making them happier, healthier, and wealthier.

In fact, for a while I took my knowledge of behavioral science and applied it at Google. I teamed up with behavioral science great Dan Ariely to run a group at Google called the Irrational Lab, a nod to his book *Predictably Irrational*. And while I loved working with Dan and the Irrational Lab team, studying human behavior and running experiments, I had other concerns on my mind. I was single and in my early twenties. I was struggling with one of life's most essential and common questions—how do we find and sustain love?

I've long been interested in studying dating, relationships, and sex. In college I studied the porn-watching habits of Harvard under-graduates for a paper I wrote called "Porn to Be Wild." (Hint: Harvard students watch lots of porn.) For my first job at Google—years before I ran the Irrational Lab—I managed the Google Ads accounts for porn and sex toy clients, including Bangbros, Playboy, and Good Vibrations. People referred to our group by its unofficial name: "the Porn Pod."

I trace my curiosity about relationships to my own childhood. I had a happy, loving family growing up, but my parents suddenly divorced when I was seventeen. My "happily ever after" bubble burst, and I no longer took long-term marital success for granted.

At the time, I was single. Dating apps had just come out, and I was spending a lot of time swiping. I saw people all around me were struggling, too. We'd gone from the first iPod ("a thousand songs in your pocket") to ubiquitous smartphones with a thousand possible Tinder dates in your pocket. Instead of marrying Bobby or Belinda on our block, we could pick from thousands of singles online.

With that in mind, I launched a side project called "Talks at Google: Modern Romance," a speakers' series that explored the challenges of modern dating and relationships. I interviewed world-renowned experts about online dating, communication in the digital age, monogamy, empathy, and the secrets to a happy marriage. Within hours, thousands of Googlers joined the Modern Romance email list to receive updates on these talks. Once the interviews went online, millions of viewers watched on YouTube. Clearly, my friends and I were not the only ones struggling.

One night a stranger came up to me and said, "I saw your talk on polyamory. I didn't realize that relationships could work like that. It changed my whole world." At that moment I realized the impact of my work. I'd found my calling.

But I didn't want to be just another love guru, offering unscientific advice. I thought, *What if I take the behavioral science tools I honed at Google and apply them to help people make better decisions in their romantic relationships?*

IRRATIONALLY EVER AFTER

After almost a decade in tech, I quit my job and set out to help people find and maintain lasting relationships. I believe our natural errors in decision-making cause us to stumble. Behavioral science is the missing piece that can help people change their behavior, break bad patterns, and find lasting love.

Selecting a partner is already an incredibly daunting task, one weighed down with cultural baggage, bad advice, and societal and familial pressure. But until now no one has applied behavioral science to help people find love. Maybe that's because we think love is a magical phenomenon that defies scientific analysis. Or perhaps there's fear of this critique: *Who wants to be rational in love?* But that's not it. I'm not trying to turn you into a hyper-rational super-computer that analyzes all possible matches and spits out a soul mate solution. I'm helping you overcome your blind spots that are holding you back from finding love.

Behavior change is a two-step process. First we'll learn about the invisible forces driving your behavior, those errors in judgment that lead to costly mistakes. Mistakes like refusing to commit because you always wonder if there's someone better out there (Chapter 4), pursuing the prom date instead of the life partner (Chapter 7), or staying in bad relationships after their expiration date (Chapter 14).

But awareness on its own doesn't lead to action. (Knowing you shouldn't date "bad boys" or "manic pixie dream girls" doesn't make them any less appealing.) You have to actually do something about it. That's where the second part of behavioral science comes in. Tried-and-tested techniques can help you jump from knowing that information to doing something about it. Step two is designing a new system that helps you shift your behavior and achieve your goal. Each chapter includes evidence-based frameworks and exercises to help you navigate important dating decisions.

HOW THIS BOOK CAN HELP

In this book you'll discover you're not alone. You're not the only one struggling with these doubts. You and your questions and concerns are totally normal.

There's no certainty in relationships, but you *can* approach your decision-making in a more strategic way, pulling from research that understands the strengths and weaknesses of our brains (and our hearts). Intentional Love is informed by both relationship science (what works for long-term relationships) and behavioral science (how to get us to follow through on our intentions).

I will give you a process. And process creates peace.

It's worked for my clients, and I know it can help you.

Section 1: Getting Ready

We'll start with an exploration of why dating today is harder than ever before. Then you'll take a quiz to figure out your dating blind spots—tendencies in your life that are holding you back, likely without you even realizing it. Then I'll explain how your tendencies affect your dating life and what you can do to overcome them. Next we'll talk about attachment theory and how it affects whom and how you love. I'll set you straight about what to look for in a long-term partner. It's likely not what you think.

Section 2: Getting Out There

We'll take a deep dive into dating apps. I'll help you identify and overcome the common pitfalls of modern dating. We'll have you swiping better, meeting people in real life (IRL), and going on dates that don't feel like job interviews. You'll learn a better system to decide whom you should see again.

Section 3: Getting Serious

Then we'll talk about how to handle major decision points in your relationship, including how to define the relationship (DTR) and determine if you should move in together. I'll walk you through how to decide if you should break up, how to break up with someone, and how to get over heartbreak. If things progress, you may find yourself asking, "Should we get married?" The last chapter of this section will help you answer that question. Finally, we'll end with techniques to make your long-term relationship successful by investing daily attention and designing relationships that shift and change as the people in it grow, too.

COMMIT TO TRYING SOMETHING DIFFERENT

You're reading this book because you want to find love. Perhaps you've dated a series of people who haven't brought out the best in you, who left you disappointed and alone. Or maybe you haven't been dating at all. School and work and family and all the complexities of life have gotten in the way. But you know deep down that you want to find someone.

I'm here to help you get to that next step. I want you to think of yourself as my dating-coaching client. Here's my ask of you: Commit to doing the exercises. (They really work!) And allow me the chance to change your mind. You've done things your way for your entire life. Why not try something different? A lasting, loving relationship may very well be waiting for you on the other end.

GETTING READY

CHAPTER 1

WHY DATING IS HARDER NOW THAN EVER BEFORE

How to Understand the
Challenges of Modern Dating

Each generation faces its own set of challenges—wars, recessions, shoulder pads. The same holds true for dating. While people of every era have bemoaned their love lives, today's singles might just be right: Dating is harder now than ever before. And the next time your mom pesters you about finding someone nice to settle down with, you can tell her I said that.

In this book, I'll offer solutions to some of life's most difficult dating decisions. But before I get to the tactical advice, I want to set the stage and explain the factors conspiring against modern daters. If looking for love has left you feeling incredibly stressed out, here's why.

WE SHAPE OUR OWN IDENTITIES

Religion, community, and social class dictated the lives of our ancestors. Expectations were clear, and personal decisions were few. Based on where and into what kind of family you were born, you knew, for example, that you'd work as a textile merchant, live in Bucharest, eat kosher food, and go to the synagogue. Or you'd work as a farmer, live on the outskirts of Shanghai, and eat livestock and crops from your land. When it came to finding a partner, the answer often came down to the dowry—who could offer the best acres of land or the largest caravan of camels.

Today all these decisions are up to us. Modern life is a path that we must chart on our own. Whereas our predecessors didn't have to weigh where to live or what to do for a living, we make those choices now. That gives us incredible freedom to shape our identities—to pick Nashville over Atlanta, to choose whether to work as a meteorologist or a mathematician—but that freedom comes at the cost of certainty. Late at night, our faces lit by the blue glow of our smartphones, we wonder, *Who am I?* and *What am I doing with my life?* The dark side of all this freedom and endless choice is the crippling fear that we'll screw up our lifelong pursuit of happiness. If we're in charge, then we have only ourselves to blame. We could fail, and then it would be our fault.

And one of the biggest questions left up to us—a decision that used to be made by our parents and our community—is *Who should I pick as a romantic partner?*

WE HAVE TOO MANY OPTIONS

We're experiencing a seismic shift in dating culture. Dating itself only began in the 1890s. Online dating started in 1994 with Kiss.com, followed shortly by Match.com a year later. And we've been swiping for love for less than a decade. If it feels like we're in the middle of a gigantic cultural experiment, it's because we are.

We're no longer limited to the single people we know from work or church or our neighborhood. Now we can swipe through hundreds of potential partners in a single sitting. But there's a downside to these seemingly infinite options. Psychologists, including Barry

Schwartz, professor emeritus at Swarthmore, have shown that while people crave choice, too many options can make us feel less happy and more doubtful of our decisions. They call this the **paradox of choice**.

People are struggling. Like that obnoxious person in front of you in the fro-yo line who can't pick a flavor ("Can I try them all one more time?"), we're crippled by analysis paralysis. And this is especially true when it comes to choosing a life partner.

WE YEARN FOR CERTAINTY

What's the last purchase you researched online? Which electric toothbrush to purchase? Which wireless Bluetooth speakers to get your brother for his new apartment? We live in an information-rich society that offers the false comfort of research. It can feel like the perfect decision is only a few more Google searches away. Whether we're selecting the most authentic taco place or the best-performing vacuum cleaner, we can consult endless rankings and reviews. It feels like if we can research all our choices, then we can select the right one.

We've gotten hooked on this feeling of certainty, and we crave it in our romantic lives. But when it comes to relationships, that kind of assurance doesn't exist. There is no "right answer" to questions like *Who should I be with?* and *How much should I compromise?* and *Will they ever change?* No amount of Googling will reveal if James or Jillian will make a good spouse. We can't achieve complete certainty before any big relationship decision—and luckily, we don't have to in order to be happy. Great relationships are built, not discovered. But our minds are often stuck in a trap, thinking that by combing through hundreds of options, we'll be closer to knowing whether the one in front of us is "right."

SOCIAL MEDIA LEADS US TO
COMPARE AND DESPAIR

Years ago, people lived in communal villages. They witnessed other couples being affectionate, fighting, and making up. There was no such thing as a private problem. Today our primary view into other people's relationships is staged, curated, Instagram-filtered social media feeds—excited mid-hike engagement announcements, vacation pictures with a snoozing baby strapped on someone's chest. This leads us to feel like we're the only ones experiencing heart-wrenching struggles in our love lives (just in much less flattering lighting). Feeling like everyone else's relationship is perfect when yours is floundering (or nonexistent) exacerbates that pain. I find this is especially true for men, who tend to have smaller social networks and fewer people with whom they can share their fears. They're even less likely to talk to their friends about their problems and learn that everyone, at one time or another, experiences relationship hardships.

WE LACK RELATIONSHIP ROLE MODELS

We want to find the best possible partner and build the best possible relationship, yet many of us have witnessed few functional relationships firsthand, especially when we were young.

Divorce rates peaked in the 1970s and early 1980s. And while they've gone down since then, many of us are what couples therapist Esther Perel calls "the children of the divorced and disillusioned." Around 50 percent of marriages in the United States end in divorce or separation, and about 4 percent of married people report feeling miserable in their relationships. Put it all together, and a majority of married people have either chosen to end their relationship or are enduring it unhappily.

This is a problem. Study after study demonstrates the power of role models. It's much easier to believe something is possible when you've seen someone else do it, whether that's running a four-minute mile or eating seventy-three hot dogs in under ten minutes (#life-goals). For example, women are much more likely to become inventors if they grew up in a zip code with many female patent holders. In fact, they're more likely to patent in the *same categories* as older female inventors in their neighborhood.

The same is true with relationships. We all want to build lasting and fulfilling partnerships, but it's harder to do that when you lack relationship role models. Many of my clients confess fears around not knowing what the day-to-day looks like in a strong relationship—*How do healthy couples resolve conflict? How do happy spouses make decisions together? How do you successfully spend the rest of your life with one person?*—because they didn't observe those behaviors in their own parents.

Even those of us with the best relationship intentions may struggle because many of us haven't seen a functional relationship in action.

THERE ARE FAR MORE WAYS TO BE IN A RELATIONSHIP

Many of the relationship questions we tackle today never would have crossed the minds of our camel-herding ancestors, such as *Are we dating or just hooking up?* or *Should I break up now or wait until after wedding season is over?* We agonize with our close confidants over not knowing whether we're in love with a new boo or feeling burned out from first dates that go nowhere.

Now, thanks to advances in reliable birth control and fertility science, people can ask themselves about new trade-offs, such as *Do I want kids, and if so, when?* (It's unlikely that hunter-gatherers lost a lot of sleep over that one.)

Beyond scientific advances, we're expanding our models for dating and long-term relationships. We're pondering questions such as *Are we monogamous?* and *How do we define monogamy?*

In some ways, these questions are exciting. Who doesn't want to feel free and in control of their destiny? But at a certain point, all these options and opportunities can stop making us feel free and start making us feel overwhelmed.

WE FEEL PRESSURE TO GET THIS DECISION "RIGHT"

To top it all off, we're bombarded with messages imploring us to get this decision right. Everyone from public figures like Facebook COO Sheryl Sandberg (who said: "I truly believe that the single most important career decision that a woman makes is whether she will have a life partner and who that partner is.") to our own parents ("Don't make the same mistakes I did!") reinforces how critical it is that we don't mess this one up.

It can feel like our entire lives hinge on the one major decision of whom to marry. This is especially true for women, who face more time pressure to pick a spouse if they want to have children by a certain age.

BUT THERE'S HOPE!

We can take control of our love lives by better understanding ourselves: what motivates us, what confuses us, what gets in our way. And that's where behavioral science—and this book—comes in.

KEY TAKEAWAYS

1. **Dating is harder now than ever before.** And you can tell your mom I said that.

2. Here's why:

   - **We define our own identities,** unlike our ancestors, whose lives were defined by their communities.

   - We have **thousands of options at our fingertips,** which causes us to question our decisions.

   - We're **uncomfortable making big decisions when we can't research our way to the right answer.**

   - **Social media leads us to believe that everyone else is in healthier, happier relationships** than we are.

   - Far too **few of us have good relationship role models.**

   - There are **far more models for dating and long-term relationships.**

   - We're **bombarded with messaging that we need to get this decision "right"**—and that a right answer exists at all.

3. But there's hope. **Using insights from behavioral science, we can take control of our love lives.**

CHAPTER 2

THE THREE DATING TENDENCIES

*How to Discover
Your Dating Blind Spots*

Have you ever looked around and wondered, *Why has everyone found love except me? I like my job, I like my friends, I like myself. Why hasn't this one piece of my life fallen into place yet?*

I've heard versions of this from nearly all my clients. I've discovered many of them suffer from **dating blind spots**—patterns of behavior that hold them back from finding love, but which they can't identify on their own.

I've categorized the most common blind spots into a framework called **The Three Dating Tendencies.** Each group struggles with unrealistic expectations—of themselves, of partners, and of romantic relationships.

The following quiz will reveal your dating tendency. It will help identify what's holding you back, so you can break your bad habits and develop new ones. Your tendency impacts your behavior at every stage of the relationship, so it's crucial to learn yours as the first step along your journey to finding love.

THE THREE DATING TENDENCIES QUIZ

Instructions

Read each statement and decide how much it describes you. Circle the number that corresponds to your answer:

1. Very unlike me
2. Somewhat like me
3. That's so me

Question	Answer	
1	1 2 3	I don't want to go on a second date with someone if I don't feel the spark when we meet.
2	1 2 3	When I'm on a date I might ask myself, *Is this person up to my standards?*
3	1 2 3	I'll be ready to date when I improve myself (for example, lose weight or feel more financially stable).
4	1 2 3	I'd prefer if my partner and I had a romantic "how we met" story.
5	1 2 3	I usually read reviews before I make a significant purchase.
6	1 2 3	I don't have time to date right now.
7	1 2 3	I believe there's someone out there who's perfect for me, I just haven't met them yet.

8	1 2 3	When making a decision I tend to go back and forth weighing all the possible options.
9	1 2 3	My friends tell me I need to put myself out there more.
10	1 2 3	I find the apps unromantic because I want to meet my person in a more natural way.
11	1 2 3	I pride myself on never settling.
12	1 2 3	I rarely go on dates.
13	1 2 3	I don't believe the spark can grow over time. Either you feel it in the beginning, or you don't.
14	1 2 3	I'll know I've met the right person because I'll feel completely sure about them.
15	1 2 3	If I want to attract the best possible person, first I need to *become* the best possible person.
16	1 2 3	Love is a gut feeling. You know it when you feel it.
17	1 2 3	My friends think I'm too picky.
18	1 2 3	I'm focusing on my career now and I'll think about dating later.

Scoring Key

The Romanticizer: Add up your scores for every third question, starting with question 1 *(sum of answers to questions 1, 4, 7, 10, 13, 16)* _____

The Maximizer: Add up your scores for every third question, starting with question 2 *(sum of answers to questions 2, 5, 8, 11, 14, 17)* _____

The Hesitater: Add up your scores for every third question, starting with question 3 *(sum of answers to questions 3, 6, 9, 12, 15, 18)* _____

On which one did you score the highest? That's your dating tendency.

The Romanticizer

You want the soul mate, the happily ever after—the whole fairy tale. You love *love*. You believe you are single because you haven't met the right person yet. Your motto: It'll happen when it's meant to happen.

The Maximizer

You love doing research, exploring all of your options, turning over every stone until you're confident you've found the *right* one. You make decisions carefully. And you want to be 100 percent certain about something before you make your choice. Your motto: Why settle?

The Hesitater

You don't think you're ready for dating because you're not the person you want to be yet. You hold yourself to a high standard. You want to feel completely ready before you start a new project; the same goes for dating. Your motto: I'll wait until I'm a catch.

Although they seem quite different, the **Romanticizer, Maximizer,** and **Hesitater** have one major thing in common: unrealistic expectations.

The Romanticizer has unrealistic expectations of *relationships.*

The Maximizer has unrealistic expectations of their *partner.*

The Hesitater has unrealistic expectations of *themselves.*

If you scored highly on more than one tendency, reread the descriptions and select the one that best describes you. If you're still struggling, send a picture of these three options to a trusted friend. In validating this quiz, I discovered that friends were able to identify the dating tendency at play even more accurately than the person taking the quiz. Remember, these are blind spots. Friends can often recognize patterns in our behavior that we don't see.

My tendency is (circle one):

The Romanticizer   The Maximizer   The Hesitater

In the next few chapters, I'll share more about each of the three tendencies, including the struggles they encounter and how to overcome them. I recommend reading all three chapters because they contain helpful lessons for everyone, and they'll help you understand daters you encounter who have a different tendency from your own.

KEY TAKEAWAYS

1. **Many people suffer from dating blind spots**—patterns of behavior that hold them back from finding love, but which they can't identify on their own.

2. I've categorized the most common blind spots into a framework called The Three Dating Tendencies. Each group struggles with **unrealistic expectations.**

   - **The Romanticizer** has unrealistic expectations of *relationships*. They want the soul mate, the happily ever after—the whole fairy tale.

   - **The Maximizer** has unrealistic expectations of their *partner*. They love to explore their options and want to feel absolutely confident they're making the right decision.

   - **The Hesitater** has unrealistic expectations of *themselves*. They feel like they're not ready to date.

3. Understanding your dating tendency helps you **discover what's holding you back and how you can overcome these blind spots.**

CHAPTER 3

DISNEY LIED TO US

*How to Overcome
the Romanticizer Tendency*

Twenty minutes into our first session and the tears were already flowing.

"I know he's out there," Maya said. "He just hasn't found me yet."

He? Her soul mate. The peanut butter to her jelly. The one. Maya couldn't stop talking about this man who would make all of her dreams come true. She believed the perfect guy was waiting for her just around the corner.

"I want to meet him organically," she explained when I asked about her current approach to dating. "The apps feel too unromantic to me. Why mess with fate?"

Maya has long black hair that she spends an hour blow-drying every morning before work. When she tells a story, every detail seems slightly more dramatic because she lifts her dark eyebrows in surprise or grins to show her sparkling teeth. (Makes sense—she's a dentist who runs her own practice.) She's the child of Iranian immigrants, and her parents are in year thirty-five of what she describes as a "very happy marriage." She wants what they have.

She's had a few boyfriends—one in college, two since—but nothing's stuck. She's always broken up with these guys. "When it's right, I'll know," she says, arching an eyebrow. She grew up watching and rewatching Disney movies like *The Little Mermaid* on VHS, and is waiting for her happily ever after.

Maya is a quintessential Romanticizer. Romanticizers believe that love is something that happens to you, and that the reason they're single is they just haven't met the right person yet. Romanticizers might not consciously identify with fairy tales, yet they expect their lives to resemble one. They believe the perfect person will walk into their lives one day. All they have to do is wait for that moment. And once that Prince Charming or Cinderella appears, love will be effortless. Of course! Cue the Céline Dion soundtrack!

THE PROBLEM WITH FAIRY TALES

Who cares if you're a hopeless romantic? I do, and you should, too.

In behavioral science, we know **mindset matters**. Our attitudes and expectations create the context for our experience, which in turn affects how we interpret information and make decisions.

When it comes to romantic relationships, psychologist Renae Franiuk found that people have either a **soul mate** mindset, the belief that relationship satisfaction comes from finding the right person; or a **work-it-out** mindset, the belief that relationship success derives from putting in effort.

Unsurprisingly, Romanticizers fall into the soul mate mindset category. This impacts how they act at every stage of the relationship. First, it affects the way they approach finding a partner. When I asked Maya why she thought she was single, she said, "It just hasn't happened to me yet." In Maya's mind, love is something that happens *to* you, like lightning striking. So why try? Romanticizers *wait* for love and won't put effort in to *create* love. (I once worked with a woman who would dress up for every flight in case her "future husband" was on the same plane, but then refused to approach anyone lest she be perceived as trying too hard.)

Second, this mindset influences whom you're willing to go out with. People with soul mate beliefs tend to have a very specific vision of how their partner will look. When we met, Maya rattled off a list of her future husband's physical traits: "Light-haired, light-eyed. Fit. Muscular but not *too* muscular. Tasteful tattoos. Medium-length hair. Pretty face but slightly rugged, bad-boy-looking. Tall—five-ten and up. Good hands, no short nails."

Since Romanticizers are confident they know what their future partner will look like, when they meet someone who doesn't match that image, they won't give that person a chance. They end up missing out on great potential matches.

When they start dating someone they believe is "the one," their sky-high expectations can propel the relationship forward. But when the couple hits an inevitable obstacle—say, for instance, a particularly heated fight—they give up on the relationship rather than trying to overcome it.

Maya's Romanticizer tendency helps explain why she struggled in her previous partnerships. "In all my relationships, I end up thinking, *Wait a minute. Why is this so hard?*" she said. "Love is supposed to be effortless, right? This can't possibly be 'the one.'"

In comparison, those with the work-it-out mindset believe that relationships take effort, that love is an action you take, not something that happens to you. People with the work-it-out mindset tend to fare better in relationships because when they stumble, they put in the work needed to get the relationship back on track, rather than giving up.

If you're a Romanticizer who wants to find a lasting relationship, it's time to move on from fairy tales and start a new chapter with a work-it-out mindset.

OUR FAIRY-TALE EXPECTATIONS

Romanticizers aren't the only ones who think marriage holds the promise of a great love story filled with explosive passion. Many of us feel that way.

But it wasn't always like this.

In fact, for most of history, the idea of marrying for love would have seemed silly. Marriage was about economics and convenience. You married someone because their father's land was adjacent to your father's land. Or because you were poor and someone offered your family a dozen cows in exchange for your hand in marriage.

As marriage historian Stephanie Coontz explained, "Until the late eighteenth century, most societies around the world saw marriage as far too vital an economic and political institution to be left entirely to the free choice of the two individuals involved, especially if they were going to base their decision on something as unreasoning and transitory as love."

We know from ancient poetry that humans have always experienced love. In the four-thousand-year-old Sumerian "Love Song for Shu-Sin," considered the world's oldest love poem, the author declares: "Lion, let me caress you / My precious caress is more savory than honey." (And I know what you're thinking, but no, that isn't a Beyoncé lyric!) But for most of human history, love was simply not part of the marriage equation. Love was something you might experience *outside* of the marriage. Perhaps you'd have a love affair with a neighbor or develop a major crush on the local blacksmith.

Alain de Botton studies how our views on love have changed over time. He's a philosopher who runs the School of Life, a crash course in how to design a meaningful existence. He's also written two profound novels on relationships—*On Love* and *The Course of Love*.

When I spoke with him, he explained how our ancestors used to view love: "It was seen as a very exciting moment, akin to a kind of illness, a kind of ecstatic moment. Love stood outside of ordinary experience . . . almost like a religious visitation. And it might have occurred to someone only once in their life. It was not generally seen to be something that you should act upon in any practical way. You let it wash over you, you let it guide an intense summer in your youth, but you certainly didn't marry according to it."

It wasn't until around 1750 that the idea of marrying for love took hold. It all dates back to the age of Romanticism, an ideological movement that began in Europe, with philosophers waxing poetic about love, and eventually took over the world. Romanticism elevated love from "a kind of illness" to the new model for what we have come to expect from long-term relationships. The Industrial Revolution propelled this model's adoption by mainstream society. With greater mechanization and more widespread wealth, marriages could finally focus more on personal fulfillment than on meeting basic needs.

Several centuries later, Romanticism still rules our ideas about love. Take a look at this list of Romantic ideals. How many of these do you relate to?

- Love is a gut feeling. You know it when you feel it.

- When we meet our soul mate, we will feel an immediate attraction to them. We will be attracted only to them, and vice versa.

- Our soul mate will intuitively understand us and know what we need before we do.

- We will remain passionately in love with our partner throughout our marriage.

- Our soul mate is the only person we really need. They can fill every role in our life, from best friend to travel partner to passionate lover.

- Good sex marks a good marriage. Bad or infrequent sex (or worse, infidelity) means the relationship is doomed.

- It's not sexy to talk about money. Love isn't meant to be practical.

The more these ideas resonated with you, the more you've been brainwashed by the principles of Romanticism. (And if all of them did, I'd love to borrow your glass slippers and pumpkin carriage.)

When people expect romantic relationships to unfold this way, they develop soul mate beliefs, just like Maya did. They waste years waiting for "the one," rejecting anyone who doesn't meet their unrealistic expectations of love.

HOW TO FIGHT BACK AGAINST THE IDEALS OF ROMANTICISM

Movies and TV shows have long perpetuated the syrupy ideals of Romanticism (read: Life isn't *The Notebook*). Not only are these messages about love and long-term relationships incorrect, they're also harmful. Plus, kissing in the rain is so much colder and more uncomfortable than it seems. Here are the main culprits:

Romanticizer Intensifier #1: Disney's Prince Charming

Soul mate belief Disney perpetuates

"The one" is out there, and he or she looks just like you imagined.

Disney tells us that one day we'll get swept off our feet by our own Prince or Princess Charming. This tendency plagues more than just straight women; I've met Romanticizers of all different genders and sexual orientations. And they're all out there waiting for this perfect person. He's an architect who also mentors foster children. She's a model with a PhD. This person has every positive quality they want and none of the bad ones.

In animated Disney movies, people fall in love without even knowing each other. In *The Little Mermaid*, all Prince Eric knew about Ariel was that she was an attractive redhead with the upper-body strength to pull him safely to shore when his boat capsized. And he loved her for that? In *Cinderella*, the heroine falls for the prince because he can dance and makes an effort to return lost items to their rightful owner. Seems a little shallow, if you ask me.

Work-it-out mindset shift

Even Prince Charming has morning breath.

No one is perfect, including you. Don't know what I'm talking about? Think about the last time you really let someone down. (If you're having trouble thinking of your flaws, try giving your siblings a call for inspiration. I'm sure they'd be more than happy to remind you.)

It's time to give up on this idea of perfection.

Like Maya, you may have in your mind a vision of your future wife or husband. Perhaps this is informed by an early crush on the boy across the street or your favorite movie star. It's time to realize that the package this person comes in might be different from what you were expecting. Maybe this person is shorter or taller or rounder or slimmer or darker or lighter or hairier or smoother than you expected. That very narrow view of this person's looks holds you back from seeing the possibilities in front of you. If you're not perfect, why should this person be? Stop the double standard: You're not a movie star. (And if you are, cool! Thanks for reading my book!)

Romanticizer Intensifier #2: Disney's Happily Ever After

Soul mate belief Disney perpetuates
The hard work of love is finding someone. Everything after that is easy.

Disney movies depict everything a couple goes through leading up to the marriage—the courtship, the conflict, the evil witch standing in their way. But once they vanquish their foes and can finally be together, the couple's challenge ends. After that, happily ever after, right?

Wrong. I call this the **Happily-Ever-After Fallacy**—the false notion that the hard part of love is finding someone.

Work-it-out mindset shift
No relationship is easy all the time. Even the healthiest, most rewarding marriages require effort.

Finding someone can be hard, but often the real challenge comes later. *The hard part* is the daily work you put in to grow and sustain a great relationship. *The hard part* is feeling excited to see your spouse at the end of the day, after thirty years and two kids, long after the honeymoon period is over. *The hard part* is remembering why you love someone during all the logistical, financial, emotional, and spiritual challenges life throws at you.

Romanticizer Intensifier #3: The Rom-Coms' "Meet-Cute"

Soul mate belief rom-coms perpetuate
Don't worry, love will find you, and it'll probably happen in a really great meet-cute way you'll want to tell your friends about.

Rom-coms are Disney fairy tales for people old enough to buy their own movie tickets. And who find bumbling English men attractive. (Colin Firth is like Brussels sprouts; you don't appreciate him until you're older.) We all know rom-coms are not real life. Yet they've still surreptitiously bored their way into our collective subconscious. Especially when it comes to the meet-cute. In a rom-com, the meet-cute is the hero and heroine's first encounter, and it often happens as the two characters are just going about their day—visiting the farmers' market, for example. And you think that it could happen to you, too. You'll reach for that perfect-looking tomato at exactly the same moment when the handsome stranger next to you goes for it, and BAM! your eyes meet. He explains he needs the tomato to make his grandmother's bruschetta (pronounced with the proper Italian flourish). You offer to let him keep it. He asks if he can buy you a cappuccino to thank you. You say yes. Eleven months, one major fight, and one grand gesture later, he's chasing you down the terminal at JFK Airport, flanked by TSA agents, begging you not to get on your flight to Seoul for your new job at an advertising agency.

The rom-com promotes the idea that love finds you and not the other way around. That love at first sight is real. That all you have to do is live your life (and consume vast amounts of tomatoes while hanging out at the farmers' market) and one day your future husband or wife will magically appear. While I acknowledge that people do meet in real life all the time—at parties, events, even protests—the problem with this idea is that it gives people permission to be *overly passive* in their love lives.

Work-it-out mindset shift

Love takes work—from finding it to keeping it alive. Waiting around at the farmers' market just won't cut it. You need to put in effort to find someone. (Don't worry, I'll show you how in Section 2.) The magic of a relationship doesn't depend on a serendipitous or cinematic meeting. The magic lies in the fact that two strangers come together and create a life. It's not important where or how they met.

Romanticizer Intensifier #4: Social Media

Soul mate belief social media perpetuates

Relationships are effortless, sex-filled love fests (in great lighting).

At least Disney movies and rom-coms are up front about the fact that they're fictional. Social media is in many ways a more dangerous culprit because its lies disguise themselves as real life. On social media, we see curated images of the perfect relationship—from the romantic beach walk captured at sunset to the kiss over a masterfully plated homemade dinner. By contrast, we find our own partnership lacking. We compare and despair.

Work-it-out mindset shift

First off, don't believe what you see on Instagram. Images are cropped, blurred, and distorted to send a message. And when it comes to relationships, the pictures you see on social media are only one heavily filtered view of that partnership. Just like people don't post pictures of themselves crying or picking their nose, no one puts up photos of blowout fights with their girlfriend or nights spent wondering whether they should stay with her. Social media tells us that everyone else is experiencing a blissful, effortless, passionate, picture-perfect relationship, which contributes to our sky-high expectations for our own partnership.

Relationships go through periods of highs and lows. If you're working hard at your relationship, that's a good sign, not a bad one! Many hours of a marriage are spent on the everyday, rarely posted minutiae of life: changing dirty diapers, doing laundry, and washing dishes. Love happens *in* these moments, not in spite of them. Love is so much more than a filtered photo captured at sunset.

FROM FAIRY-TALE ROMANCE TO REAL-LIFE LOVE

I explained to Maya how Disney, rom-coms, and social media had triggered her Romanticizer tendencies. If she wanted to find love, she needed to change her expectations.

She crossed her arms over her chest. "Do you get it?" she asked me, her eyebrows furrowed. "I feel like you're telling me to give up on my dream. I have this vision of love, and now you're saying it doesn't exist. That I have to settle or give up. Why do other people get to have this epic relationship and I don't? Why am I not good enough?"

I did get it. "Maya, no, that's not it," I said. "I want you to be open to a love that is different from the one you thought you'd have. I'm not telling you to settle. That would imply that Prince Charming is the prize and I'm asking you to date a runner-up. But that's not true, because Prince Charming doesn't exist."

Same goes for you: It's time you gave up on Prince Charming and started looking for someone real. Let's call him Larry.

Because that's the name of the guy Maya wound up with. She met him when she was filling in for another dentist who went on vacation. Through our work together, she learned to let go of her soul mate beliefs, which were holding her back from finding real love. Her now live-in boyfriend is nothing like she expected. He's a divorced dad with two little kids.

"He slouches, he wears sweaters with holes in them," she said. "He doesn't open doors for me." She smiled, surprised that she no longer cared about those superficial traits. "But he makes me laugh. He's kind, and I feel like myself around him. He makes me feel smart and funny. I know it sounds cheesy, but I'm honestly much happier than I've ever been."

They fight. About where to spend Thanksgiving, whether or not they really need to go to her frenemy's wedding, and the amount he spends on his dog's super-premium food. But now Maya believes those fights are a sign that things are right, not wrong.

"We're passionate! We care about stuff. We talk openly. We're not the same person, so of course we're going to fight. I know all relationships require work. And I'm choosing to invest in this one."

KEY TAKEAWAYS

1. Our mindset matters! The ability to shift your mindset from **soul mate** to **work-it-out** beliefs could mean the difference between finding a life partner or not.

   - **People with soul mate beliefs reject promising partners because they don't match their vision for what love should look and feel like.** They think that love will just happen to them. They expect love to be effortless. If it's not, they must be with the wrong person.

   - **People with a work-it-out mindset know that relationships take effort and that building a successful relationship is a process.**

2. **Our belief in fate and fairy tales**—caused in part by Disney movies, rom-coms, and social media—**creates unrealistic expectations for finding and sustaining relationships.** Remember, no one is perfect, including you. Even Prince Charming has morning breath.

3. **The Happily-Ever-After Fallacy is the mistaken idea that the hard work of love is finding someone.** In reality, that's only the beginning. Staying in love takes work, too. If you expect relationships to be easy, you'll be caught off guard when they hit an inevitable rough patch.

4. It's time to embrace (and seek out) real love, scuffs and all!

CHAPTER 4

DON'T LET PERFECT BE THE ENEMY OF GREAT

*How to Overcome
the Maximizer Tendency*

Steven told me he couldn't remember a time when he'd just known *instinctively* what to do. Extensive research preceded every major— or minor—decision. Every few months, he interviewed at a different company ("to keep my options open," he told me) only to stay in his current job. He pored over Scotch reviews for two hours before buying his dad a bottle for Father's Day. He saw every decision as a problem to dissect, analyze, and fret over. Pro/con lists filled the Notes app on his phone. Why risk making a merely okay decision when a perfect one was only a few hours of research away?

While his behavior was occasionally annoying to his friends— and job recruiters—no one but Steven really suffered from his indecision. No one except his girlfriend Gabby.

Gabby loved Steven. Steven loved Gabby. They had dated for four years and lived together for three of them. But Steven often wondered: *Who else is out there?* He knew Gabby's good qualities. She worked as a nurse and fostered cats from the local animal shelter. She was loyal, warm, caring, attractive, kind, and intelligent. Yet that wasn't enough. He wished she were more social.

He wanted dinner parties and deep conversations about abstract ideas.

Gabby felt ready to get married and start a family. True to form, Steven wasn't so sure.

After a year of waiting for Steven to make up his mind, Gabby had had enough. She was tired of going to the weddings of friends who had met *after* she and Steven started dating. Late one night, she told Steven, through tears, "I can't wait around anymore. I want to get engaged or break up."

For the next few months, Steven had no idea what to do. He *wanted* to want to get engaged, but he could never actually get himself to propose. He debated with his friends. He went on long swims to meditate on the question. But he never felt any closer to knowing what he really wanted.

He couldn't stop himself from asking, *Could I be 5 percent happier with someone else?*

MAXIMIZERS VERSUS SATISFICERS

Steven is a **Maximizer**. Maximizers obsess over making the best possible decision. American economist, political scientist, and cognitive psychologist Herbert A. Simon first described this personality profile in a 1956 paper. According to Simon, Maximizers are a special type of perfectionist. They're compelled to explore every possible option before they feel like they can choose. Yet this compulsion becomes daunting, and ultimately unfeasible, when they face a vast number of possibilities.

On the other end of the spectrum are **Satisficers** (a portmanteau of "satisfy" and "suffice"). They have standards, but they aren't overly concerned that there might be something better out there. They know their criteria, and they hunt until they find the "good enough" option. It's not that they settle; they're simply fine making a decision once they've gathered *some* evidence and identified a *satisfactory* option.

Imagine you're on a two-hour flight. The plane takes off and you begin scrolling through the movie options. Do you A) select the first movie that appeals to you? Within five minutes, you're reclining in your seat, eyes glued to *Good Will Hunting*. Or do you B) spend twenty-five minutes scrolling through every single new release, comedy, drama, documentary, and foreign film, as well as all the TV shows, before committing to the absolute best option?

If you chose A, you're likely a Satisficer. If you selected B, you're clearly a Maximizer. (You can fall on the spectrum between these extremes, or you may be a Maximizer in some parts of your life and a Satisficer in others.)

Maximizers obsess over their decision-making. They trust that careful analysis will ultimately make their life better. But that's not true. Not only are Satisficers able to make *good* decisions, they tend to wind up happier about them. That's because—and it's worth repeating—satisficing is *not* about settling. Satisficers may have very high standards and stop only after those standards have been met. The difference is, once they stop, they don't worry about what else is out there. Maximizers, on the other hand, may find an option that meets their standards, but they feel compelled to explore all possibilities.

When it comes to relationships, Maximizers—like Steven—mistakenly believe that with the right amount of exploration, they can find the perfect person and have absolute confidence in their decision. But this perfect person (and complete certainty) doesn't exist. That's why maximizing leads to anguish, delays in decision-making, and missed opportunities. In other words, it's better to be a Satisficer.

WHY ARE MAXIMIZERS LIKE THIS?

Anxiety plagues Maximizers. It's not just FOMO (fear of missing out). They also suffer from the less catchy FOMTWD (fear of making the wrong decision). They think maximizing will help them make the perfect choice and alleviate their anxiety. But FOMTWD creates an immense amount of pressure. Anything less than perfection feels like failure.

This happens to me when I travel. Even if a trip unfolds almost perfectly, when I make a mistake—like booking a hotel far away from the center of town—I can't help but feel like I failed. I think, *If only I'd done just a little more research*. I have to fight to prevent this feeling from ruining the trip.

Hardly anything exacerbates the Maximizer tendency more than choosing a long-term partner. Maximizers fear making a mistake. *What if I get divorced and have to raise my children on my own? What if I dread coming home after work because I have nothing to say to my wife? What if I'm so bored that I have an affair?*

For most of human history (and to this day, in many societies), our families, communities, or religious leaders told people what to do—what to wear, what to eat, how to act, what to believe, and, yes, whom to marry. Now, in our increasingly individualistic and secular culture, we each define our own identity. *Do I eat meat? Do I work on Shabbat? Do I baptize my child? Do I get married in a synagogue? Do I identify as a man or woman or neither?*

Our life, once scripted by culture, religion, and family, is now a blank page. This grants us the freedom to express ourselves more fully. But we're also burdened by the pressure to get it right. When we are the authors of our own story and that story sucks, we have no one to blame but ourselves. No wonder we can get trapped in analysis paralysis.

When everything is up in the air—and up to us—we yearn to stand on solid ground. "I want to feel a hundred percent certain before I walk down the aisle," Steven told me.

But that's exactly the problem. Steven believes it's possible to "pro/con list" his way to the correct answer, no different from purchasing the optimal vacuum (Dyson V11 Animal, 160 five-star reviews) or planning the optimal day (five a.m. surfing, coffee from the little stand that people love but no one knows about, sprint triathlon, meeting up with two different friends, beach meditation, home-cooked meal, and board games). But this assumes there *is* a right answer for whom to marry. And there's not.

THE PROBLEM WITH MAXIMIZING

Do Maximizers obtain better outcomes?

We can think about this question in two ways—the objective *result* and the subjective *experience*. In other words, the quality of your choice and how you feel about it.

Imagine you're a Maximizer who's sick of spending money on your morning coffee. You spend hours conducting research into home espresso makers. You read Amazon reviews and study product comparison websites like Wirecutter. You select Wirecutter's number one pick: the elegant Breville Bambino Plus. As soon as it arrives, you notice it doesn't fit as easily into your kitchen as you thought it would. You wonder if you should've gotten a smaller one. Just as the review warns, it doesn't capture the brightness of your coffee bean. As your cup brews, you stew, and regret not going with a different option.

Meanwhile, your Satisficer friend is also on the market for an espresso maker. She goes to the mall, pops into a Nespresso store, tells an employee what she's looking for, and walks out with a reasonably priced machine. She tells you how much she adores the process of making her daily latte, from selecting the fun-colored pods to steaming her milk.

In this scenario, you selected the best espresso machine available. Several websites compared your machine to hers, and yours won. But who feels better about the decision?

Satisficers report feeling happier with their choices, even when they select an objectively worse option. (I mean, come on. Your friend's Nespresso machine didn't even make Wirecutter's top picks!) That's because Maximizers constantly second-guess themselves. They suffer doubly: first in the agony leading up to the decision, and again every time they worry they've made the wrong one.

Psychologist and *The Paradox of Choice* author Barry Schwartz explains that what separates Maximizers and Satisficers is not the quality of their decisions, it's how these decisions make them feel: "Maximizers make good decisions and end up feeling bad about them. Satisficers make good decisions and end up feeling good."

What's your goal? To have the world's best coffee machine or to be happy? If it's happiness you're after, it's the subjective experience, not the objective result, that really matters. While the quality of coffee is important, how we *feel* about that coffee is paramount.

THE WISDOM OF SATISFICING

Maximizers want to turn over every stone before they make a decision. That presents a particularly tough challenge when it comes to dating. You can't go out with every eligible single in your city, let alone the whole world. If you hope to get married or commit to a long-term relationship, eventually, you'll need to make a decision with the information you have.

If you're a Maximizer, that idea might make you nervous. What if you aren't happy with what you pick? Here's the good news: We have an incredible tool working on our behalf to make us happy—our brain! Once we commit to something, our brain helps us rationalize why it was the right choice.

Rationalization is our ability to convince ourselves we did the right thing. Imagine you buy an expensive winter coat that you can return within thirty days. You take it home and weigh its pros and cons. Even if you keep the coat, you can't shake that list of cons in your head. But when you buy a coat on final sale, you immediately commit to liking it. You can't return it, so why worry about its drawbacks? That's the power of rationalization. Embrace it.

This works for dating, too. When you commit to someone, your brain will do its best to convince you it was a good decision. Satisficers inherently understand this idea—and benefit from it.

Now, perhaps you're thinking: *I'm not looking to make a merely "good" decision. I refuse to settle.* But this is a common misunderstanding about satisficing. Remember, Satisficers can have very high standards. They may look around for a while until they find an option that meets their expectations. The difference is, once they find something that meets their standards, they are happy with it. They don't wonder what else is out there.

And that's why I want you to work toward becoming a Satisficer. The best choice of all is choosing to be happy.

THE SECRETARY PROBLEM

You can learn to date like a Satisficer by studying the decision-making riddle known as the **Secretary Problem**. Imagine you are hiring a secretary. And let's be sure to make him a male secretary, because I know you were envisioning a woman and #fuckthepatriarchy. There are a hundred possible candidates whom you must interview one by one. After each interview, you decide whether to hire that person or keep looking. If you reject a person, he's gone. You can't change your mind later and hire him.

How should you maximize your chances of picking the best candidate? You don't want to decide too early in the process, because you might miss out on a strong candidate at the end of the line. But you don't want to make it too far without choosing, because what if the final options aren't very good? It turns out there's a mathematically correct answer to this problem. You should interview 37 percent of the candidates and then pause. Identify the best person from this first group. Now you have a meaningful *benchmark*. After evaluating the first 37 percent, you should be prepared to hire the first candidate who is better than the standout from the first group.

This logic applies to dating, too. In the Secretary Problem, you know there are a hundred possible candidates. In dating, you have no idea how many possible matches are out there. Even if you did, you couldn't meet all of them. Life, logistics, and geography all get in the way.

Instead of thinking about the total *number* of people you might date, consider how *long* you're likely to actively look for a partner. Apply the rule of 37 percent to that time period. In the book *Algorithms to Live By*, authors Brian Christian and Tom Griffiths discuss a single man who wants to get married. "Assuming that his search would run from ages eighteen to forty, the 37% rule gave age 26.1 as the point at which to switch from looking to leaping."

That means that by the age of 26.1, he should set a meaningful benchmark from his first 8.1 years of dating—that is, the single best person he's dated thus far. He should then marry the *next person* he meets whom he likes *more than that benchmark*.

I explained the Secretary Problem to Doug, a software engineer who'd recently sold his business to a major tech company. Doug had been in several three- to six-month relationships. He always found something lacking with the women he dated. This one laughed at his jokes, but she wasn't funny. That one worked too hard. The next one didn't work hard enough.

When I began to describe the idea of the benchmark, he nodded and interrupted me. "I get it. I get it," he said. "I'm thirty-one, and I've probably already dated someone who would make a great wife." It clicked.

I followed up with a homework assignment. "Put together a spreadsheet of all the women you've gone out with in the last year. Make a column for their name, how you met them, how you felt when you were with them, and what values you shared. You can include other details, too, but I don't want a laundry list of their flaws or a ranking of their hotness."

"I'll do it."

During our next session, Doug pulled up his laptop and showed me his work. "Brielle," he said as the page loaded. "She's the one."

"The one? You mean like the *one* the one?" I asked. (I know: I temporarily suspended my distaste for that term.)

"Not the one I'm going to marry, but the benchmark. She was smart, funny, fun to be with, ambitious, and pretty. Ugh, why did I break up with her? Anyway, it's too late for that. Brielle is my benchmark. I'm going to commit to the next girl who I like as much or more than Brielle."

Now it's your turn. To determine your dating window, count the number of years from when you started dating to when you'd like to enter a long-term relationship. Now, what's 37 percent of that number? Add that to the age when you started dating. That's your 37 percent mark. If you're in your thirties, you've probably already passed it. Complete the assignment I gave Doug to determine your benchmark partner.

Don't worry. I'm not telling you to marry the next person you go out with, nor am I implying that it's too late if you're past the 37 percent mark. I'm merely suggesting that you likely already have enough data to generate a reasonable, well-informed benchmark. *You do not need more research.* The next time you meet someone whom you like as much or more than that benchmark, commit to them.

GENDER INEQUALITY AND
RELATIONSHIP TIMELINES

I am a feminist. I believe men and women are and should be equal. However, that does not mean we are the same. We're separated by real biological differences in our reproductive systems. (I recognize these categories don't contain everyone and that trans and genderqueer folks face unique challenges while dating.)

Women's fertility declines in our thirties. Men can have kids until their late sixties and beyond. (Robert De Niro was sixty-eight years old when his youngest child was born—though I'd encourage any man who thinks he has infinite time to imagine playing catch when he's seventy, with arthritic hands.)

To my beloved female readers: If you want to have kids, and you hope to carry them yourself, it's important to incorporate that goal when you consider your dating window. While you don't need a partner to have a kid, this may affect the age by which you'd like to find someone.

Although it's expensive, you may want to consider egg freezing. While it's certainly not a *guarantee* that you can have kids later, it may buy you some time. I froze embryos, fertilized by my partner's sperm, the month I turned thirty-one because we weren't ready to have kids and wanted to put the decision on ice. Pun intended.

As unfair as it is, you will likely hit that 37 percent mark before men your own age. I really wish it weren't this way. But I'd rather you recognize the situation and plan for it, rather than being caught off guard later in life and wishing you'd made different choices.

This brings me back to Steven, who was still asking himself: *Could I be 5 percent happier with someone else?* A few months after Gabby gave Steven her ultimatum, she confronted him once more. He admitted he'd made no steps toward buying a ring.

She told him it was over. Enter moving boxes, breakup sex, new profile pictures on social media.

Steven sat alone in his half-empty apartment. No couch, no TV, no dresser. Just a bed, some chairs, and his painstakingly researched ultralight camping gear.

At that point, I didn't expect to hear from Steven again. Based on my experience with other Stevens, I figured he'd meet new women—people he'd get excited about and then leave when he didn't feel 100 percent certain about them.

Then, about a year later, he called me.

"I met someone," he told me. "Someone I want to spend the rest of my life with."

I was surprised but thrilled. "Tell me more."

"The other weekend we went away together. We rode bikes, we cooked, we had sex. And I just felt like this was the person I was going to marry."

I was so happy to hear that he was happy. But I had to ask: "What about those Steven voices in your head, wondering, *Could I be five percent happier?*"

He laughed. "Look, it hasn't been easy. But I worked on that. I'm grateful for what I have with her. I'm not wondering what I could have with someone else. All I know is that I could build a life with this person. An amazing life."

Steven had learned to satisfice. To feel uncomfortable with uncertainty. To make a decision based on a less than exhaustive search. Through this work, he'd changed the punctuation of his life: from the anxious question mark of a Maximizer to the confident period of a Satisficer.

At first I thought Steven's story would serve as a warning: **Don't let perfect be the enemy of great.** But now I can share it as a tale of victory. Maximizers, give yourself the gift of happiness. Give yourself the gift of satisficing.

KEY TAKEAWAYS

1. **Maximizers obsess over making the right decision.** They want to explore every possible option before they make a choice. Even when they decide, they constantly wonder what they're missing out on. **Satisficers figure out what they want and stop looking once they've met their criteria.** They don't *settle*, they merely stop worrying what else is out there once they've made a decision.

2. Research shows that **Satisficers tend to be happier**, because in the end, satisfaction comes from how you *feel* about your decision, not the decision itself.

3. **The current dating climate creates Maximizers out of many of us.** No one ever seems good enough, and we wonder if we could be happier with someone else. Maximizing tendencies in relationships can lead to mental anguish, costly delays in decision-making, and missed opportunities.

4. Maximizers assume there is a right answer for whom to be with. And there's not. **We can apply lessons from the Secretary Problem to see that we likely already have enough dating experience to select a great partner.** This knowledge can help us commit without worrying about what else is out there. **The power of rationalization can also help us embrace our decisions.**

CHAPTER 5

DON'T WAIT, DATE

*How to Overcome
the Hesitater Tendency*

I met my new client Shea on a hidden patio in downtown San Francisco, several blocks from his office. He was thirty-five and over six feet tall. (He later told me this gives him a big advantage in the Jewish dating market in San Francisco.)

I knew very little about Shea going into the meeting. He seemed confident and charming. Sitting at our table while he stood in line to order us coffees, I tried to guess why he'd contacted me for help. Was he having trouble deciding whom to date? Did he need help ending a bad relationship? Was he trying to get back out there after a tough breakup?

He walked back over and handed me my latte. "Well, I guess I'll start at the beginning," he said. "I've never had a girlfriend. Okay, maybe one in high school, but not since then."

I was surprised to hear how little dating experience he had. "Why do you think that is?"

"I've never felt ready," he said. "First I wanted to make sure I had my job in order. Then I found a great job, but I wanted to make sure I had enough money saved to support a wife. I got close, but then I started therapy and wanted to work on myself first. I recently switched jobs, and now I feel like I won't be ready to date until work is more settled again."

He explained that he ultimately wanted a wife and a family, but he didn't think he was ready for that yet. He'd reached out to me only because his parents had pressured him to get some help.

You might be nodding along, thinking, *That makes sense. Good for him. He'll date when he's ready.*

Except when I pushed him for more details, I discovered that Shea *was* ready. He had worked as a lawyer at a big firm for ten years and was financially stable. He was self-aware and mature. He had hobbies (he played guitar—poorly, he said). He had friends. He enjoyed a close relationship with his family.

I've encountered a lot of clients like Shea. They seem like they'd be a great catch, but they aren't actively dating. I call this bunch the **Hesitaters**. They come to me because they *feel* like they should be dating, but they're having trouble taking action. When I ask why they haven't been going on dates, their "I'll be ready when" excuses start tumbling out:

"I'll be ready when I lose ten pounds."

"I'll be ready when I get promoted."

"I'll be ready once I finish grad school."

"I'll be ready when I have new pictures for my dating profile."

"I'll be ready when things calm down at work."

We all want to improve along some dimension. But these aspirations can turn into excuses. And I get it—dating is scary. Fear paralyzes the Hesitaters: fear of rejection, fear of failure, fear of not being good enough. No wonder they avoid dating. You can't fail at something you never attempt, right?

But people who wait until they are 100 percent ready underestimate what they're missing out on.

WHY IT'S A MISTAKE TO WAIT

You'll never be 100 percent ready for anything, including—and perhaps especially—dating.

The urge to wait until you feel fully self-actualized is understandable. What if you meet your ideal mate too early and they reject you?

For Hesitaters, there's a story in your head that one day you'll wake up and feel ready. That story is fiction. That's not how life works. Everyone feels awkward sometimes. Most people feel nervous in high-pressure situations. Many of us have a part of ourselves we don't want to reveal to others. And yet these very same people still go out on dates and kiss people and fall in love and break up and fall in love again and get married. Eventually, you just have to get out there and start dating, imperfect as you are. Everyone else is imperfect, too—even the person you'll end up with.

And, by the way, let's say you do reach this so-called state of perfection you've envisioned for yourself—by earning that promotion or shedding ten pounds—and then enter into a relationship. Will you worry that their love is conditional? That they'll leave you if you lose your job, tailspin, develop a ravenous cheddar cheese addiction, and gain twenty-five pounds?

When you wait to date, you're missing out on more than you think. Economists often refer to the **opportunity cost** of decisions—the price you pay when you choose one option over another. If you're facing two mutually exclusive choices, Option A and Option B, your opportunity cost is what you give up from Option A if you choose Option B, and vice versa. A quick example helps illustrate the concept.

Imagine you're deciding between Option A, attending grad school, or Option B, continuing to work in your current job. The tuition plus living expenses for two years adds up to two hundred thousand dollars. If I asked you how much grad school costs, what would you say? "Two hundred thousand dollars," right?

Wrong. You've neglected to include the opportunity cost. If you go to grad school, you can't keep working full-time, so the total cost of grad school includes forgoing your current salary. Therefore, the real cost of grad school is two hundred thousand dollars in tuition and expenses *plus* the money you would've made over two years if you'd worked instead of going to school. That's two hundred thousand plus two times your current annual salary.

Or let's say you're deciding between going to your friend Samantha's birthday party at a bar or your coworker David's housewarming party. When you consider the cost of going to Samantha's party, it's not just about the time it would take to get there, the money you might spend at the bar, or how bad your hangover might feel the next day. It's also the opportunity cost of not being able to get to know David and your coworkers better at his party.

When it comes to dating, Hesitaters wait until they have more confidence, more money, more *whatever*. But they're neglecting the opportunity cost of not starting.

MISSING OUT ON THE CHANCE TO LEARN

The first opportunity cost is losing the chance to learn. You can't figure out what you like (and what you don't) if you don't date different people. So much of dating is iterative—making incremental changes as you learn over time—especially because you're probably wrong about what you like or value in a partner (more on that in Chapter 8). You think you want something, you try it, turns out you *don't* want it, so you learn and move on. Maybe you fall for someone mysterious: the aloof bohemian Cirque du Soleil performer who once hitchhiked across Madagascar and sews their own pants. After a few months of dating, though, you realize that while the mystique is attractive at first, you want a partner who is warm and affectionate (and owns nice pants). If you're not going on dates, you're not getting closer to knowing the kind of person you want to be with long term.

Take my client Jing, for example. At thirty-one, she's dating for the first time. Her family moved a lot when she was growing up, so she never established a group of lifelong friends, much less a girlfriend. In college, she was studious and shy. She made new friends, but the dating and mating rituals of college seemed impossibly foreign to her. "I didn't know how to flirt," she confessed. "I just never learned."

After college, she joined an advertising agency as an intern. She worked her way up to lead copywriter. She transformed herself into someone she liked—sophisticated, funny, passionate—but she still didn't date. She put off trying because she already felt so behind.

Now she realizes that her lack of experience complicates her search for a good match: "I missed out on experimentation. I don't know my likes and dislikes. And now it feels a lot harder to find a partner without that information."

GETTING IN YOUR DATING REPS

Hesitaters who delay getting out there also miss the opportunity to improve their dating skills. I'm constantly surprised by how many of my clients think they should naturally know how to date. Dating is hard! And it takes time to master, just like anything else.

I tell my clients they need to get in their reps. A "rep" is a single movement (or repetition) of an exercise. At the gym, you get stronger by doing multiple reps. In dating, you get stronger by going on more dates.

When you wait to date, and sit at home thinking about how you're not ready yet, someone like you is going on a first date.

They're practicing their storytelling abilities, their listening skills, and their French-kissing technique. They're getting in their reps.

Jing still feels like a beginner, she told me. "I'm making rookie mistakes when I'm supposed to be ready for the game of my life." The fact is, everyone has to make those rookie mistakes at first. You're going to make them no matter when you start dating, so you might as well start making them now.

Dating is a bit like stand-up comedy (though hopefully with less heckling from strangers). They're both an audience-based art. Comics often say that if they're at home coming up with jokes, that's just writing. It's not until they're in front of a crowd that they're truly performing stand-up. Stand-up comics know that no one brings the house down the first time they step up to the mic; they need to learn by doing. That's one of the reasons up-and-coming comedians work so hard to get stage time. Before her breakout Netflix comedy special, *Baby Cobra*, Ali Wong went to multiple open mics every night, practicing her set over and over in small clubs.

It's the same with dating. You need to practice asking interesting questions, expressing yourself in a compelling way, and going in for a first kiss. Those are your reps. And you can't work on any of these skills if you're sitting around by yourself, "preparing." The only way to get better at it is to actually *date*.

OVERCOME YOUR HESITATION AND START DATING

Behavioral science warns us of the dreaded **intention-action gap**, when we *intend* to do something but don't take the steps to make it happen. Your intention is to start dating. But you may get stuck in the gap between wanting to date and doing it. To help you get started, here are some techniques from the behavioral science toolkit. They worked for Jing, who, after a number of bumbling first dates and a handful of slightly less awkward second, third, and fourth ones, entered into a relationship with her first boyfriend.

Step 1: Make a deadline.

Deadlines are one of the most efficient ways to motivate someone to take action. Short deadlines work especially well. Imagine you get an email from your bank telling you to change your password. They don't provide a deadline. How likely are you to do it? You might *intend* to change it, but since it seems like you can do it anytime, you'll likely forget about it before taking action. You'll fall into the intention-action gap.

Now imagine your bank emails you and says, "Change your password by the end of the day." In this case, you have a short, concrete deadline. To avoid missing it, you're likely to either change your password immediately or set aside specific time later in the day to do it. Either way, with the short deadline, you're far more likely to take action.

Researchers have studied the effects of the well-timed deadline—short while still doable. Behavioral scientists Suzanne Shu and Ayelet Gneezy looked at how often people redeemed gift certificates to a bakery. When the certificate was good for two months, fewer than 10 percent of people redeemed it for a pastry. (The rest were too flaky!) But when the certificate was good for only three weeks, suddenly, more than 30 percent of people redeemed the coupon. In the first scenario, people held off on taking the action because they figured they could do it later. With the shorter deadline, people were more aware that they could miss the window, so they took more immediate action.

Hesitaters, it's time to set a deadline for when you're going to start dating. I suggest three weeks from now. That's enough time to do what you need to do first—the pre-dating work I've listed below—but not so long that you lose momentum.

Step 2: Prep.

Once you've set the deadline, start doing the pre-dating work. Download the apps. Assemble a few solid date outfits. Consider going to an improv class to learn how to listen carefully and play well with others. Pay attention the next time you're having dinner with a friend: How much are you focusing inward (*How am I coming across?*) versus really listening and being curious (*What is this person trying to communicate?*)?

And if you've been out of the dating game for a while: Take some flattering photos. I had a client who was terrified of online dating. She'd always say, "I just don't have good photos for my profile." I convinced her to invest in beautiful new headshots. Once she got the pictures back, she finally felt ready to start. She downloaded the apps, received positive reinforcement about her pics, and went on a date the next week. You certainly don't need to splurge on professional photography. Some flattering lighting and a friend with a decent phone (oh, hey, portrait mode!) will do.

As part of your preparation, you may want to start seeing a therapist or coach. What's been holding you back? What are your unspoken fears? What in your past is preventing you from moving forward? But going to therapy isn't an excuse to not start dating. It's not a quick fix. Don't expect it to turn you into some more perfect version of yourself in a few weeks, after which you'll be "totally ready" to date. Commit to doing your therapy work *in parallel* with dating.

Step 3: Tell others.

If you publicly announce your goals to others, you're more likely to stay focused on them. A team of researchers led by social psychologist Kevin McCaul demonstrated this in a fascinating experiment. They took students who had a particularly hard test coming up and divided them into different groups. They asked one set of students to share their target test score with their group. They instructed a different group of students to keep their goal private. They found those who had shared with others felt more committed to the goal, spent more time studying for the test, and were 20 percent more likely to reach their goal and earn their target score.

Tell two to three of your closest friends or family members that you're going to start dating. Share your deadline with them. You'll feel more motivated to act once you've made this public pronouncement because now your reputation is on the line. (Bonus benefit: Sharing your dating goals with your community opens the door for people to set you up on dates. In Chapter 9, you'll find practical tips on asking to be set up.)

Step 4: Commit to your new identity.

We all have different identities: daughter, friend, Beyoncé fan, runner, and so on. We act differently depending on which of those identities we lean into at any given moment. A group of Stanford and Harvard researchers found that we can actually shift people's behavior simply by reinforcing one of those identities. They surveyed registered voters the week of an election. They asked one group: "How important is it to you to vote?" For the other, demographically identical group, they phrased the question slightly differently: "How important is it to you to be a voter in the upcoming election?" They later analyzed voting records to see who had actually shown up at the polls. They found the people who had been asked about *being* a voter were 11 percent more likely to have voted than those who were simply asked about the *act* of voting.

While people in both groups may have *intended* to vote, the people who were nudged to think of themselves as voters were more likely to follow through on their plan. They considered themselves voters, not just people who vote. Once that identity was reinforced, they were more likely to show up and vote.

You can use this lever to motivate yourself to start dating. Reinforce your own identity as a dater, not just someone who goes on dates. Stand in front of a mirror and say out loud: "I am looking for love. I am a dater." Does this seem ridiculous, especially before you've been on a date? Of course! But you should do it anyway.

I once worked with a client named Jacob who described himself on our first call as "very fat." He told me, "My mom is fat, my dad is fat, we're all fat."

He worked at a nonprofit on their learning and development team. He welcomed new employees to the company and trained them during their first week on the job. "I meet new people all the time. That's not the problem. I just hate the idea of dating because I can't imagine getting naked in front of anyone. So what's the point?"

Jacob said in the past he would try to lose weight, but then he'd fall off the wagon and end up right back where he started—unhappy with his weight and still single. Every week I tried to help Jacob see himself as a dater, not someone who would start dating once he lost weight. He did the mirror exercise. He hated it, but he did it.

One day, instead of our normal session, and perhaps inspired by a recent *Queer Eye* marathon, I took Jacob shopping. It was time to show his body some love.

He walked out of the dressing room and said, "Wow, I almost look good."

I laughed. With the help of a trendy teenage sales associate, we learned that he'd been buying his clothes two sizes too big. He bought some flattering new jeans, jackets, and shirts.

Over the months that followed, we found ways to improve his self-esteem by focusing on his best qualities—like his beautiful eyes and wicked sense of humor—instead of waiting for a new body that might never come.

With time, his identity as a dater grew stronger. He continued to do the mirror exercise and started to hate it a little bit less. He downloaded a dating app and tried to go on at least one date a week. One weekend, he reconnected with an old friend from college who was visiting San Francisco from Denver. When they went for a walk, he told her stories about his dating adventures. For the first time, she saw him as a potential romantic interest.

During her next trip to San Francisco, they went on a date. And then another. He visited her in Denver. And she came back to San Francisco. Fast-forward one year: He had just relocated to Denver to be with her. The last time we spoke, he was elated. He finally had the one thing he never thought he'd find: a happy, healthy relationship.

He didn't lose weight; he lost a limiting identity. He saw himself as an active dater, not a future one. The trick was changing how he saw himself.

Start thinking of yourself as a dater, and the world will see you that way, too.

Step 5: Start small.

You're not the Beatles—you don't have to go on eight dates a week. (Get it? Like the song "Eight Days a Week"? Forgive me my dad jokes.) Psychologists Edwin Locke and Gary Latham found that setting specific goals not only makes you more likely to *achieve* your goals, it also leads to greater motivation, confidence, and self-efficacy.

In general, I recommend that clients go on at least one date a week. You should proactively save time in your schedule for dates. One of my clients has a goal of going on a date every Wednesday after work. It's consistent, breaks up the week, and gives her something to look forward to. Plus, if the date goes well, she can meet up with them again that weekend.

Step 6: Be compassionate with yourself.

Look, I know this is hard. You're putting yourself out there, perhaps for the first time. It's scary. You might get hurt. Or hurt someone else.

When a date doesn't turn out how you hoped it would, talk to yourself the way you'd speak to your best friend. Imagine that friend called you and said, "What's the point? This will never work. I'm just not good enough."

How would you respond? You wouldn't pile on the negativity,

right? You'd try to give a pep talk: "Come on. It's just one date. Good for you for getting out there. I bet you learned something, even if the date sucked."

Learn to be your own cheerleader. Learn to use that compassionate tone with yourself.

This was the key for Shea, our Hesitater from the beginning of the chapter. Through our work together, and his weekly sessions with a therapist, he learned to accept himself for who he is now instead of focusing on the person he hopes to be in the future. He's currently single and dating. (And if you know anyone special who might like a tall, thoughtful amateur guitar player, let me know!)

Now it's your turn. Start today. If not now, when?

EXERCISE: Complete the Getting Ready Checklist

☐ I will start dating in earnest on the following date: _____.

☐ I've downloaded at least one dating app.

☐ I have at least five photos I could use for my profile.

☐ I have two outfits I could wear on a date.

☐ I've told at least two friends that I am starting to date.

☐ I've stood in front of the mirror and said, "I'm looking for love. I'm a dater" (or at the very least, "I *think* of myself as a dater!").

☐ I'm committed to going on at least one date per week.

☐ I'm practicing talking to myself compassionately—the way I'd speak to a small child or best friend.

☐ If I hit a roadblock and lose momentum, I commit to trying again instead of indulging my Hesitater ways.

STOP TALKING TO YOUR EX

One last thing—I've found that many of my Hesitater clients struggle to commit to dating in earnest because they're hung up on an ex. But this advice holds true for all daters: Stop talking to your ex.

We can think of keeping in touch with an ex (in a romantic or potentially romantic way) as keeping a door open. You want the option to change your mind about the relationship. That instinct, like so many others explored in this book, is wrong. Keeping our ex around makes it harder, not easier, to move on.

Research bears this out. As part of an experiment, Harvard psychologists Daniel Gilbert and Jane Ebert created several two-day photography workshops for students. Students shot photos around campus and developed their film with the help of an instructor. At the end of the workshop, the instructor told the students they could choose one of their developed photos for a special art exhibition in London. One group of students were told they had to choose a photo to send that day and couldn't change their minds later. Another group was told to choose a picture now, but that someone would phone in the next few days to see if they wanted to change their selection.

When the instructors asked students in the second group if they wanted to change their photos, very few of them did. But when the researchers surveyed the students, the group that couldn't change their minds about their pictures was much more satisfied than the group that could. Why would those students be any less satisfied, especially since most of them stuck to their original selections?

While we instinctively prefer reversible decisions to irreversible ones, this flexibility often make us less happy in the long run. We'd rather be able to change our minds—return our new phone, switch our flight to a different day, reply "maybe" to an event. But it turns out, just like the students who could switch their pictures, we're less committed to choices we think we can reverse, and commitment is crucial for happiness.

As we discussed earlier, once you commit to something, your brain starts the magical process of rationalization, convincing you that you made a good choice. You retroactively ascribe more positive traits to things you chose and more negative traits to things you didn't. The students who had to choose a final photo committed to their picture right away, immediately launching the rationalization process. Those who had the chance to change their selection spent the week going back and forth, weighing the different options. This led to feelings of doubt, so that even when they stuck with their original photo, they felt less sure about it. When your brain accepts something and you move on, you aren't left agonizing over the decision.

In other words, we want reversible decisions, but irrevocable ones make us happier in the long term. Keeping your ex around as a potential love interest turns your breakup into a *changeable* decision. Allow yourself to move on by making it an *unchangeable* one.

So, did you slide into your ex's DMs last night? If you're still carrying a torch for them and secretly wondering if you'll get back together, try these **Seven Simple Steps to Block 'Em Like It's Hot:**

1. Take a deep breath.
2. Grab your phone.
3. Delete their number.
4. Block them. Block them on everything. Social media, email,

your bed, etc. If their mom or sister follows you, block them, too. (It might seem harsh, but you're protecting your future self against mom postings of your ex with a new boo under the mistletoe.)

5. Actually delete their number this time. I know you have it saved elsewhere. I'll wait.
6. Burn your phone. (Just kidding, but you honestly might want to limit your screen time during this initial separation phase.)
7. Oh, and don't forget the payment app Venmo. Seeing your ex send Venmo money to some new fling for—*Oh, God, is that an eggplant emoji?!?! THEY NEVER SENT ME AN EGGPLANT EMOJI!*—is doing nothing for your emotional wellness.

Maybe this seems like too much. How harmful could it be to check their Instagram or Facebook once in a while? Here's even more evidence from psychologists Tara Marshall and Ashley Mason. In one research paper, Marshall wrote that "exposure to an ex-partner through Facebook may obstruct the process of healing." Mason found that talking to an ex *worsens* your psychological health. And for goodness' sake, don't sleep with your ex! Mason also discovered that "having SWE (sex with ex)" makes it harder to move on. In other words, creeping on (or sleeping with) an ex only slows down the process of getting over them.

So do yourself a favor and shut that door. Stop talking to your ex! Make your changeable decision unchangeable.

KEY TAKEAWAYS

1. **Hesitaters delay dating because they don't feel 100 percent ready yet** and want to put their best foot forward. **But no one ever feels 100 percent ready for anything.** At a certain point, you just have to start.

2. **Perfection is a lie.** Everyone else is imperfect, too—even the person you'll eventually end up with.

3. **By waiting to date, Hesitaters miss out on a chance to develop their dating skills and figure out what type of person they want to be with.**

4. **Here's how you can learn to overcome your hesitation:**

   - Set deadlines for yourself.

   - Do prep work for your new dating life.

   - Tell others about your plan.

   - Commit to your new identity as a "dater."

   - Start with small goals.

   - Be compassionate with yourself.

   - STOP TALKING TO YOUR EX!

CHAPTER 6

LEARN YOUR ATTACHMENT STYLE

How to Manage Your Attachment Style

I met Vivian at a barre workout class. She was always the first one there, doing enthusiastic butt clenches and micro squats before class even started. I also like to arrive early to workout classes, mainly to alleviate my anxiety about getting a good spot. Week after week, we'd see each other, both of us clearly trying not to look annoyed when our teacher arrived late.

One of those mornings, we started talking, and I learned how much we had in common. We shared several close friends from the East Coast. We'd moved to San Francisco the same year. We also loved the same neighborhood café, which we began visiting together after class.

It was in that café where she confessed: "All of the guys I like don't like me back, but all of the guys who like me, I think are boring." As we waited in line to order, she glanced around and whispered, "What am I supposed to do? Am I going to have to settle?"

Vivian didn't like to think of herself as someone who settled. She worked in corporate PR at a large company, handling what's known as "crisis comms." That year and the years before it, the crises had been relentless. She was expected to be battle-ready at all times, prepared for any lawsuit or hit piece. She exercised five times a week, ate a strictly vegan diet, and had just obtained her sailing license. The woman was in control of everything. Everything *but* her dating life.

Vivian knew I worked as a dating coach and matchmaker. She had shared a little bit about her dating life in our previous conversations, but this was the first time she had really opened up.

"So, let's take a step back. What's your dating history like?" I asked her.

"In a word: disappointing," she said. "I had a thing with this guy for two years. I don't even know if I should really call it a thing. He sure wouldn't. He lived in my apartment building in New York, and we'd hook up whenever he felt like it. Then there was this guy at work when I first moved here, but he sent a lot of mixed messages, and it sort of fizzled. Lately, I've been on the dating apps, and I've been on what feels like a million dates, but as soon as someone says they like me, I immediately lose interest. Tell me the truth. Am I cursed? Am I going to die alone?"

I laughed. "No, you're great. You're beautiful and interesting, and you know how to sail a friggin' boat. I just think you might be looking for the wrong things." I was trying to stay on my side of the mat but felt myself slowly veering into coaching mode. I wanted to help.

"The wrong things? I didn't say anything about going after tall guys or rich guys."

"That's not what I mean," I said, interrupting her. "Have you ever heard of **attachment theory**?"

ATTACHMENT 101

Of all the relationship science insights I share with my clients, attachment theory is one of the most powerful. It's a popular framework that helps explain why we're attracted to certain types of people, why past relationships haven't worked out, and why we're plagued by certain bad habits.

You can read entire books on the topic, including *Attached*, by Amir Levine and Rachel Heller, and *Hold Me Tight*, by Sue Johnson, but attachment theory has made such a difference to my friends, my clients, and my own life that I wanted to include it here, too. I've worked with people who struggled with dating for years, learned about this framework, and used it to completely shift their approach. It's not easy, but the results can be powerful. I know more than a handful of people who owe their marital success to what they learned from attachment theory. (Clearly, I'm very *attached* to this theory.)

After ordering our drinks, Vivian and I sat in a cushion-filled nook at the back of the café. I began to explain what attachment theory is and why it matters.

It all dates back to the work of developmental psychologist John Bowlby. He believed that children have an innate attachment to their mothers. Later, psychologist Mary Ainsworth investigated how attachment might vary between children in a now-famous experiment called "The Strange Situation." She invited mothers and babies (between twelve and eighteen months old) into her lab and observed them in a series of different scenarios.

First the mother and baby entered a room filled with toys. The baby felt safe to play and explore because the mother functioned as the secure base—someone who could provide help if they needed it. Then the lab assistant instructed the mother to leave the room, and observed how the baby responded to both the mother's absence and her return a few minutes later. The experiment explored a baby's ability to trust that their needs would be met, even with the temporary absence of their secure base.

Some babies showed signs of distress as soon as their mother left. When she returned, these babies would be temporarily soothed and stop crying but then angrily push the mother away and begin crying again. Ainsworth called these babies "**anxiously attached.**"

Another group of babies cried when their mother left but stopped as soon as she returned. They quickly resumed playing. These were the "**securely attached**" babies.

A third group did not respond to their mother leaving the room; nor did they acknowledge her when she returned. They pretended they weren't bothered by the situation, but the researchers could tell from their elevated heart rate and stress levels that these babies were just as upset as the ones who cried. These were the "**avoidantly attached**" babies.

Ainsworth and her team concluded that we all have the same need for attachment and attention, but we develop different coping strategies to deal with our particular caregivers.

Years later, researchers found the same theory applies to our adult attachment style—whom we're attracted to, how we relate to them, and why many of our relationships succeed or fail. But don't blame your mom for your relationship issues just yet. Our relationship with our parents is one of only a number of factors that determine our adult attachment style.

"Which one am I?" Vivian said.

"Well," I said, "those anxiously attached babies who cried when their mothers left the room and continued to cry when the mother returned? As babies, they worried their needs would go unmet, and lashed out with anger and frustration. As adults, they're afraid of abandonment and want to be in constant contact with their partners."

"That is so me."

I smiled at Vivian because she *had* sent me seven rapid-fire texts in a row when I hadn't shown up to class the week before.

When people are anxiously attached, their brains flood with "activating strategies," thoughts that compel them to regain closeness. For example, they might think about their partner nonstop. Or they may dwell on their partner's good qualities while undervaluing their own. This distortion leads to panic. And when they don't hear back from their partners immediately, they worry they're being abandoned. They can shake their anxiety only when they're actively communicating with their partner. This also leads them to jump into relationships and stay in them past their expiration date because they fear being alone and worry that this is their only shot at love.

"Anxiously attached folks," I said, "and I'm not pointing any fingers here, also engage in '**protest behavior.**'"

People with **anxious-attachment** styles often act out in order to get their partner's attention. They might call or text an excessive number of times, threaten to leave to make the other person jealous, or withdraw and ignore phone calls to underscore a point.

And what about the avoidantly attached babies who acted uninterested when their moms returned to the room, even though they were upset? They felt like they couldn't rely on their caregiver, who met only some of their needs. They develop into avoidantly attached adults: They try to minimize the pain of rejection by pretending they don't actually want to connect. They don't believe they can rely on others to meet their emotional needs, so they avoid getting too close to anyone. When intimacy increases, they try to pull away. Those attempts to disengage are called "**deactivating strategies.**" If you've heard someone say, "I'm not ready to commit" or "I just need space" or "My job is really demanding so I can't see you right now," then you've experienced avoidantly attached behavior.

People with this attachment style also tend to dwell on their partner's imperfections and use those as an excuse to exit the relationship and regain independence. They fantasize about how much happier they'd be if they were single or with someone else.

When I outlined the avoidant-attachment style, Vivian nodded. "That sounds exactly like everyone I've ever dated," she said.

"Don't be too hard on yourself," I told her. This pattern is actually extremely common. It's called the "anxious-avoidant loop." Anxiously attached people expect that the person they love will pull back and they in turn will need to chase them. It's what happened with Vivian's ex who lived in her apartment building.

"It was so exciting," Vivian said. "I'd wonder: *Will he call me back? Can I see him this weekend?*" That possibility of rejection created anxiety, a feeling Vivian confused for butterflies. And when the guy started pulling away, she felt it even more intensely.

The avoidantly attached guy, meanwhile, was probably experiencing something else entirely. People with this attachment style fear losing their independence. So when Vivian started pulling closer, it likely reinforced his unhealthy view of relationships—and made him want to withdraw even further.

"If you think about it this way," I said, "the anxious-avoidant loop makes sense. Avoidantly attached people are so good at pushing other people away, the only time they end up in a relationship is when the other person is especially persistent."

"I am nothing if not persistent," Vivian said.

The server finally arrived with our drinks. Vivian looked out the window, watching a couple on the bench outside the café. "What about that last group of babies, who stopped crying when their mom returned?" she asked.

"Those are the securely attached babies, who felt confident their mothers would meet their needs. People with a secure attachment style make ideal partners. They're reliable and trustworthy. They tend to avoid drama and, if not, are able to defuse it when they see it coming. They're flexible, forgiving, and good at communicating. They behave consistently. They create healthy boundaries. They're comfortable with intimacy. People with secure-attachment styles end up reporting higher levels of relationship satisfaction than avoidant or anxious folks."

"I have literally never dated anyone like that," Vivian responded. "Are secure people, like, one percent of the population?"

In reality, 50 percent of the population is secure, 20 percent is anxiously attached, 25 percent is avoidantly attached, and the remainder fall into a group called anxious-avoidant. That might seem like good news. The problem is that while securely attached people make up 50 percent of the general population, there are far fewer in the single population. That's because secure people tend to get snatched up quickly. They're good at building healthy relationships, so they tend to stay in them. That's why the dating pool is full of anxious and avoidant daters.

When I explained all of that to Vivian, she sighed. "I give up," she said, sipping the last of her smoothie.

She said that, but she didn't.

EXERCISE: Determine Your Style

If you're curious about your own attachment style, answer these questions:

1. How comfortable are you with intimacy and closeness? How much do you tend to avoid intimacy?
2. How anxious do you feel about your partner's love and interest in you? Do you constantly worry about the relationship?

You may be anxiously attached if you crave closeness but are insecure about your relationship's future and your partner's interest in you. You may be avoidantly attached if you feel uncomfortable when things get too close, and you value freedom over connection. You may be secure if you are comfortable with intimacy, spending time alone, and don't often worry about the relationship.

You can take the online quiz linked from my website, loganury.com, to confirm your attachment style.

LOOK FOR A SECURE PARTNER

Despite what Vivian had said about giving up, in the months following our conversation, she made an effort to approaching dating differently. She started looking for secure partners. It took time. She'd go out with someone new and complain that they were "boring." When I dug deeper, I discovered this usually meant the person was being nice to her. For example, she told a guy with whom she'd been on two dates that she was visiting Seattle the next weekend. He then sent her a list of restaurant recommendations. When she told me that story, she ended by saying: "And that's why I never want to see him again."

"Wait, what?" I said.

"He clearly likes me way too much. It's pathetic."

I did my best to help her see the situation differently. This guy was trying to be helpful because he liked her. It was a secure act and not a pathetic one. We worked on helping her break that anxious-avoidant loop.

If you relate to Vivian's story, and believe that you're anxiously attached, that's your homework, too. Now, I'm not suggesting that *everyone* you find boring is secretly secure. They might actually be boring. But it's time to stop pursuing the chase. That was the challenge I gave Vivian: Try to date secure partners. The ones who text when they say they will. Who let you know what's on their mind. Who don't play games and avoid or even de-escalate drama.

The same goes for you, my avoidantly attached readers. Find yourself a secure partner!

LEARN TO SELF-REGULATE

At the same time, you can work to become more secure yourself. Attachment styles are relatively stable over your lifetime, although about a quarter of people change their attachment style over a four-year period. It takes effort, but you can shift your attachment style.

Vivian was determined to make a change, which for her meant learning to **self-regulate**—managing disruptive impulses and emotions. She trained herself not to panic when she didn't immediately hear back from someone. In those moments, she practiced quieting her anxieties by either taking a walk or calling a friend. (Both healthier options than sending fourteen texts to the guy she'd met in the elevator at work the day before.)

And for those of you who are avoidantly attached, pay attention to your feelings when you sense yourself withdrawing. Learn to *ask* for space instead of disappearing *into* space. Or when you sense yourself focusing on your partner's shortcomings and wanting to leave because of them, try a different technique: Practice looking for the positive qualities instead. Remember that no one is perfect, and if you leave, the next person you meet won't be perfect, either.

Changing your attachment style on your own can be challenging. There are so many unconscious reasons we are the way we are, and mining the past may bring up unexpected and difficult questions. How does our relationship with our mom relate to our attachment style? If we find a healthier attachment now, does that mean we're betraying or abandoning her? You may have to face that you didn't get what you needed from the person you most needed it from. Many people find it helpful to talk through these issues with a therapist.

Vivian and I continued to discuss her love life after each class. Soon she stopped calling guys "boring" when they began to express interest in her. She proudly texted me when she told a clearly avoidant suitor to buzz off. And guess what? After about six months, she met a great-looking guy who had just relocated to San Francisco from Houston. After their first date, on a Friday night, he called her and said, "I really like you, and I want to see you again tomorrow." Instead of deeming that "pathetic," she found herself at breakfast with him the very next day, just as he'd asked. Breakfast turned into a walk. The walk turned into meeting up with her friends at a brewery. The brewery turned into a drunken cab ride back to his house, followed by a long nap. Two years later, they're still napping together.

KEY TAKEAWAYS

1. **Attachment theory is a popular framework for understanding relationships.** It can help explain why you're attracted to certain people, why past relationships haven't worked out, and why you're trapped in a pattern of bad habits.

2. You may be **anxiously attached if you crave a lot of closeness but are insecure about your relationship's future and your partner's interest in you.** You may be **avoidantly attached if you feel uncomfortable with intimacy and value independence over connection.** You may be **securely attached if you are comfortable with intimacy, spending time alone, and drawing clear boundaries.**

3. **Securely attached folks make up 50 percent of the population but not the dating pool,** since they tend to get into relationships and stay in them. **Anxiously attached and avoidantly attached people often date each other, reinforcing their worst tendencies.**

4. If you're anxiously attached or avoidantly attached, you can **help yourself develop better relationship skills by looking for a secure partner and learning to self-regulate—managing disruptive impulses and emotions.**

CHAPTER 7

LOOK FOR A LIFE PARTNER, NOT A PROM DATE

*How to Focus on What Matters
in a Long-Term Partner*

Brian looked like Keanu Reeves's more attractive brother.

We met at Burning Man, the annual art and psychedelics festival in the Nevada desert. That first night, dressed head to toe in white linen, dust goggles draped around his neck, he whispered, "Can I kiss you?" I nodded, adjusting the cream-colored fur hat I'd paired with a spotted onesie to complete my snow leopard look. We kissed as Paul Oakenfold DJed. Thousands of Burners danced around us. When the beat dropped, the crowd cheered, and we kissed harder.

Later, a stranger in a wizard's robe handed us a Polaroid capturing our embrace. "You just looked so in love." And I was sure we were. I was swept up in the romance of falling for him while exploring this otherworldly desert moonscape.

I was still interested in Brian when we returned to San Francisco. One afternoon we sat on a bench at Google headquarters, where we both worked, and traded stories about our "decompression"—the experience of adjusting back to real life after Burning Man. Brian had swapped his linen for jeans and a T-shirt.

We swiped some beers from a microkitchen and hopped on the

Google shuttle back to San Francisco. I grinned as I slid onto the seat next to him. We shared headphones. Left earbud in his ear, right earbud in mine, he played "The Trapeze Swinger" by Iron and Wine. I closed my eyes and remembered our deliriously happy moment dancing in the desert. *This is what love feels like*, I thought.

Brian was hot, spontaneous, and fun. But also unreliable. I never knew if he'd text me back or come over when he said he would. He knew how much I liked him. He'd act interested one day and aloof the next. I never asked myself questions like this: *Is he kind and thoughtful? Do I trust his judgment? Would he remember to take our kids to the dentist?* (If his own dentist-going habits were any indication, no, he would not.)

Looking back, I wonder why I, someone who wanted to find a serious partner and create a long-term relationship, desperately tried to convince him to date me. Why did I keep falling for guys like Brian? My choices weren't helping me create the relationship I wanted. Instead of dating for long-term partnership, I was optimizing for short-term fun.

THE PROM DATE VERSUS THE LIFE PARTNER

Many of us struggle to make good choices for our future selves—and not just when it comes to dating. We're guilty of this when we procrastinate on household chores (although we know we have to do them eventually), when we don't exercise (although we know it's important for long-term health), and when we spend money frivolously (although we know we should save it). These are all moments when we fall prey to the **present bias**, an error in judgment that causes us to place a disproportionately high value on the here and now and an inappropriately low value on the future.

Many of us don't date for long-term viability. I certainly didn't when chasing Brian. I call this pursuing the **Prom Date**. What's an ideal prom date? Someone who looks great in pictures, gives you a night full of fun, and makes you look cool in front of your friends. Many of us finished high school more than a decade ago, and yet we're still using the same rubric to evaluate potential partners. Do you really want to marry the Prom Date? To worry if your partner is going to help you take care of your aging parents? Or show up to your kid's parent-teacher conference? Or nurse you back to health after contracting a case of Montezuma's revenge?

Those probably aren't the questions you ask yourself when you first meet someone. The answers have little bearing on whether you want to kiss the person or go out with them again. (And who wants to think about diarrhea on a first date!?) But when you're looking for a long-term partner, you want someone who will be there for you during the highs *and* the lows. Someone you can rely on. Someone to make decisions with. The **Life Partner**.

I'm lucky to count the brilliant couples therapist Esther Perel as a mentor. She once explained to me the difference between a love story and a life story. There are many people with whom you can share a tryst but far fewer with whom you can build a life. When you're thinking about who to marry, she says, don't ask yourself: *What would a love story with this person look like?* Instead, ask: *Can I make a life with this person?* That's the fundamental distinction.

Most of us start developing crushes on the Prom Date around the time we go through puberty. And it makes sense! When you're a teen, you're thinking about whom you want to smooch, not who will make a good coparent.

But you're not fifteen anymore. If you really are seeking a long-term relationship with a committed partner, you need to stop looking for a Prom Date and start seeking a Life Partner.

WHEN TO DITCH THE PROM DATE

When should you make this shift? There isn't one answer for everyone, but in a conversation I had with behavioral economist

Dan Ariely, we came up with a helpful rule of thumb for those of you who want to have children: You should deliberately change the way you evaluate potential partners around six to eight years before you want to have kids. Now, that's not a scientific number but, rather, a framework for thinking through when to make this shift.

I imagine many of you—like many of my clients—are already in that critical window. I don't mean to make you feel behind. I just want to encourage you to take yourself seriously and start dating someone who has the potential to be a serious partner.

Be honest with yourself. Do you tend to date Prom Dates or Life Partners? A client once told me she'd gone on several dates with a guy who lived alone. When she visited his apartment and used the bathroom, she was met with a sink full of beard hair trimmings, an overflowing trash can, and no toilet paper. This woman is a successful, talented professional. She's thirty-four, and she told me she wants to have "many kids." I'm not saying that a guy with a filthy bathroom couldn't make a great husband and father. But if she's thirty-four and wants to give birth to a brood of children, she realistically needs to start soon. And who's more likely to be ready to start a family—a guy with a clean bathroom or a man who still acts like he lives in a dorm? I advised her to say goodbye to this Prom Date and focus her energy on finding a Life Partner.

To shift toward pursuing the Life Partner, you must learn to recognize the present bias and deliberately work against it.

WHAT WE GET WRONG ABOUT WHAT MATTERS

In addition to coaching, I also work as a matchmaker and set my clients up on dates. I started this work when I learned how many of my friends and clients were struggling on the apps. As a matchmaker, I've met with dozens of people to learn what they're looking for in a partner. Hundreds have filled out the matchmaking form on my website to join "Logan's List." Through this process, I've collected enough data to understand what people *think* matters most in a serious partner. We can compare that to what the academic field of relationship science tells us *actually* matters for long-term relationship success.

We can thank John Gottman for many of these relationship science insights. He spent more than four decades studying romantic relationships. For years, he and his colleague Robert Levenson brought couples into an observational research laboratory dubbed the "Love Lab" by the media. There, he recorded them discussing their relationship. He asked couples to share the story of how they met and then recount a recent fight. He even invited couples to spend a weekend in an apartment he'd decked out with cameras to observe how they interacted during everyday moments.

Years after they participated in the apartment study, Gottman followed up with the couples to check on their relationships. They fell into two camps: the "masters," couples who were still happily married; and the "disasters," couples who had either broken up or remained together unhappily. He studied the original tapes of these two types of couples to learn what patterns separated the masters from the disasters.

When we look at Gottman's findings, and the work of other relationship scientists, we can see clearly which qualities contribute to long-term relationship success. In other words, the research tells us what makes a good Life Partner. However, these are not the traits my matchmaking clients tend to ask for. Instead, they focus on short-term desirability—or the characteristics of a good Prom Date.

WHAT MATTERS LESS THAN WE THINK

Not only do we undervalue the qualities that matter for long-term relationships, we overvalue irrelevant ones. In part, we can blame a cognitive error called the **focusing illusion**—our tendency to overestimate the importance of certain factors when anticipating outcomes, like our future happiness.

Behavioral economists Daniel Kahneman and David Schkade explored this phenomenon. They asked people attending college in Michigan and Ohio who they thought were happier—Midwestern students, like themselves, or students in California. They asked students in Southern California the same questions.

Both groups predicted that the California students were happier. Yet researchers found the overall life satisfaction for Californian and Midwestern students was nearly identical.

It turned out that both sets of students overestimated the impact that living in a warmer climate has on daily satisfaction. That's because the climate is an "easily observable and distinctive" difference between these two places. They ignored all the other factors that contribute to happiness, which both sets of students shared: concerns about grades, social status, family issues, money, career prospects, and more. Those things are the same no matter the weather. However, when asked to compare life in those two places, the students focused on the weather and assumed it had a greater impact than it really does.

Kahneman summarized this research finding perfectly: "Nothing in life is as important as you think it is while you are thinking about it." Merely thinking about something accentuates the differences.

We're guilty of falling victim to the focusing illusion when selecting potential mates. The people I coach often list requirements such as "I need someone who loves to dance." In that moment, they're focusing on the fact that they themselves love to dance. Then, because of the focusing illusion, just *thinking* about it causes them to overestimate its importance. The truth is, even if they're notorious for sweating through their shirt on salsa night, they likely don't spend more than a few hours a month on the dance floor. But people tend to fixate on these insignificant characteristics and ignore the far more important factors that are correlated with long-term relationship happiness (more on those in a moment).

The same is true of looks, money, and more. These things make a difference, just much less than we tend to think.

1) Money

Don't get me wrong, money matters. When couples below the poverty line struggle to meet their basic needs, their marriage suffers. Texas Tech University psychologists studied married couples in therapy and found that low-income couples were far more dissatisfied with their relationship than middle-income couples. In fact, low-income couples felt about as unhappy as divorced couples did in the month before they broke up.

It's no secret that financial woes cause marital stress. It's one of the main reasons why couples divorce. If you have enough resources, you won't constantly face the strain of hard financial decisions, like having to choose between getting your oldest child braces and sending your youngest to a math tutor. What's more, research from Harvard Business School found that couples who can afford to outsource time-intensive tasks like cooking and cleaning enjoy greater relationship satisfaction because they can spend more quality time together.

But that doesn't mean that in order to be happy, you should pursue the richest partner you can. While it's difficult to determine an exact threshold beyond which more money will no longer buy you more happiness, research by behavioral economists Daniel Kahneman and Angus Deaton famously found that there is no increase in "emotional well-being" (economist-speak for happiness) once salaries exceed $75,000 a year.

In fact, additional research suggests that the extent to which you can derive happiness from money in the first place depends on the wealth of those around you. In other words, it's not really the size of your house that matters. It's the size of your house *in comparison* to the size of your neighbors' houses.

That's because we acclimate to our conditions. We often forget about **adaptation**—the process of getting used to a situation. No matter how wonderful something is, the novelty eventually wears off, and we stop paying much attention to it. And once we stop paying attention to it, it doesn't bring us the same level of joy, or misery, that it did when we were focused on it. This explains the results of a 1978 study led by psychologist Philip Brickman, in which he and his team surveyed lottery winners a year after their windfall. Lottery winners, it turns out, are less happy in the long term than you'd think. They're about as happy as non–lottery winners, and actually have an even harder time enjoying the small pleasures in life than people who haven't won anything. Lottery winners *adapted* to their environment, and their wealth had a much smaller than anticipated effect on their overall life satisfaction.

Key tip for your dating search

When we make a decision, we tend to focus on the immediate joy or misery it will bring. But remember: We are bad fortune-tellers! We often can't account for how those feelings will change over time. Money matters, but only up to a certain extent. You're not wrong for considering that element of your future relationship, but don't prioritize wealth above all else.

2) Good Looks

It's no secret that looks make a difference in many realms of life. Attractive people tend to earn higher salaries and beat their less attractive opponents in political races. In multiple studies investigating attractiveness, researchers noted that good-looking people are perceived as more persuasive, trustworthy, outgoing, socially competent and powerful, sexually responsive, healthy, intelligent, and likable.

And when it comes to dating, there's a historical and evolutionary reason for prizing good looks. Early on, life was a constant struggle for survival. Physically attractive traits—like clear skin or thick hair—indicated health and vitality. That was important for mate selection because it meant that not only would this person *pass on* these desirable quality traits to your kids, they'd also be more likely to *stay alive* long enough to help raise them. No wonder our brains trained us to go for the hotties.

In today's world, thanks to the miracle of modern medicine and industrialized food production, we're not plagued by the same issues. Our offspring have a very good chance at surviving, so it no longer makes sense to prioritize reproductive fitness—the ability to pass on genes to future generations—when choosing a partner. Your kid will be fine even if his dad had acne in his teens.

What's more, focusing on attractiveness to the exclusion of other traits ignores the fact that lust inevitably fades over time (and remember, we're going for long-term success here). In his book *The Science of Happily Ever After*, psychologist Ty Tashiro analyzed a fourteen-year longitudinal study of satisfaction in marriages over time. He found that over the course of seven years, "lust" (sexual desire) for a partner declined twice as fast as "liking" (friendship characterized by loyalty and kindness).

Biological anthropologist Helen Fisher helps explain why that happens. Lust is incredibly intense in the beginning and then fades. When we fall in love, it feels like we're addicted to the other person, as if they're a drug. Fisher found that cocaine and falling in love light up the same regions of the brain.

The fading of our lust is also a strategic evolutionary move. Our "addiction" to our partner keeps us around long enough to have a baby and raise him or her together until the child is around four years old, old enough to be somewhat independent (at least on the ancient savanna) and survive. Once our work there is done, lust fades, and our brain frees us to create new children with new partners, increasing the chance that at least one of our children will live to adulthood and carry on our DNA.

If you're judging your relationship during a stage when you have sex all the time, how well can you predict what the relationship will be like when that slows down?

And if it's good sex you're after, there's no guarantee someone who is attractive will even *be* good in bed. There may be skills that beautiful people never develop because they don't need to. An episode of the TV show *30 Rock* called "The Bubble" takes this idea to the extreme. Jon Hamm plays a character who is insulated by his own handsomeness. He's a former tennis pro who can't serve, a doctor who doesn't know the Heimlich maneuver, and as Tina Fey's character complains, "He's as bad at sex as I am." Her suave boss knows this phenomenon firsthand: "That is the danger of being super-handsome," he tells her. "When you're in the bubble, nobody ever tells you the truth." So yeah, don't assume that the best-looking people make the best lovers.

Finally, remember what we just learned about adaptation. Even if you marry the most attractive person, eventually, you'll get used to how they look. That initial pleasure will fade. A big part of our sex drive is associated with novelty. So no matter how hot your partner is, it's likely that your sexual interest in them will decrease over time, simply because they are no longer new to you. To paraphrase some Internet wisdom: "For every hot person, there is someone out there tired of having sex with them."

Infatuation fades! Lust fades! All that matters is that you feel attracted to the person, not that you scored the hottest possible person.

Key tip for your dating search
Physical attraction can obscure long-term compatibility. Pay attention to whether or not *you're* attracted to someone and focus less on how *society* would evaluate that person's looks. Don't prioritize lust over more important long-term factors.

3) A Personality Similar to Yours

My clients often complain that they need to find a partner with a personality similar to theirs. I hear: "I'm so extroverted and he's so introverted. It would never work." Or: "I'm really neurotic and nothing ever seems to bother him. We're just not a match."

I've found this sentiment especially common among my older clients. When we're younger and we enter a relationship, it's like a start-up—two people coming together to build something. We're more flexible and still figuring out what we want. When we're older and thinking about long-term relationships and, eventually, marriage, the process is more like a merger: two complete beings coming together. The older we get, the more set in our ways we are, and the more we crave someone who will easily fit into our lives. We assume that the more similar we are, the easier the merger will be.

But that assumption is wrong. Research tells us that similar personalities are not a predictor of long-term relationship success. In my interview with Northwestern professor and marriage expert Eli Finkel, he said, "There is no correlation between how satisfied or how happy you are with a relationship and how similar your personalities are." In other words, we make our potential pool of partners smaller by mistakenly eliminating people who are not similar enough to us.

The question is: Would you *really* want to date yourself? I know I wouldn't!

A client of mine is the life of the party. He's an event promoter with a big personality. He was dating someone calm and caring who liked to be in bed before ten p.m. on most nights. He wondered, *Wouldn't my life be better if I dated someone more like me?*

I sat him down and told him that two of him would be too much for one room, let alone one relationship! They'd fight to be the center of attention. "Do you know the show *The Amazing Race*?" I asked him. The show follows couples or pairs of friends or family members who travel to exotic locations to complete missions. "The pairs that are too similar fight," I said. "They get stuck on the same things. The most successful duos complement each other. They don't have identical traits. When they miss a flight, one partner finds another route and soothes the other's panic. That's what makes them win. You want the same thing with your life partner."

Over the course of a year, he worked on appreciating his partner's differences rather than wishing she were more like him. They recently decided to have a baby together.

Key tip for your dating search

Find someone who complements you, not your personality twin.

GENETICS!

Many people say they want to find someone with a similar personality. Yet when Michigan State University researchers William Chopik and Richard Lucas studied more than twenty-five hundred married couples who had been together for an average of twenty years, they found that couples with similar personalities aren't any more satisfied with their relationships.

And when it comes to our genes, we may have evolved to prefer people who are genetically *dissimilar* to us. There's a theory that we feel attracted to the smell of people who are genetically different from us because if we reproduced with them, we'd pass on two very different sets of genes—making our offspring more robust and more likely to survive.

Swiss biological researcher Claus Wedekind explored this in his famous T-shirt study. He collected DNA samples from male and female students. To capture their smell, he instructed male students to wear the same cotton T-shirt for two nights and to avoid smell-producing activities like sex. Then he asked female students to smell six T-shirts—three from genetically similar men and three from genetically dissimilar ones—and rate each one based on intensity, pleasantness, and sexiness. He found women preferred the smell of the men whose genes were *more dissimilar* from theirs.

(Coincidentally, the effect reverses for women on oral birth control. Things can get awkward when a couple marries, the woman goes off birth control, and suddenly, she's attracted to different people.)

4) Shared Hobbies

Once, when I was on a road trip with an old friend, we started talking about how she and her husband love tennis. That conversation carried us all the way to the gas station. She got out of the car and browsed her phone while filling up the tank. When she climbed back in, she thrust her phone in my face and said, "Look. Aren't my in-laws cute?" Her screen showed a blurry, poorly executed selfie of a couple in their sixties.

As she started the car, she said, "Honestly, it's surprising my husband's parents have been married for so long. They have nothing in common."

"People often think shared hobbies matter more than they do," I responded. "It's possible you're underestimating all the things they do share." By then she had already heard me talk about the Gottmans. (Along with obscure Weird Al trivia, I usually mention the Gottmans before the first pit stop on a road trip.)

John Gottman, whom I mentioned earlier, is married to Julie Gottman, a noted clinical psychologist. John chose to spend many years of his life in a lab, coding the micro-expressions of couples. Unsurprisingly, he considers himself "an avid indoorsman." He jokes that he's the kind of person who can think of a thousand ways to die at a picnic. Julie shares his passion for helping couples. But Julie's idea of fun is spending time in the wilderness. She was a competitive skier in college. For her fiftieth birthday, she dreamed of hiking to Everest Base Camp. Imagine John, the guy afraid of picnics, ice-picking his way up Mount Everest with Julie.

Of course, John and Julie knew about these differences before they got married. Yet, because of their work, they also understood that couples do not need to share hobbies to create a successful long-term relationship. And they've been happily married for more than thirty years.

Here's the key: It's fine to have different interests, so long as the time you spend pursuing your favorite activities doesn't preclude you from investing in the relationship. If you love wine and your partner couldn't care less about it, that's okay; you don't need to marry a sommelier. What matters is that when you drink wine, or go on a trip to Napa to try a new prized cabernet sauvignon, your partner doesn't try to make you feel guilty or say something like "Why do you *always* have to drink?" A good relationship has space for different people with different hobbies.

Key tip for your dating search

Don't worry about finding someone with the same hobbies. It's fine to enjoy different activities as long as you give each other the space and freedom to explore those hobbies on your own.

THE OTHER SIGNIFICANT OTHER (OSO)

One technique for managing different hobbies is the "other significant other" (OSO), a phrase coined by relationship scientist Eli Finkel. Modern couples often assume they can get all of their needs met by their romantic partner. They expect this one person to wear many hats—in fact, almost all of the hats; hats that had been dispersed among our social network before we were married.

Expecting our partners to fulfill all our needs puts a lot of pressure on relationships. OSOs help alleviate that pressure. Think of it this way: If you try to pile dozens of hats on one person's head, the pile (and maybe the person) will topple over. Instead, you can give the baseball cap to your sports-loving cousin and call *her* when you want to talk RBIs. You can give the cowboy hat to your friend who loves country music and make plans with *him* the next time you want a two-stepping partner.

Research from social psychologists Elaine Cheung, Wendi Gardner, and Jason Anderson supports this idea. They found that having multiple people you can turn to for emotional needs—rather than just one or two—leads to an increase in your overall well-being. For example, you might talk to your roommate when you're angry and depend on your sister when you're sad.

When you're in a relationship, here's how you can incorporate OSOs into your life. Consider what roles you've asked your partner to play that they are uninterested in fulfilling: for example, insisting they go to a party with you when they much prefer smaller gatherings. Or wishing your partner would suggest visits to museums and art galleries when it's just not their thing. Remember, just because they don't share all your interests doesn't make them a bad partner! And for those roles your partner isn't suited for, find a friend or family member who can fill in. In the long run, this will make *you* happier because your needs are being met. And it will make *your partner* happier because they can focus on roles that match their skills and interests.

WHAT MATTERS MORE THAN WE THINK

When I work with clients, I rarely hear them say their number one goal is to find someone who's emotionally stable. Or good at making hard decisions. Sometimes they'll mention kindness, but usually *after* telling me their height minimum and maximum. And yet these are all examples of qualities that relationship scientists have found contribute much more to long-term relationship success than superficial traits or shared interests.

It's not that people don't know that this stuff matters; rather, they just tend to underestimate the value of these attributes when deciding whom to date. (One reason is that these qualities can be hard to measure. They may be discernible only after spending time with someone. This also explains why dating apps focus on the easier-to-measure, matter-less-than-you-think traits, but more on that in the next chapter.) If you want to find a Life Partner, look for someone with the following traits:

1) Emotional Stability and Kindness

In his book *The Science of Happily Ever After*, psychologist Ty Tashiro digs into the existing research on what matters when choosing a partner. He found that emotional stability and kindness are two of the most important and yet underrated characteristics. He defines emotional stability as being able to self-regulate and not give in to anger or impulsivity. The combined emotional stability of a couple predicts the satisfaction and stability of their relationship.

In his 2017 TED Talk, Tashiro notes that "Kind partners are awesome. They're generous, they're empathic, and they want to be supportive of you." Kindness and emotional stability also allow us to treat our partner with care and compassion, which research from John and Julie Gottman suggests is the key to long-term relationship success.

Key tip for your dating search

You can get a sense of how kind someone is by paying attention to how they treat people from whom they don't need anything. Are they nice to the waiter? Do they give up their seat on the subway? Are they patient with new team members who are learning the ropes at work? Do they treat their friends and parents with compassion?

One way to get a sense of someone's emotional stability is to pay attention to how they respond to stressful situations. Do they freak out or keep their cool? Emotionally stable partners are measured in their responses. They take time to thoughtfully *respond* rather than impulsively *react*. When I explain this concept to my clients, I quote Viktor Frankl, a Holocaust survivor and celebrated psychiatrist. He wrote: "Between stimulus and response there is a space. In that space is our power to choose our response. In our response lies our growth and our freedom." Someone who is emotionally stable takes advantage of that space.

2) Loyalty

You know those fair-weather friends who are with you when life is going great but forget your number when you need help? A fair-weather friend may be fine in certain situations, but you don't want a fair-weather partner. Find someone who will be there for the good and the bad. Loyalty matters.

I often think about a passage my sister read in a speech at her wedding. (I also often think about how she rejected my multiple bids to officiate—who wouldn't want a modern-day yenta with them under the chuppah?) It's from an article by Robin Schoenthaler, a doctor who treats cancer patients, called "Will He Hold Your Purse?"

Schoenthaler explains that she's observed thousands of couples going through a crisis, which has taught her what really matters in a relationship: "It's a privilege to witness these couples, but the downside is I find myself muttering under my breath when my single female friends show me their ads for online dating. 'Must like long walks on beach at sunset, cats,' they write, or 'French food, kayaking, travel.' Or a perennial favorite: 'Looking for fishing buddy; must be good with bait.' These ads make me want to climb onto my cancer doctor soapbox and proclaim, 'Finding friends with fine fishing poles may be great in the short term. But what you really want to look for is somebody who will hold your purse in the cancer clinic.' "

My sister found a wonderful man who will hold her purse whenever she needs him to. In other words, she married someone who shows up for her, who takes care of her when she's down. Look for loyalty. Look for someone who's there for you whether you've won an industry award or are stuck in the cancer ward.

Key tip for your dating search

One easy way to estimate someone's loyalty is to see if they have friends from different stages of their lives. How many old friendships have they carried with them over the years? Did they ditch their college bestie when they got depressed, or do they still meet up for monthly movie matinees? Do people from their past seem to rely on them for companionship and support? Of course, there are exceptions to this rule, since some people have moved around a lot or lived in places where they didn't fit in. But in general, old friendships indicate loyalty.

3) A Growth Mindset

Stanford psychologist Carol Dweck has spent decades studying what she calls "fixed" and "growth" mindsets. People with a growth mindset believe that they can improve their intelligence and skills. They love to learn. They're motivated by challenges and see failure as a sign that they need to stretch their abilities. They're resilient and comfortable taking risks. Someone with a fixed mindset believes the opposite: that talent and intelligence are assigned at birth and taking a risk only presents an opportunity to embarrass yourself.

You want to align yourself with someone who has a growth mindset because when problems arise, which they inevitably will, you'll want a partner who will rise to the occasion, not throw up their hands in defeat. A person with a growth mindset is much more likely to buckle down and work on improving things rather than give up on the relationship and assume things can't be fixed.

Key tip for your dating search

You can spot people with a growth mindset by paying attention to how they handle themselves in different situations.

HOW TO SPOT A GROWTH MINDSET		
Situation	Fixed	Growth
How they approach challenges	Avoid them	Embrace them
How they respond to setbacks	Give up	Persist
How they view learning new skills	As a chance to embarrass themselves	As a chance to grow
How they respond to someone else's accomplishments	Feel threatened	Feel inspired
How they speak to themselves	With condemnation from a loud inner critic	With self-compassion

4) Personality That Brings Out the Best in You

In the end, a relationship is not about who each of you is separately, it's about what happens when the two of you come together. What does this person bring out in *you*? Does their kindness make you feel relaxed and cared for? Or does their anxiety provoke your anxiety?

You must understand what qualities they bring out in you, because this is who you'll be whenever you're with them.

A client met a guy who seemed perfect on paper. He had everything she thought she was looking for, especially in terms of intelligence and career success. Unfortunately, whenever they were together, he made her feel small. He'd ask her why she chose a certain recipe that was clearly above her cooking skill level. Or he'd make fun of the framed Picasso posters that hung on her wall. She'd leave dates with him questioning her decisions—and herself. At first, she thought his criticisms made her stronger. She tried to convince me he was merely trying to "up her game." But through our work together, she realized that he was actually very insecure and that *his* insecurity triggered her own insecurity. It didn't matter what he looked like on paper. In person, he made her feel bad about herself. She refused to choose a lifetime of self-doubt and ended things with him.

One of my friends says his girlfriend makes him feel competent. She asks for his advice—and takes it. She relies on him in a way that makes him feel important and capable. He loves the side of him that she brings out.

Key tip for your dating search

Pay attention to how you feel when you're around this person or right after you finish spending time together. Energized? Deflated? Bored? Challenged? Happy? Desired? Smart? Stupid? Select someone who brings out the best side of you.

It could also be helpful to get a third-party view by going out with a group of friends. Instead of asking, "What did you think of him?" ask, "What did you think of *me* around him?"

5) Skills to Fight Well

Fights aren't fun, but they don't necessarily spell disaster. If you lacked relationship role models who demonstrated how to fight and how to make up, don't fret. You can learn to fight well.

Fights—anything from a small disagreement to a screaming match—are a chance to deal with things as they come up instead of letting resentment build. A friend of mine prided himself on *not* fighting with his girlfriend. She had decorated their house, and he felt like there was no room for him. His interests and his stuff were not represented. He wanted to bring it up, but because he believed that avoiding conflict was a sign of a healthy relationship, he didn't. He grew more and more resentful of her over time. The lack of physical representation in their shared space started to seem like a metaphor for their whole relationship—he didn't see himself in it. He stopped investing in their partnership and began to spend most of his time at work, where he had his own office. By the time he finally broached the issue, it was too late. Too much space and resentment had grown between them, and they decided to end their five-year relationship.

The first step in fighting well is understanding that there are two types of problems in relationships: solvable problems and perpetual ones—unsolvable, permanent features of your partnership. John Gottman discovered that 69 percent of all relationship conflicts are perpetual.

Common examples of perpetual problems include situations where one person likes to go out while the other prefers to stay in, or where one person is neat and the other is messy. These might include differing opinions on work, family, ambition, money, and sexual frequency.

Imagine that you're someone who arrives five (okay, ten) minutes late to everything, and your significant other grew up in a family with the slogan "Early is on time, on time is late, and late means don't bother showing up." You'll inevitably fight over punctuality. You may find solutions to *manage* this difference, like going to the airport separately, but it's unlikely that you'll *solve* the problem. The goal is *not* to convince each other to change or even to come to an agreement—it's to find a productive way to live with this difference.

As the late couples therapist Dan Wile explained in his book *After the Honeymoon*: "When choosing a long-term partner, you will inevitably be choosing a particular set of unresolvable problems." The goal isn't to find someone with whom you don't fight. It's to choose a partner with whom you fight *well*, and who doesn't make you worry that the fight will end the relationship. The second element to fighting well is being able to recover from a disagreement. John Gottman writes about "repair attempts," statements or actions that prevent a fight from escalating. Successful couples are able to break the intensity of a fight by making a joke, conceding a point, or telling their partner what they appreciate about them.

Key tip for your dating search

Remember that you'll inevitably have disagreements with whomever you choose. Pay attention to how you fight. Are you able to get your point across? Do you feel heard? Does your partner make repair attempts to de-escalate the disagreement? The goal is to fight well, not to avoid fights altogether.

6) Ability to Make Hard Decisions with You

You and your partner will, at some point, face tough choices. What do you do if one of you gets an unbelievable job offer in another city? Or if you need to raise a child with a disability? How will you handle aging parents who need around-the-clock care? You want to be with someone who can make hard decisions with you.

One of my clients dated someone who lost her job the first month they were dating: She had to simultaneously mourn the loss of her dream job *and* look for new work. If she couldn't find something good quickly, she had to decide if she wanted to stay in San Francisco or move back east. While this was challenging, my client said that helping her through these tough choices revealed how well they functioned together in a challenging situation. It certainly wasn't fun, but it demonstrated their compatibility and strengthened their relationship.

Key tip for your dating search

The best way to know what it will be like to make decisions with someone is to actually make decisions together. Real decisions (read: not whether to order Chinese or Thai food). It's critical to stress-test your relationship. I am *not* recommending that you artificially create a crisis (such as texting: "HELP! Grandma's been kidnapped!"), but I *am* recommending you pay attention during shared experiences that challenge both of you. For example, what happens when you try to cook a complicated meal or travel internationally? Or when you're driving together and your car breaks down in the middle of the road? What do you do when you're each invited to a different wedding on the same weekend? How do you react when you're stuck deciding between two equally good (or equally bad) options?

Dan Ariely offers something called "the canoe test." Share a canoe. Yes, an actual canoe. Can you find a rhythm together? Is one of you comfortable leading and the other following, or do you both want to be in charge at all times? Most important, how much do you blame your partner when things go awry? Pay attention to how you literally navigate choppy water together as a team.

LEAVING THE PROM DATE AT THE PROM

As you've seen, the things that matter less than we think for long-term relationship success tend to be superficial traits that are easy to discern when you first meet someone. And the things that matter more usually reveal themselves only when you're in a relationship or have gone on at least a few dates. That's why you have to intentionally shift your approach in order to focus on what really matters.

Making that shift is hard. I know because I did it.

A long time ago, on a Saturday night about four months after Burning Man, I texted Brian to see what he was doing that night.

"I'm going to Bootie," he texted back, referring to a local dance party where DJs dress up as robots or pirates and drag queens vogue onstage. I wanted to join him but he didn't invite me.

My counteroffer: dinner, on me, beforehand. I figured that if I could remind him how much fun we had dancing in the desert, he'd ask me to join him.

After dinner I talked my way into joining his friends' pregame. Several drinks deep, I insisted on accompanying them to Bootie.

We stood outside as his friends entered the club. I was freezing, in a short leather skirt with a silk tank top tucked in (I'd chosen this outfit hoping to score an invite, and without considering San Francisco's notoriously cold summer nights). I shifted my weight back and forth on my wobbling heels.

He put his hands on my bare shoulders and looked me in the eyes. "Please don't follow me in. I want to go out with my friends and meet girls. You need to go home."

I cried and pleaded, but thirty minutes later, he walked away to join his friends inside the club.

Where had I gone wrong? No dating advice I'd encountered had covered that moment in your life when you're on the street, alone, outside of a lame club, eyeliner and snot dripping down your face, pining after someone who sends mixed messages and makes you feel foolish.

This wasn't my first time pursuing someone like Brian. I knew I was going after the wrong people, but I didn't know how to fix it. A week later, desperate to feel like I was still moving forward, I hired Nadia, a new age dating coach. (I didn't yet work in the business of love.)

Nadia and I sat cross-legged on the rug in her office/living room/ Zen garden/energy nexus. She helped me understand that I liked Brian because he was fun and exciting to be around but that he wasn't really what I was looking for in a husband, and I didn't like the anxious side of me he brought out. In her stern Russian accent, she said, "Your homework is to focus on how you want to *feel* in your relationship."

During our next meeting, I shared my response: "I want him to make me feel smart, funny, appreciated, and secure in our relationship."

Nadia nodded approvingly.

On the long walk home from that session, homework in hand, I felt frustrated. As much as I appreciated Nadia's help, I was still obsessing over Brian. Even in that moment, I wondered where he was and what (or whom) he was thinking about.

I checked my phone and considered sending him a text. In that moment, a calendar invitation popped up. It was from a guy at work named Scott.

We'd met eight years earlier, when we'd had lunch together in college with some mutual friends. The summer before this one, he'd reintroduced himself at the Google shuttle stop. Shortly after that, I'd invited him to another lunch—this time a Harvard alumni gathering at work. During that meal, I'd announced that I wanted to learn the statistics coding language R. He said he'd just dropped out of a math PhD program and offered to tutor me.

We started meeting weekly at work. He was a natural teacher—kind, patient, funny. "Based on the visualization you produced in R, what can you say about the distribution of eruption times for Old Faithful?" he asked me in one tutoring session.

"It's bimodal?"

"Yes!" he cheered, high-fiving me.

Unfortunately, he undermined our budding flirtation by mentioning his dislike of exotic travel and the Burning Man crowd. I wrote him off.

But that was before. On that walk home, I realized Scott had many of the qualities that I'd told Nadia I was looking for. And he made me feel smart, funny, appreciated, and secure in our relationship.

When I reevaluated Scott through the new lens of what mattered, I realized those initial surface-level preferences were distractions. I loved how I felt around him, even if he shuddered at the idea of staying up all night and partying in the desert. In the years since, I've discovered that Nadia's advice was not just smart—it was backed by mounds of research.

That fateful Saturday, walking through Dolores Park, looking down at the San Francisco skyline, I replied "yes" to his invitation for lunch.

That lunch turned into a weekly—and then daily—activity. We started calling each other to commiserate after our terrible online dates with strangers. He and his friend recorded a YouTube show—a parody of tech called "Silly Valley"—near my house, and we'd meet up for a few minutes before or after their tapings.

One day, as we said goodbye to each other after yet another lunch, he retrieved a white flower that had escaped a tree and put it into my hair.

"It feels like we're in a haiku," he said.

I told him I was free that Friday, and he asked me out. (So, technically, I asked him out.)

Scott was nothing like Brian. He made his interest in me clear. I felt excited to see him and spend time with him. There wasn't that voice in the back of my head wondering, *Does he like me?* because I knew he did. He'd send me texts like "I'm excited to spend time with you today"; "I like your brain"; and "I just want to rush into things with you."

Two weeks after our first official date, I sent him an aggressive text, annoyed about something he'd said. I knew from past relationships that this would launch us into a fight. I would sit on my couch, angrily poking at my phone, heart racing, eyes unblinking, as I rage-typed my disappointment in a volley of short, combative texts. I knew what would happen next: We'd go back and forth until I got so upset that I'd revert to some trusted old protest behaviors, likely ignoring his calls and texts. (Let's hear it for anxious-attachment styles!)

But we never went down that road. Instead, Scott wrote back, "Let's chat in person about this one." It was my first time dating someone so secure. It was a completely new experience. We discussed issues instead of careering headfirst into arguments. (It doesn't hurt that his mom is a therapist.)

It's been six years since I invited Scott to that lunch at Google.

We've now shared two Burning Mans (he eventually came around to it), a five-day scuba diving trip in Thailand, and an apartment. We've killed one basil plant and three succulents.

We're happy. We say R is our love language.

KEY TAKEAWAYS

1. Relationship science can teach us what really matters for committed long-term relationships. **Seek Life Partners: people who are trustworthy and reliable and who will stay with you for the long haul. Avoid Prom Dates: individuals who are fun in the short term but ultimately let you down.**

2. **Superficial qualities like looks and money matter less for long-term relationship success than people think they do** because lust fades and people adapt to their circumstances. The same goes for shared hobbies and similar personalities.

3. **A great long-term partner is loyal, kind, and emotionally stable,** a person with whom you can grow, make hard decisions, and fight constructively.

4. In the end, a relationship is about what happens when the two of you come together. **Focus on the side of you this person brings out,** because that's who you'll be whenever you're with them.

GETTING OUT THERE

CHAPTER 8

YOU THINK YOU KNOW WHAT YOU WANT, BUT YOU'RE WRONG

How to Avoid the Pitfalls of Online Dating

I once swiped left on Scott on Tinder.

I told you how I met him—in college and then years later at the Google shuttle stop. What I neglected to mention is that before he started tutoring me, I saw him on Tinder. I flipped through his photos and then rejected him.

It was 2014, and I was heading home from work on the shuttle bus, stuck in San Francisco's dreary traffic, when Tinder served up a photo of a guy who looked vaguely familiar. We had enough friends in common that I knew we must have gone to the same college. Backward baseball hat. Tank top. Unsmiling eyes squinting harshly into the sun. He looked like a bro. Not my type. I swiped left.

Why did I reject this person—someone who has made me very happy—when I saw him online? How did I come to such an inaccurate conclusion about him?

I thought I knew what I wanted and what would make me happy in a long-term relationship. And I believed I could accurately evaluate someone based on a few photos.

I was wrong on both counts.

I'm not the only one prone to these kinds of errors. Many of my clients have everything going for them—great personalities, friends, hobbies, and so on—but remain perpetually single. Why? They're dating wrong. It's not their fault, and it's not yours. We can often blame it on the apps.

According to research by Stanford sociology professor Michael J. Rosenfeld, "met online" is the most common way romantic partners connect today, followed by "met in a bar or restaurant" and then "met through friends." (Less common responses included: "at the rodeo," "while complaining to random strangers about how much I hate these f**king dating apps," and "Red Lobster.")

In the last twenty years, digital dating has exploded: Rosenfeld found that while only 2 percent of couples met online in 1995, 39 percent now meet that way. And as more couples connect digitally, fewer meet through social connections—like friends, family, and work—or through communities like school and church.

Much like we've seen with all social media giants, while apps create many thriving relationships, they can also perpetuate harmful cognitive biases among their users. Since so many people are meeting this way—and even people who don't use the apps often go out with people who do—app makers have a subtle but astonishing amount of power over our love lives. They are designing the environment in which we make decisions about dating. And, by extension, they deeply influence the decisions we make.

Traditional economics assumes people have consistent, static preferences. But behavioral scientists know that's a lie. The truth is, our **environment matters**. We're impacted by the setting in which we make our decision, whether that's a physical location or a digital landscape. What we choose is highly affected by how the options are displayed. We may think preferences are permanent, but they're actually rather pliable.

Here's an example of how that plays out with our food choices. A few years ago, Google diagnosed its employees with "an M&M

problem." To nudge them into making healthier food decisions, an internal team of behavioral scientists changed the environment in which the snacks were presented. They stopped offering M&M's in giant clear bins that enticed snackers with the multicolored chocolate treats. They moved the candies to clearly labeled but opaque containers, where they would be less tempting. Healthier snacks, like dried figs and pistachios, sat nearby in clear glass jars.

These were bright tech workers who had known the healthy snacks were available the whole time. But merely changing the *environment* in which food choices were presented resulted in employees eating 3.1 million fewer M&M calories over seven weeks in the New York office alone. According to the *Washington Post*, which covered the experiment, "that's a decrease of nine vending machine-size packages of M&M's for each of the office's 2,000 employees." In the Google office, nothing changed about the employees' preferences. But those opaque containers made all the difference. That environment had a huge impact on employees' choices.

When it comes to modern dating, our decision-making environment is the dating app. We're affected by the way the app presents certain matches and the order in which those matches appear on our screens. That's why my clients tell me about swiping no on someone on one app and then swiping yes on that same person on a different app a few weeks later. These small contextual differences have a big impact on our decisions.

To be clear, I am not anti-app. Apps have introduced millions of happy couples who may not have met otherwise. Dating apps have been especially meaningful for singles in so-called thin markets, including the LGBTQ+ community; people in sparsely populated areas; and daters over the age of fifty. And not all dating apps are the same. I'm a fan of those that focus on helping people get off the app and on real dates.

(In fact, after writing this book I took a job as the Director of Relationship Science at Hinge. Not only is Hinge singularly focused on getting their users off the apps and on real dates—as evidenced by their slogan "Designed to be deleted"—they also hired me to do exactly what I hope to accomplish with this book: help millions of people around the world learn how to date more effectively.)

But unfortunately, the way that certain dating apps present information can cause us to focus on the wrong things.

It doesn't have to be that way. I'll teach you how to make the apps work for you so that you can take advantage of digital dating while avoiding possible pitfalls.

WE'RE DATING WRONG

I was in the middle of writing an email when Jonathan knocked at my door, fifteen minutes late for his first session. I had figured he wasn't going to show.

"Sorry, sorry!" he said, extending his giant hand to me. "I got stuck at work."

Jonathan was tall, fit, and charming. His dimples appeared when he smiled or pronounced the letter "c," as in "CEO," his current title. He was from the Midwest and had lived in San Francisco for about five years. He'd been single for most of them, save for a few connections that had seemed promising but then fizzled. After years of struggling on dating apps, he'd come to me for help.

During our first few sessions, I learned what a high standard Jonathan held himself to and how successful he'd been in other areas of his life: student body president in college, winner of major international awards, Rhodes Scholar, and more. He was ambitious but also thoughtful and funny. (You know, the kind of person your parents would longingly compare you to.)

He said, "I've been using the apps, and I've been on a ton of dates. I know what I want, but I just haven't found him yet. I'm looking for an in-shape business executive who's at least six-four. Can you help?"

"Yes, I can help," I responded. "But not in the way you think."

Jonathan didn't need an introduction to the *right* tall business-man. He needed to completely reset his mindset for dating. That began with understanding all the ways in which the apps were affecting him.

Issue #1: Our brains focus on what's measurable and easily comparable. Apps display superficial traits, making us value these qualities even more.

As we discussed in the previous chapter, decades of relationship science have revealed what matters for long-term relationship success: things like if the person is emotionally stable, kind, and loyal, and how that person makes us feel.

Yet current dating apps don't let you search for *any* of those qualities. How could they? It's hard enough to accurately measure personality traits, let alone what those traits would elicit in *you*. Instead, dating apps are limited by the information they can reliably capture and catalog: height, age, college, job, and how good someone is at selecting flattering pictures that make them look cool yet approachable, sexy but playful.

This is a problem. As management consultants love to say, "You are what you measure." In a column on this topic for the *Harvard Business Review*, behavioral economist Dan Ariely wrote: "Human beings adjust behavior based on the metrics they're held against. Anything you measure will impel a person to optimize his score on that metric. What you measure is what you'll get. Period." If you create a frequent-flyer reward system where you measure miles flown and tell customers that this number matters, Ariely explained, customers respond. They start booking absurd flights from faraway airports to maximize their miles. In other words, we're suggestible—show us a metric and we'll assume it's important. While people have always prized certain superficial traits, the apps make us think they're even *more* important simply by measuring, presenting, and emphasizing them.

University of Chicago professor Chris Hsee writes about a related concept called **evaluability**: The easier it is to compare certain traits, the more important those traits seem.

Imagine this scenario (and for the sake of this thought experiment, imagine you're interested in men). I walk up to you on the street and say: "You can go on a date with one of these two single men. One guy is five-nine and one is five-ten, but the shorter one makes more money. Who do you want to go out with?"

Most likely, you'd walk away slowly, confused why a stranger was asking you such a weird question. If you decided to stick around, I'd follow up with another question: "How much more money per year would a shorter guy have to make for you to find him as attractive as a taller man?"

At that point, you might laugh awkwardly and tell me it was impossible to come up with such a number. But thanks to research from Dan Ariely, we know it's not. He discovered that there is, in fact, a quantifiable correlation between height, income, and finding success on the dating apps. And it's not small. Using data from a popular dating website, Ariely found that a man has to earn $40,000 more each year to be as desirable as a man one inch taller.

Yes: $40,000.

Evaluability helps us understand why. In real life, you may meet guys who are five-nine and five-ten and barely notice their height difference. (And you certainly won't know their income—unless they tell you, unprompted, which is gross.) But as we just learned, the more a quality can be compared, the more important that trait seems. Apps make it easy to compare height. While women have long favored tall men, the digital world exacerbates this preference. Because of the explicit height comparison across online dating profiles, shorter men are at a much greater disadvantage than they would be in the real world. No wonder Jonathan was so focused on the height of his potential husband!

You may be asking yourselves, how much does a *woman's* income affect her desirability? Turns out it doesn't. High earners don't inspire single men on that dating website the way they inspire single women. Instead, the quality that men cared about most when evaluating attractiveness was body mass index (BMI). They preferred a woman whose BMI was 18.5—slightly underweight—and didn't care about her salary or her level of education. Again, it's not that men actually value thinness in potential life partners above all else— they're just stuck working with a limited set of comparable qualities. (Also, ughhhhh.)

Which brings me back to why I swiped left on Scott on Tinder. I was selecting potential partners based on the superficial traits featured on the dating apps, and I'd created an image of an ideal partner that he just didn't fit. If you'd asked me when I was swiping what I'd wanted in a partner, do you think I would've said "five-eight redheaded vegan engineer"? No, probably not. I easily could have set a height minimum of five-nine and never even seen Scott. Yet—after dating more than my fair share of people—I found that he is the man who makes me the happiest. (And it turns out he's nothing like the bro his pictures made him out to be.)

This is all to say that the apps may lead us astray by emphasizing measurable and comparable qualities. They can trick us into valuing these traits while ignoring the qualities that relationship science tells us matter most.

Issue #2: We think we know what we want, but we're wrong. The apps allow us to filter out great potential matches.

My clients often come to me with long checklists of all the qualities they want in a partner. But the strange thing is that most of us have not dated *that* many people. We have relatively little experience, especially where it counts for figuring out compatibility in long-term relationships. Yet we think we are experts in what will make us happy.

This is a major point! Underline this next sentence, please: Most of us have no idea what kind of partner will fulfill us long term.

Yes, we *think* we know what we want. Yes, we have that long checklist. But those are likely *not* the qualities possessed by the person we fall in love with. Our eventual partner may be completely different from what we expected. Remember, I wasn't looking for a vegan engineer.

Being wrong about who would make you happy long term is not a new problem created by technology. But in real life, you're exposed to all kinds of potential partners: tall and short, fat and thin, intellectual, funny, introverted, religious, atheist, whatever. If you're looking for a partner in the physical world—at a book club, a pottery class, your friend's birthday party—you meet people who aren't your so-called type. You could develop a flirtation, and then a relationship, with one of them. You might be pleasantly surprised by how wrong you were about needing to date someone who, say, is taller than you or grew up religious.

But dating apps never give you the chance to be proved wrong, because you can weed out people who aren't your "type." I once conducted in-person interviews with folks who met their husband or wife offline. I asked, "If you had seen your current spouse online, would you have swiped right or left?" Many people told me they wouldn't have seen their future partner at all because their app settings would've shut them out. "My age limit was up to one year older than me, and she's five years older than me," one guy told me. "My app setting was for Jewish men only, and he identifies as Buddhist," another said.

Many digital services require you to go through an onboarding process when you sign up. Netflix, for example, asks what kinds of movies you like. For dating apps, it's what kind of people: What's the youngest person you'd date? What's the oldest? What's the tallest or shortest person you'd date? Do you care if this person smokes? Does drugs? Drinks?

From a practical perspective, it makes sense that apps use the onboarding process to limit the number of potential matches. Dating apps can't show us an infinite number of people. They have to narrow things down somehow. But most people aren't making these decisions carefully. You see, during the onboarding phase, users are in a rush to see potential matches as quickly as possible. They answer the questions with about as much forethought as they'd use when filling out a make-your-own sandwich form at the grocery store. But unlike smoked turkey, Dijon mustard, and extra-sharp cheddar, the ingredients we hastily select for our dating profiles may or may not make us happy.

These decisions have a huge impact on our dating experience. The constraints we set filter out potentially great matches. This would be like rushing through your sandwich order because you're hungry for lunch, marking off a box that says "Turkey only," and then finding that every time you went to get a sandwich in the future, you could look at only turkey sandwiches.

Of course, we *could* change our preferences on the dating apps after we sign up, but most people don't. This is because of something called the **status quo bias**—our tendency to leave things as they are, to not rock the boat. That's why businesses with subscription-service models tend to be lucrative. If you sign up for a gym membership and it's automatically renewed each month, you're much less likely to make the call to cancel than if you had to decide every month whether you want to keep the service.

The same thing happens when people sign up for a dating app. Once people set app preferences during onboarding, they're very unlikely to change them. The apps show us people who meet our initial criteria—the type of people we *think* we want. If you believe that you'd hate dating a woman who's taller than you are, and the apps offer you only short women to choose from, you never get the chance to be proved wrong.

Issue #3: Apps promote "relationshopping"—searching for potential partners like potential purchases.

Many of us conduct extensive research before making a purchase. If you wanted to buy a camera, for example, you might compare and contrast along every potential axis—megapixel count, image quality, weight, battery life, cost, and so on. Dating apps create the illusion that we can do the same comparison shopping with potential partners.

In fact, while researchers once called the process of transitioning from strangers or friends to romantic partners as "relationshipping," they now speak of a new phenomenon—"relationshopping"—searching for our mate like we'd search for a new pair of shoes. But treating potential partners like potential purchases gets us into trouble.

A team of behavioral economists, including Michael Norton and Dan Ariely, explained in a research paper that many consumer items are "searchable goods": things like cameras, laundry detergent, and big-screen TVs that can be measured based on their objective attributes. These differ from "experience goods," which they define as being "judged by the feelings they evoke, rather than the functions they perform. Examples include movies, perfume, puppies, and restaurant meals—goods defined by attributes that are subjective, aesthetic, holistic, emotive, and tied to the production of sensation. Most importantly, people must be present to evaluate them; they cannot be judged secondhand." We've all seen a movie that got bad reviews but made us laugh. Or tasted wine that earned amazing reviews but didn't taste good to us. We've been pleasantly surprised or surprisingly disappointed by experiencing these goods ourselves. The process of evaluation was more personal than just knowing that we wanted a wide-angle lens.

People, the authors of this paper tell us, are experience goods. We are not like cameras. We are much more like wine. (If you're like me, you're also full-bodied, a little dry, and getting better with age.) We cannot be understood by comparing and contrasting our parts. Yet dating apps have turned living, breathing, three-dimensional people into two-dimensional, searchable goods. They've given us the false belief that we can break people down into their parts and compare them to find the best one.

Apps primarily give us a list of résumé traits and nothing more. Only by spending time with someone can you appreciate that person for the "experiential good" they are.

Issue #4: Apps make us more indecisive about whom to date.

The first night I downloaded Tinder, I spent six hours swiping. Yes, that's longer than it would take to binge-watch the entire first season of *Fleabag*. I went through hundreds, possibly thousands, of profiles. As if it weren't enough that dating apps can confuse us about what's important, they can also make it harder to choose whom to go out with. Our brains aren't set up to select a partner from so many options.

Remember what psychologist Barry Schwartz discovered about the paradox of choice: We assume that more choice will make us happier, but that's often not the case. In fact, too many options make us *less* happy, in part because of choice overload. It can feel so overwhelming to compare our options that we may give up and make no decision at all.

Columbia professor Sheena Iyengar and Stanford professor Mark Lepper demonstrated this in a now-famous study. They entered a gourmet grocery store and set up a table of free gourmet jam samples. When they offered twenty-four types of jam, people were more likely to approach the table than when they offered six jams. However, customers who sampled from among the twenty-four jams were far less likely to buy any jams than those who encountered only six options. The researchers hypothesized that when you have six options, it's possible to make a confident decision about which jam you'll like the most. But twenty-four options are so overwhelming that people often make no decision at all.

In a grocery store, that might mean leaving with no jam. In the world of dating apps, that means not finding a relationship (also, sadly, no jam). And selecting a potential partner is way harder than selecting a jam out of twenty-four options: choosing from not just twenty-four but thousands of people and perhaps committing to one for the rest of your life. In dating, we may feel so overwhelmed by the options that we decide not to go on any dates at all. Even if we do, it can feel impossible to know whom to date seriously.

It's not just that too many choices make it hard to decide. Schwartz tells us that even when we're able to overcome choice overload and make a selection, having so many options to choose from makes us less satisfied with what we choose. (This effect can be amplified when you're a Maximizer, as discussed in Chapter 4.)

We start to think: *What if I'd chosen something else? Would that have been better? Would I be happier?* That train of thought leads down a dark path toward regret. And the effect multiplies. The more options you have to choose from, the more chances you have to feel regret about your selection. This can even lead to feelings of depression.

In this case, *more is less*—or at least less fulfilling.

I've worked with all kinds of daters. I know that not everyone experiences the paradox of choice in dating. It depends on factors like race, age, gender, orientation, and location, which all affect the size of your dating pool. (Plenty of my clients *wish* they had too many options to choose from.) But if you're someone who's getting a lot of matches, or you're caught up in the game of seeing how many people you can swipe on, you might already understand the impact of the paradox of choice. Remember, the point of a dating app is to go out on an actual date, not to spend all of your evenings swiping.

Issue #5: When we see only a rough sketch of someone, we fill in the gaps with flattering details. We create an unrealistic fantasy of this person, which ultimately leaves us disappointed.

In *Clueless,* one of my all-time favorite movies, Tai, the new girl, asks Cher, the most popular girl in school, what she thinks about their classmate Amber. Cher says, "She's a full-on Monet. It's like a painting, see. From far away, it's okay, but up close it's a big ol' mess."

I call this error in judgment the **Monet Effect**. When we have only a rough perception of someone, our brain, hoping for a great outcome, fills in all the gaps optimistically. People seem way more desirable than they actually are. It's only later, when they transform into real people standing in front of us, that we see the flaws.

We can see this play out in the corporate world. When companies search for a new CEO, they can choose between promoting an internal candidate or hiring an external one. Research into these decisions found that companies who decide to hire externally have sky-high expectations of the candidates. When you evaluate external candidates, you know only the broad details about them. They tell you about their wins. Internal candidates, you know more intimately; you are familiar with their successes *and* their failures. The Monet Effect helps explain why, when compared to internal candidates, external CEOs are often paid more but perform worse.

The same thing happens with dating. Looking at a dating app profile is the equivalent of seeing someone from very far away. All you get are a few carefully selected photos and some basic information. You go out on the date, and maybe the pitch of their voice bothers you or they have bad table manners or you are not aligned on the time and place for dad jokes (them: always; you: on *Full House* reruns only). Instead of those flaws seeming normal—because they are, and everyone has some—they leave you greatly disappointed. There goes the perfect person you built up in your mind. In the bathroom, you can't help but open Tinder. Time for the ol' swipe-and-wipe. You give up on the date you're on and start fantasizing about the next person on your screen, who seems perfect because of the Monet Effect. But as soon as you meet *that* match in person, you realize they have flaws, too, and the cycle continues. This creates a grass-is-always-greener reaction: You always think the next thing will be better than what you have. You're dooming yourself to an endless cycle of unrealized connections.

DATE SMARTER

All of these issues are working against you, making it harder to meaningfully choose whom to date. You're focusing on factors that are less important than you think and comparing people in ways that don't reflect their true potential. But there are ways to use the apps to date smarter.

Change Your Filters

The people you see on the apps are a reflection of the restrictions you set up when you joined. Think back to that time. There you were. You'd just downloaded the app. You were full of hope. Birds were chirping. When asked to choose your settings, such as height and age preferences, you likely rushed through this step, because you knew hundreds of potential love interests were waiting for you on the other side.

And, for all the reasons above, you might have made a mistake. While you may *think* you know what you want in a partner, you're probably wrong. Therefore, I want you to be more open-minded about whom you allow the apps to show you. Take out your phone and update your settings. Yes, on all the apps. Yes, right now. For the people you're filtering out, whom you once thought were too young or too old, could you be more flexible? And would you really not date a great person outside your stated height range?

Also think about your non-numerical requirements, like "must have graduate degree" or "must be Catholic." Those yes/no switches probably represent preferences for deeper values—intellectual curiosity or a connection to tradition—that the apps have difficulty capturing.

Do this now. Seriously, I'll wait. (I've been craving a smoked turkey, Dijon mustard, and extra-sharp cheddar sandwich for the last fifteen minutes anyway.)

I completed this exercise with Jonathan. He broadened his height requirements and immediately saw way more men than before. Intelligence and sense of humor were still must-haves, but Jonathan recognized that he'd have to look for those qualities by reading people's profiles, messaging with them, and getting to know them on actual dates. The apps couldn't filter those for him.

Change How You Swipe

You've updated your selection *settings*. Now it's time to update your selection *process*.

Challenge your assumptions. One time I observed my client making her way through an app. We came across a guy who looked cute and had a funny bio. She swiped left. I asked her why, and she said, "He was a consultant, and consultants are boring." What?! All consultants? Every single one? She was assuming she knew everything she needed to know based on one fact about this person's life. What you do isn't who you are. And people with the same job can be completely different.

Here's another example: I worked with a client who loved traveling and wanted someone who had also traveled extensively. I helped her understand that adventure and curiosity were the underlying traits that mattered to her, not how many countries he'd been to.

Fast-forward a few months. She met a lovely guy who had never left the country before because he'd lacked the financial means to travel. However, he shared those values we'd identified. For him, that had manifested in starting his own business. She helped him get his first passport. Now they travel together constantly. If she had filtered only for people with a passport full of stamps—as she'd originally intended—she never would've given him a chance.

Just because you know where people have been or where they are now doesn't mean you know where they're going.

Look for reasons to say yes. It's tempting to approach dating apps as an exercise in discovering what's wrong with people or finding a reason to say no. Instead, try to be less judgmental. I've seen people swipe no when they read something like "teacher" ("Oh, he won't make enough money for me") or "yoga instructor" ("I don't want to date someone who worships crystals and wants to activate my chakras"). You don't know these people. You're seeing a tiny sliver of who they are—a few photos and some basic information. If someone is a maybe, swipe right now and see what happens. As you evaluate potential matches, look for what's attractive about someone rather than what turns you off.

Deciphering traits by looking at the apps is more of an art than a science. Don't assume you know what people mean by their answers. Does checking "yes" to "occasionally does drugs" mean "I'll take an edible on a camping trip" or "I go on the occasional black-tar heroin binge"? Does checking "Catholic" mean "I was raised Catholic but am not actively practicing" or "I'm in the front pew every Sunday"? Don't presume you know exactly what people meant when they answered the same vague questions you struggled with. Why not meet them and explore these topics in person?

Go on dates with people whom you don't necessarily think are a fit. That's the only way you can *figure out* what you actually like rather than assuming you already know.

A woman I know posted a rant on Facebook about how "sad and misguided" online daters are these days. As evidence, she posted a picture of a recent profile she'd seen. In response to the prompt "My most irrational fear," he'd written, "Marrying someone with a name that isn't conducive to a wedding hashtag." She found the answer flippant and—I'm quoting her Facebook post here—thought it represented "the downfall of millennial dating." (If you're not familiar with wedding hashtags, it's when the couples combine their names into a punny phrase that people use when posting pictures from their wedding. For example, when my friend Dani married her husband, Eric Helitzer, her hashtag was #highwaytohelitzer, a reference to the AC/DC song.)

I, and many of the people who commented on the post, disagreed.

At first, I resisted the urge to engage, but then I couldn't *not* say something. I responded "My $.02: I think it's a mistake to judge someone too harshly for their response to a single question on a dating app. I've watched many people create their profiles and they complete the process as quickly as possible so they can start seeing matches right away. Perhaps this answer is a little flippant for you, but I think it's funny and tongue-in-cheek. This response suggests to me that he's been to enough weddings to roll his eyes at wedding hashtags, so perhaps he's a loyal guy with a big friend group. And if a lot of his pals are married, maybe he's feeling ready to settle down, too. His answer also suggests he loves puns and hopes to marry someone whose name is conducive to a punny hashtag."

She wrote back that she *loved* puns and was willing to rethink her original perspective on the guy. She said she wished she could go back and say yes to him.

Look, I'm not saying you should swipe yes on almost everyone. Rather, be open to the fact that someone may be far more interesting in person than a profile suggests.

Don't Go Out With Too Many People at the Same Time

At this point, you might be wondering, *Wait, isn't this the opposite of the advice you just gave me?* No. I want you to broaden your filters to see different kinds of people and go out with some of them. But—and this is a big "but"—I don't want you going on tons of dates at the same time. That will only make the Monet Effect worse.

It's easy to keep swiping, swiping, swiping, and setting up dates. If you're feeling addicted to the apps, it's not your fault. Really. Many believe Tinder was intentionally designed that way. While conducting research for her documentary, *Swiped: Hooking Up in the Digital Age,* journalist Nancy Jo Sales discovered that Tinder was inspired partly by psychology experiments—in particular, those in which famed behaviorist B. F. Skinner conditioned pigeons into thinking that their random pecks would lead to food. "That's the whole swiping mechanism," Sales said on Kara Swisher's *Recode Decode* podcast. "You swipe, you might get a match, you might not. And then you're just, like, excited to play the game." No wonder I spent six hours on Tinder that first night. (And once went on 8.5 first dates in a week. I'm still trying to figure out what that half a date was.)

Choose not to play the apps like a game. You'll make better decisions if you pace yourself and go out with a limited number of people at once. Try to really get to know them. If expanding your settings means a bigger menu, then dating fewer people at a time means savoring each dish.

One of my clients doesn't go out with more than three people at a time. She finds that's her perfect number, at which she can give each person a chance to let the relationship grow but also can compare how she's feeling with each one. If you go overboard and chat with too many people at once, or constantly fill in your calendar with first dates, you are likely to end up like the person who sampled from the table with twenty-four jams. You'll try more jams but won't know which one to buy. The result? A lonely walk home, a bellyache from all that sugar, and dry toast.

HOW TO WORK THE APPS SO THEY WORK FOR YOU

Thus far, we've talked about how you should assess other people's profiles. Meanwhile, they're also evaluating yours. If you're struggling to get the results you want, here are some evidence-based tips for getting more matches and going on better dates.

Select Great Photos

Duh, photos matter. They take up the most real estate on most apps. People will often swipe on someone based on a photo alone and scroll down to see more information only *if* they like the first photo.

Hinge researchers studied which types of photos elicited the most positive responses from its users, which it shared in a 2017 blog post. For this analysis, they randomly selected profile photos of a thousand members, tagged them based on their qualities (such as candid versus posed, smiling with or without teeth), and evaluated their performance. Here are practical tips based on their findings:

- Don't create any guessing games about what you look like or if you're single. Pictures that feature filters or possible significant others received 90 percent fewer likes than those without. That means no sunglasses and no pics in which you're posing with someone people may think you're dating. Potentially worse? A group photo with no clear indication of which person you are. I call these *Where's Waldo?* shots. Select at most one group pic and clearly mark which face is yours.

- Women see around a 70 percent boost in their chances of getting a like simply by including photos where they're standing alone, looking away, or smiling with teeth.

- Similarly, men see a boost in their chances of getting a like by standing alone, smiling *without* teeth, and looking straight toward the camera.

- Candids seriously outperform posed photos. While about 80 percent of posted pics are posed, candid shots are 15 percent more likely to receive a like.

- Selfies perform poorly, especially bathroom selfies, which decrease your chance of getting a like by 90 percent. (Pro tip: When meeting new love prospects, try not to associate yourself with the toilet.) Show us that you have a friend who can take a photo of you.

- Black-and-white photos kill. Despite making up only 3 percent of posted photos, they see a 106 percent boost in likes. Consider going monochrome for your next pic.

From helping my clients set up their profiles, I've found that most people are pretty bad at selecting their most attractive photos. I've developed a system to help. I ask my clients to send me ten to twenty potential photos. With their approval, I put them together in an online album and send them to contacts of mine around the country who are unlikely to ever meet my client. Those people rank the photos, indicating which pictures they like, which they'd delete, and which they'd use as the important first photo. There's often a consensus around which photos work best; it's almost *never* the photos my client chose for themselves. Once I see a pattern, I rearrange my client's photos to reflect the feedback.

EXERCISE: Select Better Photos

Collect ten to twenty photos of yourself (ideally a combination of photos of your face, your full body, and you doing an activity you love, like cooking or hiking) and send them to several friends. Ask which pictures they'd include, which they'd delete, and which they'd use as the first photo. Or run your own experiment on the apps: Swap out different photos to see which ones lead to the most matches.

Write a Thoughtful Profile

Present yourself accurately. I once coached a woman named Abby who claimed she was looking for an outdoorsy guy: She was attracted to "lumbersexuals"—hipster guys with beards and plaid shirts. Her photos included one of her hiking, and her profile mentioned an interest in nature. Yet the truth was, she hated spending time in nature. "Abby," I said to her, "your luggage tag literally says, 'I love not camping.' This isn't you. This is who you *want to be* for the type of guy you think you should be with." Through our work together, we crafted a profile that was much truer to her personality. We included artsy photographs of her from a recent trip to Berlin. We wrote about her passion for live jazz and overpriced whiskey. While it seems obvious, a good profile should represent *you*, not an aspirational version of yourself. Being up front about who you are will help save you heartache down the road, like Abby having to tell her hypothetical lumbersexual boyfriend that she doesn't want to join him for a five-day avalanche training course.

To spark conversations be specific. The point of a profile is to spark conversation, not come across as overly clever. Make sure your profile creates opportunities for people to follow up and connect. Let's take the Hinge prompt: "Qualities I'm looking for in a plus-one wedding date." If you write, "Someone who's not married," that's funny, but it doesn't really open the door to conversation. Instead, if you put "Knowing all the words to 'Wannabe' by the Spice Girls," that could spark a chat around nineties music or who will sing the Scary Spice part when you do karaoke. If you write, "Someone who will challenge me to a dance-off," that's a great opener for a chat about signature go-to moves. The best way to spark conversation is to be specific. Include quirky things that make you stand out. If you say, "I like music," that doesn't really tell me anything about you. Cool, who doesn't? Same with writing that you like travel, food, and laughter. That's like saying you like Tom Hanks. Yeah, dude, he's an American hero. Don't tell me you like to cook; describe to me your signature dish and what makes your Vietnamese soup pho-nomenal. The more specific you are, the more opportunities you give potential matches to connect by commenting on that quirk.

Focus on what you like, not what you don't. I've been surprised by the number of people who fill their—limited!—profile space with what they're *not* looking for. I understand the urge, but this sends a negative message. Your vibe attracts your tribe. Use the space to attract people who share your actual hobbies, not your hobby of complaining. Focus on what brings you joy, not what you hate or are trying to avoid. (By the way, have you noticed that people who say, "No drama, please," often tend to engage in the *most* drama?)

Craft Your Opening Line

Enough with "Hey" and "How's it going?" Don't ask people how their weekend was. That's boring! Good opening lines are (again) specific.

The goal of an opening line is to get a conversation going so that you can meet up with someone in person. Look at the profile and comment on something subtle, a detail that not everyone would notice. Use a touch of humor. For example, if a man is always looking away from the camera in his photos, you could say, "I see you like pictures where you're peering off mysteriously into the distance. I'm dying to know what's out of frame!" Or if someone's profile mentions a love for the show *The Office,* message with your favorite Michael Scott quote. (You can steal my personal favorite: "Make friends first, make sales second, make love third. In no particular order.") Show that you've put effort into your opener.

And for goodness' sake, send a message when you match with someone! Why are you swiping if you're not going to follow up?

Stay in Touch

You have a life to live. Don't stare at your screen all hours of the day and night. Even if you have a super-busy day, try to set aside fifteen minutes to respond to messages, maybe during your commute or when you're procrastinating at work. You want to keep the momentum going.

Cut to the Chase

Get to the actual date as quickly as possible. The point of the apps is to meet people face-to-face, not to gain a pen pal. I've seen over and over the negative consequences of messaging too much before a date. When people text nonstop before a date, they end up creating a fantasy of each other in their minds (#themoneteffect). When they meet up, the person is inevitably unlike the fantasy, which leads to disappointment, even if they would've been a good match otherwise. Great text chemistry doesn't necessarily mean you'll vibe in person. Wouldn't you rather figure that out sooner?

A good transition from texting to a date might sound like this: "I'm really enjoying this conversation. Want to continue it over a walk on Sunday afternoon?"

Make it easy to meet up. One way to do this is to propose a specific day and time for your date. "If you're as charming in real life as you are over text, we may be onto something. Drinks Thursday? Seven p.m.?" You may have to go back and forth to find a time that works for both of you, but this way, you start to narrow down your options. It kills the excitement and momentum when you spend so much time scheduling.

And sometimes that happens. It's not necessarily from lack of interest; people are often just busy. What's the best way to move from an online chat to an in-person date after a lot of back-and-forth texts? I recommend calling out the situation, but in a kind and playful manner. "I really enjoy our text banter and would love to see if we get along this well in person. What do you think about a quick drink this week?"

Or the next time they start to tell you something interesting:

"Wait, wait, wait. I need to hear this in person! When are you free this week to meet up and tell me the rest of this story?"

A BETTER WAY TO DATE

Look, I know this is hard. It may feel like the universe is against you, designed to confuse you and keep you from finding love. But there's hope. If you want a break from the apps, the next chapter covers how to meet people in real life. Yep, IRL. It's still possible, even if you've given up on that ever happening. And in the chapter after that, I'll help you find ways to make dating fun again. Imagine that.

KEY TAKEAWAYS

1. We think we know what we want when it comes to a partner, but our intuition about what will lead to long-term happiness is often wrong.

2. **Dating apps may cause us to focus on the wrong things.** We value what gets measured. Because apps can only measure superficial traits, they exacerbate our shallowness.

3. **Apps can make us more indecisive by overwhelming us with choices.** They've created a habit of relationshopping—comparing and contrasting people as if they're potential purchases.

4. We can **learn to swipe smarter** by expanding our settings to see more people, being less judgmental when we swipe, dating fewer people at a time, and transitioning to the date faster.

CHAPTER 9

MEET PEOPLE IRL (IN REAL LIFE)

How to Find Love
off the Dating Apps

"That's it!" Alicia said, throwing down her backpack and kicking off her shoes before she'd even closed the door to my office. "I'm done with the apps."

After years of swiping, my client Alicia, a twenty-eight-year-old nursing-school student, was still struggling to find her partner. Thousands of swipes had turned into very few first dates and almost no second ones.

Alicia is Black. I haven't referenced the race of my other clients thus far, but I need to mention it here because racism pervades online dating. It makes an already challenging experience that much more painful for Black women. Christian Rudder analyzed the behavior of users on OkCupid, the dating site he cofounded, on both the company's blog and in his book, *Dataclysm*. He reported that Black women receive 25 percent fewer first messages than women of other races. And when Black women reach out to men first, they receive responses 25 percent less often than women of other races. Asian men contend with similar behavior. Rudder found that white,

Black, and Latina women rate Asian men as 30 percent less attractive than they rate men of other races.

Alicia sank down into my couch. "The apps just aren't working for me. I want to meet someone in person. Am I the only one who feels like that never happens anymore?" she asked.

This was a complaint I heard often from clients, colleagues, and friends. People my parents' age shared stories about meeting at a church dance, in line at a movie theater, or at a park on a lunch break. But now those stories sound quaint.

"No, you're not," I said. "I once asked a client if he would approach a stranger in public. He said, 'And risk being rejected or accused of being creepy? No way.' Then he pointed to his phone and told me, 'This is where I meet people now.'"

"At least it's not just me."

"Definitely not," I said. "The apps are tough. We're going to figure out a way for you to meet someone awesome in person."

Whether you're feeling stuck with the apps or you just want to expand your search and fish in an additional pond, here are my four favorite strategies for meeting people IRL (in real life).

1) Go to events.

Alicia told me that she often saw events advertised online or heard about them through friends, but she didn't know which ones to choose. (Oh, hello there, paradox of choice!) Work ate up a lot of her free time, so it felt exhausting—and risky—to get dressed up and go out to an event that could easily end up being a dud. Analysis paralysis usually won out. "Why go to a potentially boring event when I could be bra off, yoga pants on, by five-thirty?" she said.

I knew events would offer Alicia the chance to find someone. My job was to help her pick the right ones. I pulled out my notebook and showed her a chart I'd designed called the **Event Decision Ma-**

trix. It helps busy people strategically choose the best events. Every time you hear about a new event, you plot it on the matrix using these two dimensions:

1. How likely is it that I'll interact with other people at this event?
2. How likely is it that I'll enjoy myself at this event?

THE EVENT DECISION MATRIX

A strategy for meeting people IRL

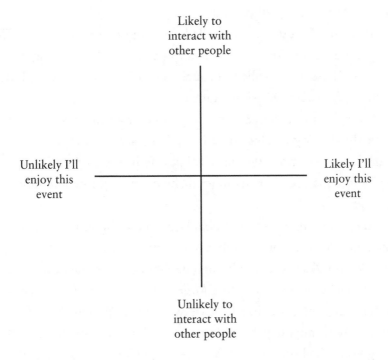

The vertical axis marks how likely the event is to have person-to-person interaction. In other words, will people attending this event have ample opportunities to meet and chat? If you hear about a silent activity with no interaction, like seeing a play, you plot this at the bottom. If you learn of one where you're likely to have a conversation—maybe even an extended one—with the majority of people there, you plot it near the top.

The horizontal axis represents the likelihood that you'll enjoy the event. Events that you're confident you'll love wind up all the way on the right. Events that you know you'll hate go all the way on the left. Here's why that matters: An event you'll enjoy—something that energizes you—is likely to bring out the best side of you. You'll be happier, more relaxed, and more yourself. That's the perfect time to meet someone. In addition, if you go to an event you think you'll enjoy, and you end up not meeting any potential love interests, you're less likely to consider the event a waste of time. You still got to do something you liked, right?

Alicia and I sat down and pulled up a popular event website. (We used SF.Funcheap.com, but you can just Google "upcoming events near me.") As we scrolled through upcoming events, we plotted them on the Event Decision Matrix.

A weight-lifting class? Alicia was more of a runner, so she didn't think she'd enjoy it. Plus, grunting side by side isn't a great way to spark a conversation. We placed that one in the bottom-left quadrant of the matrix—low likelihood she'd enjoy it, low likelihood of interaction.

Free bike-repair clinic? Probably a pretty chummy activity, but Alicia didn't own a bike, so that one went in the upper-left corner—low likelihood she'd enjoy it, high likelihood of interaction.

A movie screening of *Before Midnight*? A Richard Linklater classic for sure, but watching a movie with a group doesn't mean you connect with anyone; the only people talking are on-screen. That one goes in the bottom-right corner—high likelihood she'd enjoy it, low likelihood of interaction.

Eventually, we discovered a book club discussing Ta-Nehisi Coates, the award-winning journalist who writes about culture, politics, and social issues. Ding-ding-ding. Alicia was a huge fan of his work. And book clubs are all about interaction. She could easily extend the group conversation into a one-on-one chat if she met someone she liked. Put that in the upper-right quadrant. Finally! An event with potential.

But the Event Decision Matrix wasn't enough on its own. Alicia needed to actually attend the events that fell in the upper-right quadrant. Here's where I put my behavioral science tools to good use.

Research from psychology professor Gail Matthews shows that **publicly committing to a goal** makes people more likely to accomplish what they set out to do. So I asked Alicia, "Do you think you can attend two upper-right-quadrant events per month?" She promised to follow through, despite her busy work schedule.

THE EVENT DECISION MATRIX

A strategy for meeting people IRL

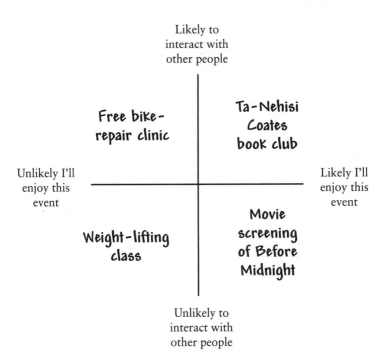

I gave Alicia a **deadline**, since deadlines help people take action and avoid the natural tendency to procrastinate: "By this weekend, can you text me the two events you've chosen?"

Alicia started using her matrix right away. Within a month, she went from going on a few dates a year to meeting six potential partners in one night. The event where she met them? The Ta-Nehisi Coates book club.

Create your own: If you're a busy person who wants to meet people IRL but struggles to decide which events to attend, start plotting your activities on the Event Decision Matrix. If an event falls in that upper-right corner, go to it! As you attend more and more of these, you'll learn how to quickly recognize events that hit the sweet spot: fun for you *and* likely to result in quality interactions.

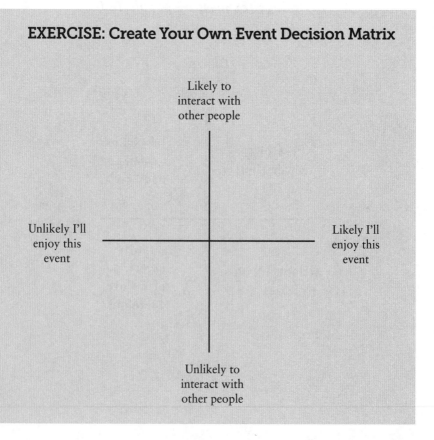

EXERCISE: Create Your Own Event Decision Matrix

Likely to interact with other people

Unlikely I'll enjoy this event

Likely I'll enjoy this event

Unlikely to interact with other people

EXERCISE: Attend Events

Commit to attending just one event in the next thirty days.

I will attend the following event this month:

_____

How to Find Interesting Events

Keep an eye on Facebook events in your area. Follow the Facebook pages of organizations you're interested in, or sign up for their mailing lists. Look through Meetup.com for upcoming gatherings that correspond with your interests. Many of these are free. You know those friends who always seem to be attending cool events? Ask them to invite you next time, or find out where they discover activities. Look up talks at local universities. Google words like "art opening" or "film festival" along with the name of your city. Churches and synagogues have websites, too! Add the events you find to your matrix, and focus on that upper-right quadrant, especially if you have a busy schedule.

One client of mine met his girlfriend at a human rights protest. Another signed up for a season as a "free agent" on a volleyball team made up of strangers, just to meet new people. She ended up dating the middle blocker, and now they play volleyball together twice a week. My friend met her husband at a meet up for listeners of a podcast they both loved.

My friends Jane and Joey met playing Skee-Ball. Joey is a three-time national Skee-Ball champion, and Jane attended a Skee-Ball night at a local bar. Now they're married with an adorable baby, and Jane is the Skee-E-O of their league.

I love hearing stories about people who meet while volunteering.

It's a great way to find people who are kind, which you now know is an underrated but supremely important quality in a partner.

How to Make the Most of Events

It's not enough to just show up to an event. To meet people, you actually have to *meet people.*

Ideally, go alone. You'll look more approachable, because it's easier to go up to someone who's alone than to wedge yourself into a group conversation. You may feel that familiar itch to reach for your phone. But seriously—keep it in your pants.

If you feel like you really can't go alone, select the right kind of wingperson: someone who's independent, caring, positive, and invested in your success. Invite someone who makes you feel comfortable and who knows you're trying to meet new people. Don't go with anyone who'd feel upset if you spent time talking to someone else.

And your mother really said it best: "You only get one chance to make a first impression." Wear something that makes you feel confident. Don't forget to flirt. Make eye contact with the people around you, smile, and then take your gaze elsewhere.

Start small and commit to meeting at least one new person per event. Introduce yourself. Say something to the people nearby about what's happening around you. You could comment on a painting, the band, their earrings or shoes, anything! The point is to practice meeting new people, even if you're not attracted to them. That way, when you meet someone you like, you'll feel confident. (Get those reps in!) In the meantime, making a new friend expands your social circle and increases your chances of meeting a new love interest.

"But how do I know if the person I talk to is even single?" my clients always ask me. Well, you don't! My friend Lucas has an in-your-face way of asking women if they're seeing anyone: "Are you in love?" If the woman pauses and then says no, he realizes that she may be casually dating someone but also might be open to going out with him.

Or you can keep it casual and say something like "Hey, I'd love to keep talking about [insert thing you were discussing]; what's the best way to connect?" Then the person can give you whatever contact info they're comfortable sharing, be that their phone number, Instagram handle, or email address. People will usually have a hunch why you're asking to follow up, and if they have a significant other, they'll find a way to mention that. (If they're taken or not interested, they may decline to give you their info at all.)

Ladies, don't worry about making the first move. Most men are thrilled to be approached by a woman, and if they're turned off by displays of boldness and confidence, they're not right for you anyway.

And gentlemen, I know you're worried about coming off as "creepy." But talking to a stranger at an event is not inherently creepy. Creeps are the ones who go from being charming to, well, creepy— making casual sexual insinuations or sexist comments, or continuing to push a conversation when the other person gives signs they're not interested, such as repeatedly looking over their shoulder or giving really brief answers. If you're worried about navigating the line between "flirty" and "creepy," stick with "friendly" and let the other person steer the conversation toward something more.

If the first-move thing is freaking you out, this trick works every time. Doesn't matter whether you need a drink, or whether you have to go to the bathroom: Get in a line, any line. People in lines are inherently bored. Even a momentary distraction—like a conversation with you—is welcome. I tried this recently while boarding a flight from Atlanta to San Francisco. And let me tell you, my jokes about boarding group E *killed*.

2) Get set up by friends and family.

According to research from Stanford, the third most common way for people to meet each other, behind meeting online and at bars/restaurants, is through friends.

Many of my clients would love to be set up, but they've told me this rarely happens to them.

To find out why, I asked a group of both single and partnered people why they don't set up their friends more. They had a range of answers. Some said it just doesn't cross their mind; or they assume if their friends wanted help, they'd ask for it. Others said they respected their friends' privacy and didn't want to interfere. Some worried their friends would be insulted if they were set up with a person they felt wasn't good enough for them.

But there's hope! Despite their hesitations, everyone I spoke to said they wanted to help. Take advantage of this instinct. Your friends are great resources because they both know you well and know people you don't.

Here are some ways you can get more people to set you up on dates:

- **Ask people to set you up.** I know it seems simple, but many people fail to ask their friends for help. Reach out to friends and say, "I am ready to find someone. Will you introduce me to some single people you know?"

- **Tell them what you're looking for, and think of the Life Partner, not the Prom Date.** For example, "I'm into people who are intellectual, artsy, and care about social justice" or "I'm looking for someone who's kind, thoughtful, and loves food. They're in good shape but aren't overly obsessed with working out." They may think of someone right away or stay on the lookout when they meet new people.

- **Send your friend some photos.** Choose flattering (but realistic!) pictures they can send along to potential matches.

- **Say yes to dates.** Seriously. If someone goes to the effort of trying to set you up on a date, say yes! Presumably, this is a friend and not someone trying to waste your time. What do you have to lose? A night? Some cash? Just do it. My friend Steph tells her friends, "If you think I'd like someone, I am willing to go out with them at least once." Because of that promise, I'm more likely to set her up, unlike some friends of mine who haven't followed up on introductions I've given them. I once had a friend who begged me to set her up on a date. I sent her a photo of the guy and told her about him and vice versa. They both agreed to the setup, but when he texted her, she never responded. She subjected this guy to unnecessary rejection. I vowed never to set her up again.

- **Give your friends feedback.** If the date goes well, send them a thank-you text. Or better yet, flowers! If it wasn't a good match, thank them for the introduction and let them know what worked and what didn't. (Choose your words carefully in case this is a close friend of theirs.) This feedback gets them closer to understanding what you want; motivates them, since feedback is encouraging; *and* provides a chance for them to let you know if you're being too picky. They might hear your reasons and encourage you to give the person another chance. Listen to them.

- **Offer incentives!** This might sound ridiculous, but it works. A former coworker told me she was offering a big chunk of change to anyone who introduced her to the man she'd marry. When I heard how much she was willing to pay— several thousand dollars—I was impressed. First, it showed me she realized how much finding your life partner was really worth. Second, while I liked this coworker (she's fun, enthusiastic, warm, and caring), I probably wouldn't have taken the time to think about setting her up with someone if not for the incentive. Suddenly, when I met eligible men, I immediately asked myself whether they might hit it off with her. Another friend's dad sends a generous order from Nuts.com to anyone who sets his daughter up on five dates (either five different guys or multiple dates with the same person). In the last year, I've received three packages. A few months ago, Scott set her up with one of his friends, whom we think she'll marry. We can't wait for our lifetime supply of premium nuts.

PAY IT FORWARD. HOW TO SET UP OTHER PEOPLE:

1. **Scan your phone contacts or Facebook friends to remind yourself who's single.** What about that great girl you used to work with? She had such a positive attitude and loved trying new things. Didn't she and her girlfriend break up recently?

2. **Once you've thought of a match, contact the person you think is pickier or the person you know better.** "Hey! I think I might have a friend who would be a good romantic match for you. Here's a picture of him. He's really thoughtful, brilliant, and fun-loving. Would you be open to me setting you two up?" A couple things to watch out for: You don't want to give too much information and overwhelm the person; nor should you provide too little information and risk triggering the Monet Effect. Just give enough so that your friend is intrigued.

3. **If the presumed-to-be-pickier person says yes, ask the other person if they're interested, using a similar text.**

4. **If the second person says no, let the first person know, gently.** You can say something like: "Turns out he's not looking to date right now. I think he just met someone." Be compassionate. It's a tough world out there.

5. **If both people say yes, connect them via group text**

or email. Keep it short. I try to say something fun or quirky. Sometimes I even suggest a date idea. Here are real messages I've sent: "Adam > Molly. Get back to me when you've come up with ten new ways to go down a slide." "Craig, Tara. Tara, Craig. Hope you two can meet up soon. May I suggest a walk through Golden Gate Park where you try to pet at least five dogs?" They don't need to follow this exact plan. My goal is to give them a silly way to connect.

6. **Give them space.** Allow the couple to go out without micromanaging them. Encourage them to start talking off the group thread. Once they've gone out, you can ask for feedback in order to get a better sense of what they're looking for, but again, be sensitive. It's up to them how much to share.

7. **Host parties!** My friend Georgina, who's responsible for several long-term relationships and dozens more friend groups, hosts a monthly brunch called the Big Gay Brunch. She reduces the pressure of trying to be a perfect matchmaker by making it a friendly event. People come hoping to meet new people, whether it's romantic or platonic. She doesn't have to figure out who will like whom; she just puts her wonderful friends in the same place at the same time and lets them take it from there.

3) Connect with people you already know.

Sometimes your person is hiding in plain sight. This might be a friend, a friend of a friend, someone on your church committee or in your running club. All you have to do is see this person in a different light. That's what happened to me! By the time Scott and I started dating, we'd been Facebook friends for eight years and real friends for one. I was able to see him with fresh eyes, thanks to the perspective I gained from working with a dating coach. (Yes, I'm proof that this stuff really works.)

All the time, people tell me how they fell for a colleague they'd known for many months or a friend they'd been hanging out with for years. One of my clients, whom I'd been working with for months, finally ended up settling down with a woman he'd known for years. He reached out to her for help preparing for a job interview, and the twenty-minute meeting stretched into a four-hour conversation, sprawling from their favorite sports teams to the recent death of his father. He realized that this woman he'd counted as a friend for so long could be much more to him.

Take a look at your friend group and see if there's someone who's single and with whom you share a lot of "friendistry"—a word I just made up that means "friend chemistry." Is there someone whom you love spending time with, whom you trust, whom you might feel an inkling of attraction to? Come on, tell me. Who just popped in your mind?

Before you start blowing up their phone, understand that the stakes are high. You don't want to make someone uncomfortable or negatively affect the dynamics of a friend group. The thought of making a move on a friend probably fills you with anxiety. That anxiety is telling you to proceed with caution.

If you go down this path, respect this person's boundaries. I'm not encouraging you to get drunk with your friend and make a move. How about grabbing beers and saying something coy, like "Have you ever considered if we could be more than friends?" or "Crazy thought: I wonder what we'd be like as a married couple." If they're interested, they'll follow you down this conversational path and tell you what you need to know. Or they may not see you that way. Regardless, it's worth bringing up. If they're not interested, what's the worst that could happen? Make a joke and move on.

4) Introduce yourself to people when you're out and about.

Imagine you're commuting to work by yourself. As you get on the train, you have two options: Sit in a quiet car or one where people are *encouraged* to talk to each other. Quiet car all the way, right? Who wants to be trapped in a conversation with a stranger about their eleven foster cats or their missing toe?

Behavioral scientists Nicholas Epley and Juliana Schroeder observed the same preference in their paper "Mistakenly Seeking Solitude." When they asked a group of commuters whether they'd like to interact with a stranger on the train or sit alone without speaking to anyone, most people chose the silent option.

Then they ran an experiment to see which experience commuters actually enjoyed more. They randomly assigned commuters on a public transit train in Chicago to either talk to the person sitting next to them, "remain disconnected, or to commute as normal." They found that those who engaged with the stranger had the most positive experience on the train, and those who sat alone with their thoughts had the least positive experience. They replicated the results in an experiment on Chicago buses.

Our instinct to avoid conversations with strangers is wrong. We only *think* we want solitude. We underestimate how much joy social connection can bring.

Open your eyes and look around. Say hi to a stranger! But don't take this as blanket advice to harass strangers in public. Test the waters. When you approach someone, see if they are open to chatting by commenting on something around you or asking a question. If they're not picking up what you're putting down, leave them alone. (Please don't get maced! That's bad publicity for me.) But you'll probably be surprised—in a good way—by what happens when you smile at a fellow traveler or start a conversation with someone who elbowed to the front of the same concert as you. The world is full of great potential matches, or people who *know* great potential matches.

Scott's parents met on the subway in New York. His future mom was holding a book from her psychology PhD program. His future dad recognized the title and said, "Oh, you're reading developmental psychology?" That comment kick-started a fulfilling marriage of thirty-five years and counting.

When I heard their "how we met" story, my initial thought was: *This wouldn't happen today, because they would've been wearing headphones.* Let this be a reminder to leave your electronics in your pocket when you're traveling through the world. Nothing screams, "Don't talk to me!" more than a giant pair of over-the-ear headphones.

One of my clients met his girlfriend in an airport lounge. They were both traveling a ton for work. He pointed out they had the same unusual heavy-duty carry-on luggage. Soon they started meeting up at different airports across the United States for dates.

Dating apps are still good for meeting a *lot* of people. You might even really like a few of those people! But don't underestimate the fun of meeting people IRL.

Alicia dated a guy from the Ta-Nehisi Coates book club for a few months. After she recovered from the breakup, she continued using the Event Decision Matrix to meet more potential matches. She's currently dating someone she met at her ten-year college reunion, an event she says she would've skipped if it hadn't landed in the upper-right quadrant of the matrix.

KEY TAKEAWAYS

1. While apps are the most common way people meet one another these days, **you can still strategize ways to meet people IRL** (in real life).

2. **Go to events.** Use the **Event Decision Matrix** to figure out the most promising ones to attend, based on how likely you are to enjoy the activity and how likely you are to interact with other people.

3. **Get your friends and family to set you up on dates** by letting them know this is something you're interested in, making the process easy for them, saying yes to dates, and giving feedback (and gratitude). You can even offer incentives.

4. **Connect with people you already know.** Your person may be hidden in plain sight. All you have to do is change your frame of mind.

5. **Introduce yourself to people when you're out and above.** Improve your chances by taking off your headphones and interacting with the world around you. If you're at an event and you don't know what to say, get in a line and start commenting on it! People in lines love to discuss lines.

CHAPTER 10

THIS IS A DATE, NOT A JOB INTERVIEW

How to Create Better Dates

Jonathan made a lot of progress in our first two months working together. He started saying yes to dates with different types of people, people he would've rejected in the past.

One afternoon, he called me to report on his latest date: "He's great. Passionate, brilliant, we share the same values. He has great taste in books. He loves his work." Jonathan paused. "But it's not a fit."

"What?" I said, confused.

"I just didn't feel the spark."

"Oh, that's too bad," I said, deciding not to launch into a tirade against the dangerous myth of "the spark." (I do that in the next chapter.) "What did you do together?"

"I'm really busy with work travel and a million meetings, so he met me at the coffee shop under my office before work."

"What time?"

"Seven a.m."

"How long?"

"About twenty minutes."

"I see. And how were you feeling at that time?"

"To be honest, I was stressed. I was scheduled to meet with a big investor at eight a.m., so I was pretty worried about that."

"And do you usually feel good in the mornings?"

"No, I hate the mornings. I'm a night owl. I'm a wreck until I grab my coffee before work."

"Hmm." I took a deep breath. I wanted Jonathan to see the situation from my perspective. "So, you're not a morning person, you're not awake until you have caffeine, you were distracted by an important work meeting, and yet you decided to meet with him for twenty minutes at seven a.m. for a coffee date?"

"Yep, and no spark."

Jonathan was trying. He really was! He was busy, and yet he made the effort to date when and where he could. But there's more to dating than simply making time for it.

ENVIRONMENT MATTERS

Remember the story of those Google employees who cut back on their M&M's consumption? They ate less candy once it moved from glass jars to opaque containers.

That example demonstrates one of the most important lessons of behavioral science: The environment in which we make our choices matters.

Jonathan left that seven a.m. date thinking there just wasn't a spark between them. That there was no romantic potential. That his date wasn't the *right* guy. But perhaps they'd merely met in the *wrong* context?

When we go on dates, we're impacted by more than just the physical location of where we meet. The *environment* of a date is also when we meet, what we do, and the mindset we bring to it. When we first started working together, Jonathan treated dating as if it were an item on his to-do list, an activity to squeeze in between going to the gym and picking up his dry cleaning. He was bringing a harried, sexless mindset into dating and was then surprised when he felt no attraction to the other person. He's not the only one. Many of my clients, desperate to find love but also busy with other commitments, have managed to drain all the flirtation and fun out of the experience of dating. Instead, they tend to engage in what I call **evaluative dating** (or "evaludating," if you want to be cute about it).

And evaluative dating isn't merely unpleasant; it's also a terribly inefficient way to find a long-term partner. In this chapter, I'll teach you how to shift your dating mindset from evaluative to **experiential**. From reviewing résumé qualities and asking, *Is this person good enough for me? Do we have enough in common?* to getting out of your own head and into the moment; to asking yourself, *How do I feel with this person?* To paying attention to what unfolds when you're together. To dating with an attitude of curiosity. To allowing yourself to be surprised.

I'll also explain how to create the right physical and mental dating environment to give yourself the best shot at finding love.

IS IT A DATE OR A JOB INTERVIEW?

Imagine yourself in the following situation: You enter the room apprehensively, worried what your evaluator will think of you. You're dressed nicely but a bit uncomfortably. You hope you're not sweating. (Damn it. You're *definitely* sweating. Back of the knees and underarms.)

You walk over to the table, put your bag down on the floor, shake hands, and slide into the seat across from them.

Would you like something to drink?

You mumble something about iced tea, no sugar. (Was that a test? What does iced tea say about me?)

The iced tea arrives.

The interview begins.

Where did you go to school?

What did you study? Why?

What's the biggest risk you've ever taken?

What's your five-year plan?

The evaluator invites you to ask her some questions.

Within forty-five minutes, the evaluation is over.

You stand up. You shake hands. You put on a friendly smile. *I look forward to speaking again soon!* You leave.

So tell me: Was this a date or a job interview? Instead of imagining it in a conference room, what if it's at a wine bar? The setting might change, but the vibe is basically the same. I'm sure you've been on sterile dates like this one. I hear this from my friends and clients all the time: "Dating isn't fun anymore. It feels like work." Look, I get it, and in a way, dating *is* work. Dating well requires time and effort, and it's not always enjoyable. It sucks to get rejected or find yourself let down yet again. If dating weren't the only way to find a long-term partner, how many of us would have given up on it years ago? But just because dating requires work doesn't mean it has to mimic what you *do* at work. This is not a networking meeting or a job interview. You should not conduct yourself the same way you do at work.

This type of date quells any sexuality that might enter the equation. Even worse, dates that are structured like job interviews put us into "press play" mode. That's how behavioral scientist Kristen Berman describes what happens when we're prompted to repeat canned responses like a robot. We launch into a story we've already told half a dozen times—likely on other dates—and start rattling off our résumé. In these moments, we're just spewing out information, not connecting with the other person.

Esther Perel characterizes the anemic state of modern dating this way: "People sit there, check their pulse, and they try to see if they're having some kind of physiological reaction—a sense of the spark. In this frozen situation, where they're interviewing each other, they want that moment to have a blip. Are you out of your freaking mind?" If you sit through a date trying to evaluate the other person *and* your own reaction, you're not present. Your date can't get a good sense of who you are, and you aren't present enough to experience the moment, let alone enjoy it.

The point of the first date isn't to decide if you want to marry someone or not. It's to see if you're curious about the person, if there's something about them that makes you feel like you would enjoy spending more time together.

TEN STEPS TO DESIGNING BETTER DATES

You can design better dates—dates that don't feel like job interviews—by shifting your mindset and selecting more intentional activities. Here's how to make dating fun again:

1) Shift your mindset with a pre-date ritual.

Your mindset doesn't just set the mood for your date—it can also determine the outcome. Richard Wiseman, a researcher from the University of Hertfordshire in the UK, wanted to find out how strongly our mindset affects our experiences. He recruited groups of people who thought of themselves as particularly lucky or unlucky. Wiseman gathered these people together and invited them to participate in an experiment. He handed out newspapers and asked everyone to count the number of photographs inside.

The self-described "luckies" took just a few seconds to correctly count the number of photographs. The "unluckies" took around two minutes. How did the luckies do it so quickly? On the second page of the newspaper, in large type that took up half the page, there was a "secret" message: "Stop counting. There are 43 photographs in this newspaper." The luckies saw this clue, wrote down the correct answer, and completed the task. The unlucky folks were so busy meticulously counting the photographs that they failed to see the hint.

Wiseman didn't stop there. He included another message, half-way through the paper, that said: "Stop counting. Tell the experimenter you have seen this and win £250." Sadly, most of the unlucky folks missed this one, too.

Why did the lucky folks spot the first sign when the unlucky participants missed both clues? It all has to do with the way these two groups of people interact with the world. Lucky people expect good things to happen. They are open to opportunities and recognize them when they appear. When they looked through the newspaper, they weren't just looking at the photographs with blinders on; they saw the hint on the second page.

People who saw themselves as unlucky tensed up—because they expected the worst—and their anxiety prevented them from noticing unexpected opportunities. A lucky break was staring them in the face in a big bold font, but they couldn't see it because of their negative outlook. Their mindset became a self-fulfilling prophecy.

I've found "unlucky daters" behave similarly. They feel burned out after years of dating and bring that negative energy into every date. This causes them to miss great opportunities. There's an old Henry Ford quote that goes, "Whether you believe you can do a thing or not, you are right." Here's my version: Whether you believe the date will go well or poorly, you are right. You're self-sabotaging if your pre-date mantra sounds something like: "Obviously, this isn't going to work. It hasn't worked the last hundred dates." You have negative-mindset blinders on! You're adopting the mindset of an "unlucky" who misses life's clues—in this case, the signs of a potential match.

Fortunately, we can change our mindset. Wiseman created a program called the "luck school," where he taught unlucky and lucky volunteers to think like a lucky person. He focused on four things: listening to their intuition; expecting to be lucky; spotting chance opportunities; and rebounding more quickly when bad things happen. Assignments ranged from keeping a diary of lucky occurrences, to "visualizing good fortune," to verbally declaring their intentions: "I am willing to put time and effort into changing my luck." After a month, 80 percent of the luck school's "graduating class" felt happier, more satisfied with their lives, and most important, luckier.

I want you to put yourself through your own version of luck school, shifting your mindset to expect great dates. To help you do this, design a **pre-date ritual**. This is something you'll do before every date to get you in the right headspace.

Here are some pre-date rituals from my clients:

- "I always plan ahead. I turn off my work notifications. I try to block off at least thirty minutes before starting my date. I usually call one of my closest friends, someone who makes me feel confident and loved."

- "I like to listen to comedy before a date. My favorite podcast is called *Good One*. On every episode, comedians share one of their all-time favorite jokes and then analyzes it with the host. It makes me laugh and puts me in a good mood."

- "I do jumping jacks to get my heart pumping. It releases endorphins and puts me in a good mood."

- "I feel so unsexy when I leave work. Baths before a date work wonders. I use a bubble bath with a great smell. I've found scent is a powerful aphrodisiac. Then I apply lotion to my body. It helps me turn my work brain *off* and *turn myself on!*"

EXERCISE: Shift Your Mindset with a Pre-Date Ritual

List two pre-date rituals you want to try before future dates:

1. _____

2. _____

Commit to trying different pre-date activities until you find one that works for you.

2) Choose the time and place of the date thoughtfully.

Time and place matter. When do you tend to feel most relaxed and like yourself? Plan your dates in those time slots. No seven a.m. dates, please.

Stop going on dates in well-lit coffee bars. If you're thinking: *If this date sucks, at least I got some caffeine out of it.* Don't. You don't want your dates to feel like a networking meeting. Choose something sexier, like a candlelit wine bar.

And try sitting next to—rather than across from—your date. Have you ever opened up to someone on a long drive? Or noticed that it feels easier to talk to a friend while walking side by side, when you're not making direct eye contact? That's because it's easier to talk when we're not looking someone in the eyes. Psychologists Shogo Kajimura and Michio Nomura at Kyoto University in Japan explored this phenomenon in a 2016 study. When participants stared into the eyes of a face on a screen looking at them (as opposed to one looking off to the side), they struggled to complete a simple word-matching game. Kajimura and Nomura attributed that difficulty to biology: Eye contact and processing language rely on the same neural circuitry. You can use this insight to your advantage on dates. Why not suggest going for a walk? This will help the date feel less like a job interview, protect your brain from overloading, and promote connection.

3) Opt for a creative activity.

Look for a fun activity you can do with your date. Dan Ariely and a team of Harvard Business School researchers ran an experiment where they sent couples on virtual dates in an online setting designed to look like an art gallery. They hoped this setting would spark conversation, and it did. Participants chatted about the artwork and discovered common interests. The art functioned as a "third object," something both people could comment on. A third object takes the pressure off. It makes awkward silence a bit less awkward.

If Renaissance paintings of the Virgin Mary or modern art sculptures of spiders aren't your thing, don't worry. It's not about the art. Third objects can include books, games, and even other people. I recommend going on dates where you can watch your companion interact with others. This is a great way to get a sense of those hard-to-measure qualities that are so important, like kindness. Perhaps that means taking a cocktail-making class in a small group. Is your date rude to the instructor? Patient while gathering the ingredients? Helpful to the woman who showed up late? Or you could suggest a date that forces you to collaborate, like working on a puzzle or visiting a Korean BBQ place where you have to cook your own meal. How well do you work as a team? You might even consider eating something messy, like dumplings dipped in sauce. Who can put up a front when they have soy sauce dripping down their chin? In any of these scenarios, you're gathering a lot more data than by talking one-on-one at seven a.m. in a coffee shop.

You can find a whole list of creative date ideas on my website (loganury.com).

Here are some outside-the-box dates that my clients and I have come up with:

- Visit a farmers' market and then cook brunch.

- Go roller-skating.

- Create a two-person hot-sauce-tasting contest.

- Watch YouTube to learn a dance from a favorite childhood music video.

- Do karaoke.

- See an old movie and then discuss it over a walk.

- Take a cooking class.

- Go for a bike ride and bring a picnic.

- Try swing dancing.

- Check out the stars at the local observatory.

- Rent scooters and explore the city. (Bring helmets!)

- Play games at a local arcade. (Bring quarters!)

- Bring watercolors to the park and paint pictures of the same tree (or each other!).

You might even enjoy stealing this idea for a "day of yes" from a friend of mine. She explained: "We went on a date in which we took turns suggesting our next move and the other person had to say yes (unless illegal or against their values). We met at the Brooklyn Heights ferry stop, where we said yes to getting on the ferry and the next person had to suggest where to get off, to which the other needed to say yes. We kept exchanging ideas of things to do, and it was an amazing date. We ended up exploring a new neighborhood together, eating a single plate at multiple Polish restaurants, and getting in some pretty deep conversation."

All right, admit it. Did you read that list and say, "Yeah, sure, cool ideas, but that's way too out there for me. Who has time for that?" I understand these dates feel far more intense than a regular ol' drinks or coffee date. But your goal here isn't to make things as comfortable as possible. It's to find a great person to build a relationship with. Going on dates like these is going to help you get there. Take a chance and suggest one of these activities. You don't have to commit to a whole day of hide-and-seek, just choose something different! The worst thing that will happen is the person will decline your offer and insist on something more traditional. That's fine, too. But a far more likely result is that your date is sick of those "job interview" dates, too, and will welcome the chance to try something new.

EXERCISE: Try Some Out-of-the-Box Activities

Take time now to think of some fun date activities. Don't be afraid to get a little zany.

1. _____

2. _____

3. _____

4. _____

5. _____

4) Show your work.

Research from Harvard Business School professors Ryan Buell and Michael Norton found that people value something more when they *see* all the effort that went into it.

Imagine if you were searching online for a flight. The quicker the results appear, the better, right? Maybe not. Norton ran an experiment where he had participants search for flights on a fake travel search engine. Participants were assigned to different experiment groups. For some, the program showed them immediate results. For others, the software took its time returning the results, with a progress bar that increased over time and a message about how it was searching for flights on this airline, and then this airline, and then that airline. Surprisingly, those in the second condition valued the system more. Even though it produced results more slowly, they felt the program was working harder on their behalf. They valued the *effort* of the program over the *speed*.

This is why Domino's Pizza lets you follow along as your pizza is "fired up," "in the oven," and "double-checked for perfection." We all know how pizza delivery works. But when you see effort, you appreciate value.

We can apply the same lessons to planning dates. Act more like that second travel search engine by letting your date know about the things you've done to make the experience special. It's not about bragging or exaggerating; it's about making your efforts apparent so your date can appreciate them more.

One great way to *show* your effort is to offer to plan the date, or to choose a place near the other person's home or work. I've found that my clients who live in big cities like New York or Los Angeles often get trapped in a back-and-forth over whose neighborhood they'll meet in. You can show effort by making the date convenient for the other person. Message them something like: "Hey, what area do you live in? I can plan something near there."

During the date, mention the thought that you put into particular decisions. Say: "I chose this Peruvian place because you wrote on your profile that it was your dream to visit Machu Picchu." People will appreciate the effort, and your thoughtfulness will help you stand out.

5) Play.

Think back to the best date you've ever had. Perhaps you met up at a tequila bar, ate perfectly cooked carnitas tacos, and sipped spicy margarita after spicy margarita, whispering increasingly flirty things in each other's ears, until it felt like you were the only people there, which, eventually, you were? Or did you go for a late-night walk, confess your fears about your fraught relationship with your brother, and then have him kiss away your tears, which transitioned to a full-on make-out, pressed up against your door?

What made your best date so great? Probably not the fact that your companion satisfied eight of your top ten criteria for a partner. You probably had fun! And yet fun is rarely something we build into our dates.

Enough with these robotic "press play" dates. Let's make your dates about *play*.

What comes to mind when you hear the word "play"? Little kids running around a playground? Maybe you think dating is serious—you want to find a partner *yesterday*—and you simply don't have time to play around.

But play isn't just for kids at recess. And playing isn't the same as playing games. In fact, it's the opposite. Playing games involves deceit and misdirection. It's a waste of time, because your love interest will discover at some point who you really are, and then what? Play, on the other hand, involves being a present, *honest* version of yourself—just a little lighter.

In an article in the *New York Times* called "Taking Playtime Seriously," Catherine Tamis-LeMonda, a professor of psychology at New York University, explained it this way: "Play is not a specific activity, it's an approach to learning, an engaged, fun, curious way of discovering your world." Play is intrinsically motivated—that means it's for its own sake, rather than achieving a goal.

Let's say you're on a date in the park. You might play by looking around and coming up with backstories for the people nearby. You could use these improvisational backstories to start analyzing which couples you think will last and which will break up—and why. Or you could run around and see how many dogs you can pet in fifteen minutes.

I understand this approach can feel a bit forced at first. Instead of pretending this is how you usually behave, try being self-deprecating about it: "Hey, this might sound a little strange, but what if we tried . . ." You'll get points for creativity even if the person declines to participate.

Have fun. Be silly. Make a joke. Humor is a great tool to create a sense of play. When we laugh, our brains release a happy cocktail of hormones, changing our psychology. Laughing releases oxytocin—the same bonding hormone released during breast-feeding—and makes us trust the other person more. (And if it's oxytocin we're after, laughing is a more socially appropriate activity on a first date than breast-feeding.) Laughter lowers levels of the stress hormone cortisol, allowing us to relax. Laughter also creates a dopamine hit, activating our brain's pleasure centers. It reinforces our behavior and makes us want to go back for more. All good things for a first date: more bonding, less stress, and an improved chance of a second date.

6) Skip the small talk.

We form stronger connections with each other when we ask questions. Questions allow people to reveal personal details about themselves, which is essential for forming close bonds. What's more, research from psychologist Karen Huang shows that being inquisitive tends to increase how much others like you.

The kind of questions you ask matter. Who cares what this person studied in college? Remember, this is a date, not an interview. Despite all the reasons to go deep, many of us spend our dates in the shallow end of the pool.

In the viral *New York Times* Modern Love column titled "To Fall in Love with Anyone, Do This," Mandy Len Catron highlights the power of thought-provoking questions. On a date, Catron and her companion answered thirty-six questions, which escalated in intensity and intimacy from "Given the choice of anyone in the world, whom would you want as a dinner guest?" to "If you were to die this evening with no opportunity to communicate with anyone, what would you most regret not having told someone?"

These weren't just random questions Catron had scribbled down on an index card on the way over. (Note: Never bring index cards on dates.) They were designed by psychologist Arthur Aron and his colleagues for an experiment in which they paired random strangers to ask each other a series of thirty-six questions. They tested the power of "sustained, escalating, reciprocal, personalistic self-disclosure." Aron and his team—and later Catron, who is still with the guy from that fateful date—found that these particular questions help potential partners bond by building connection and promoting vulnerability.

If you don't feel like asking these kinds of questions, try my favorite approach to avoiding small talk. Enter the date in media res. That's Latin for "in the middle of things." It's a literary term that describes a story opening somewhere in the middle of the action, rather than at the beginning. (You can think of it as "coming in hot.") When you walk into a date, instead of starting with the awkward "So, how's your day going?" or "Where do you live?" jump right into the middle of things: "You'll never guess what happened on my way over here!" or "I just got off the phone with my sister, and she told me about this battle she's in with her landlord over the recycling bins." By skipping the getting-to-know-you small talk and diving straight into the type of conversation that friends (or lovers!) might have, you take a shortcut to intimacy. Of course the conversation may reverse—you'll eventually cover how your day is going, where you live, and so on, but at least you will have dipped your toes into the waters of *real* conversation.

Another great approach is soliciting advice. You can ask about a real thing that's going on in your life. "My sister's getting married in a few weeks, and I don't know if I should give a roast or a toast. Have you ever given a speech at a wedding?" Or: "My boss sends me emails all weekend, and I don't know how to set boundaries with him. What would you do?"

Remember, *asking* questions is only half the equation. You need to actually *listen* to the answers, too. This allows you to see how the person thinks. Does their advice resonate with you? Are they comfortable sharing? And when you respond, do you feel heard?

7) Be interested, not interesting.

I once worked with a client named Andrea. She was charismatic, with long red hair and a big toothy smile. She performed improv on the weekends and would often make me howl with her tales of first dates gone wrong.

"Logan, I'm trying," she said, crossing her arms over her chest. "I just don't feel a connection with these people."

"Are you practicing your pre-date ritual?"

"Yes," she said, rolling her eyes.

"Are you planning creative dates?"

"You know I just went to that art class with that guy last week."

"Are you doing small talk?"

"I hate small talk."

I was struggling to see what was going wrong, so I asked Andrea to go out with a guy friend of mine to gather more information. He called me immediately afterward.

"How was it?" I asked. "Well, she talked over me the whole time, and she spent most of the date monologuing about some work drama. Oh, and she insisted on ordering for me."

A few days later, Andrea came over again. I told her what he'd said.

"I'm so embarrassed," she said. She was silent for a minute and then surprised me by grinning—as if the negative feedback had made her happy.

Turns out it had. "Wait, so it's me!" she said. "It's not something wrong with all the men in this city. It's something I can change."

Like Andrea, a lot of people think they need to perform on a first date. They want to make a good impression and come across as interesting. But good dates are about connecting with another person, not showing off. It's like this quote from Maya Angelou: "I've learned that people will forget what you said, people will forget what you did, but people will never forget how you made them feel." Instead of trying to *be* interesting, make the person *feel* interesting.

That means learning how to be a good listener. There's a lot more to it than just hearing what another person is saying. Most of us listen in order to formulate our own responses, which puts the focus back on us. The goal is to *understand* rather than merely waiting for your turn to talk.

You can become a better conversationalist by learning to give **support responses** rather than **shift responses**. Sociologist Charles Derber identified a shift response as a moment in which you *shift* the focus of the conversation back to yourself. A support response, on the other hand, encourages the speaker to continue the story. For example, if your date says, "I'm going to Lake Michigan with my family in a few weeks," a shift response would be: "Oh, I went there a few summers ago." Even though, on the surface, you're *engaging* with what your date has said, you've drawn the attention back to yourself. A support response might sound like "Have you been there before?" or "How did your family choose that location?" Support responses indicate that you're invested in their story and want to hear more. They make your date feel appreciated and amplify the connection between the two of you.

EXERCISE: Practice Support Responses

Imagine you're out, and your date makes one of the following statements. Write down a shift response and a support response to practice recognizing the difference:

Your date: "My coworker just got a goldendoodle puppy."

Shift response: _____

Support response: _____

Your date: "I'm really into Ken Burns documentaries, especially the one on the Vietnam War."

Shift response: _____

Support response: _____

Your date: "I'm thinking about going back to school."

Shift response: _____

Support response: _____

8) Limit phone use.

Please, please: Keep your phone out of sight. Research from MIT professor Sherry Turkle found two negative impacts of having a phone on the table when you're talking to someone: One, it decreases the quality of the conversation. People naturally tend to discuss more shallow topics, because there's a fear that at any moment the phone will interrupt them. Two, it weakens the empathetic connection that forms between the two people.

Despite all the evidence that phones create a barrier to connection, 89 percent of people admitted to taking out a phone during their last social interaction. Don't do it!

Try this approach. At the beginning of the date, ask the other person how they'd feel about both of you committing to putting your phones out of sight. You'll show you care *and* increase your chances of the date going well. (You might even bring up Sherry Turkle's research, because nothing screams "I'm good at sex" like a research citation.)

9) End on a high note.

An artist I know prides himself on always incorporating a happy ending to his dates. (No, not that kind! Get your mind out of the gutter and back into this book!) For example, toward the end of the night, he'll ask the cryptic question, "Have you ever been to San Francisco's secret slide?" and, if his date is curious, take them to this romantic, under-the-radar spot. He understands that the end of an experience matters.

In a famous experiment, behavioral economists including Daniel Kahneman compared the experiences of patients undergoing a colonoscopy. (Don't worry, these were all people who needed this exam, not just psych experiment volunteers.) Some patients endured thirty minutes of unpleasantness, while others experienced thirty minutes of unpleasantness with an additional five minutes of slightly less discomfort tacked onto the end. Perhaps counter-intuitively, people preferred the latter experience, even though the whole thing lasted longer. That's because of a phenomenon called the **peak-end rule**: When assessing an experience, people judge it based largely on how they felt at the most intense moment and at the end. Their memory isn't an average of their minute-by-minute experiences.

So order dessert at the end of the meal. Give the other person a meaningful compliment before you head your separate ways. Take advantage of the peak-end rule.

10) Use the Post-Date Eight to shift to the experiential mindset.

Jonathan, like many of us, had a long checklist of criteria for his potential partner. After his dates, all he could see were the ways people fell short when stacked up against his imaginary perfect man. That "Does he check all the boxes?" mentality is yet an-other example of evaluative dating. Checklists aren't inherently bad, but most people's lists focus on the wrong things—like some-one's résumé qualities. I designed a different kind of checklist for Jonathan: one that would help him shift from an evaluative to an experiential mindset. Instead of determining if a potential match met a particular requirement, he was able, with this list, to tune in to how he felt about his dates. It encouraged him to be present and to focus on what really matters.

I urged Jonathan to answer these questions on his way home from each date:

The Post-Date Eight

1. What side of me did they bring out?
2. How did my body feel during the date? Stiff, relaxed, or something in between?
3. Do I feel more energized or de-energized than I did before the date?
4. Is there something about them I'm curious about?
5. Did they make me laugh?
6. Did I feel heard?
7. Did I feel attractive in their presence?
8. Did I feel captivated, bored, or something in between?

Knowing he had to answer these questions afterward, Jonathan started paying more attention to how he felt during the date. He started agreeing to second dates with guys who weren't as impressive on paper but made him feel optimistic, attractive, and relaxed. He was able to more quickly reject guys who had impressive backgrounds but left him feeling cold. He allowed himself to experience the date rather than "interviewing" the guy for the role of husband.

EXERCISE: Answer the Post-Date Eight

Snap a photo of those eight prompts and commit to looking at them at the end of every date to help you get in touch with how the person made you feel.

KEY TAKEAWAYS

1. We're suffering from the rise of **evaluative dating—cross-examinations that feel like job interviews.** Throw out your checklist and shift to the **experiential mindset.** Stay present and pay attention to how you feel around the other person.

2. Mindset matters: **Whether you believe the date will go well or poorly, you're right. You can use a pre-date ritual** to get into the right mental state before a date.

3. With a little planning, you can design better dates. **Be thoughtful about where and when you go out.** Incorporate play. Choose more creative activities, resist small talk, stay off your phone, and end on a high note. Be a good listener by offering **support responses** that encourage your date to elaborate on a story, instead of **shift responses** that direct the conversation back to you.

4. Instead of evaluating your date against certain criteria, answer the **Post-Date Eight** questions to tune in to how your date makes you *feel*.

CHAPTER 11

F**K THE SPARK

How to Reject Myths
About Instant Chemistry

When you're going on dates, you may be looking for that instant connection. Sudden, sexy, intoxicating. It's physical, a pang of excitement in your gut, a feeling of nervousness when you look into their eyes. You can't look away. If they touch you, it's electric. Everyone else in the room fades into the background. You feel tuned in and turned on. You feel alive.

You know what I'm talking about: "the spark."

I get it, the spark is wonderful. But you know what? F**k the spark. The concept is my nemesis: I've come to see our obsession with the spark as one of the most pervasive and dangerous ideas in dating. It causes us to miss out on amazing partners because we fail to see their true potential. In this chapter, I'll bust a number of myths about the spark. By the end, I hope you'll be chanting "F**k the spark!" too.

Myth #1: When you meet the right person, you'll feel instant fireworks.

The Truth: Fireworks and instant chemistry are often absent at the beginning of a relationship. Good sex and chemistry can build over time.

Love at first sight is pretty rare. When psychologist Ayala Malach Pines surveyed more than four hundred people to ask how they fell in love with their romantic partners, only 11 percent claimed that they felt "love at first sight."

Have you ever noticed how people tend to date their neighbors? How couples form during freshman year among students who live across the hall from each other or take the same premed classes? That's because the more we see something, the more we like it. Psychologists call this the **mere exposure effect**. Exposure breeds familiarity. We're attracted to (and feel safe around) familiar things and people.

A friend of mine used to work as a hostess at an Italian restaurant. When she first started there, one of the cooks asked her out. She wasn't attracted to him, so she said no. He respected her answer, and they became friends at work. He'd drive her home from her shifts, and some nights they'd stay up late, drinking with their coworkers, after the restaurant closed. Six months after he'd asked her out, she kissed him in the car at the end of the night. He was surprised but thrilled. They went out later that week. Today they're married with two young kids.

"I wasn't feeling it at first," she told me. "But he grew on me. It took time for those feelings to develop, but now I can't imagine my life without him."

I hear stories like this all the time. Married couples love to tell me about their disastrous first (or first and second!) dates. The message is clear: The spark can grow. Sometimes it's a tiny flame, gasping for breath. If you squelch the flame before it has time to breathe, you'll never get to warm yourself by the fire of long-lasting love. (They should really hire me to write Hallmark cards.)

A few years ago, psychologists Paul Eastwick and Lucy Hunt explored this phenomenon. At the beginning of the semester, they asked straight male students to rank their straight female classmates' desirability and vice versa. When Eastwick and Hunt analyzed the responses, they found that students were more or less in agreement about their classmates' attractiveness. This initial rating, based on first impressions, is known as **mate value**.

Three months later, at the end of the semester, the researchers asked students to evaluate their peers again. Now that the students knew one another, the scores had much more variability. These new scores reflected what's called **unique value**, what you think of someone after spending time with them.

Here's how Eastwick and Hunt explained why the scores changed: When we first meet people, we evaluate them on their mate value—their overall attractiveness and how they carry themselves. As we get to know and share experiences with them, we discover their unique value—who they are on the inside. In the classroom study, the first time the students evaluated one another, their answers reflected mate value—basically how hot they found their peers—and most people found the same people hot. But by the end of the semester, they judged them on their unique value, which depended on whom they'd gotten to know. In many cases, likely because of the mere exposure effect, the students liked their peers more than they had on the first day of class. The importance of mate value disappears over time. What matters is how you feel about someone as you get to know them.

This phenomenon occurs outside of the classroom, too. When we first meet someone, we form an initial impression, based mostly on appearance. But as we get to know the person more, they often grow on us, and we start to see them differently.

That same lesson applies to sex, too. Good sex often doesn't magically happen right away. As anyone who's had a lousy one-night stand can tell you, it takes time to develop a rhythm and learn about someone else's body and preferences (and your own!).

Myth #2: The spark is always a good thing.

The Truth: It's not. Some people are just really good at making a lot of people feel a spark. Maybe they're extremely attractive. Perhaps they're best-in-class flirts. Sometimes the presence of a spark is more an indication of how charming someone is—or how narcissistic—and less a sign of a shared connection. I learned the hard way with Burning Man Brian. He made me (and plenty of others) feel the spark, and I tried desperately to convert that initial excitement into a relationship.

You may also think you feel the spark when your date is playing games or sending mixed signals. People often confuse anxiety for chemistry (I'm talking to you, anxiously attached friends out there!). It's time you learned to correctly identify that feeling, like my workout-class friend Vivian did. Then start looking for a different type of partner—someone secure who doesn't make you doubt their feelings. Stop believing that if a dependable person doesn't give you butterflies, it must not be love. It's still love, just not the anxious kind.

Myth #3: If you have a spark, the relationship is viable.

The Truth: Even if the spark leads to a long-term relationship, it's not nearly enough to keep the relationship going. I've spoken to couples who stayed together years longer than they should have, all because of the spark. Many divorced couples once had the spark.

A friend of mine went to South Korea to teach English after graduating from college. After three weeks, he was feeling homesick. He missed his family. He'd made no friends. His students barely seemed to register his lessons.

Then one day, he walked into a local bar as it was closing. He noticed a tall blond woman sitting in the corner. She was alone. He watched as she downed the last few sips of her red wine, closed her book, and stood up. She looked vaguely like a friend of his from college, a person he missed dearly.

While normally shy, he felt emboldened by the sight of an almost familiar face. He walked up to her and said, "Hi! I'm Nathan. Do you live here?"

Not expecting to hear English, she took a step back. After a moment, she said, "Uhhh, yes, I do." She stuck out her hand to introduce herself. "I'm Ava."

Nathan smiled. She was beautiful *and* she spoke English. He felt the spark instantly. "Want to find another bar and tell me about the book you're reading?" he asked.

They dated for a year in South Korea and then moved to St. Louis together. They got married the following year.

But the relationship faltered. "In retrospect, all of the warning signs were there," Nathan told me. "We were so different. Even on that first date, she was reading a book, and I was just trying to get drunk."

They'd changed the subject when certain topics came up—like the fact that he wanted children and she didn't, or that she wanted to return to South Korea and he felt ready to put down roots in St. Louis. "I guess we just ignored our differences because of that initial spark."

After less than a year of marriage, they could no longer ignore their discontent.

"I really feel like our whole relationship was propelled by our how-we-met story," he said. "If we hadn't had this picturesque story of meeting abroad, of love at first sight, I don't know that we ever would've gotten married. Our whole lives were trying to live up to that fantasy meeting."

Don't pursue the wrong relationship because you met the "right" way.

DITCHING THE SPARK FOR THE SLOW BURN

The spark isn't a bad thing in and of itself. It can be a useful signal that you're attracted to someone. Plenty of good relationships start with the spark, but plenty of bad ones do, too. The important thing to remember is that its absence doesn't predict failure, and its presence doesn't guarantee success. As my mathematician client said to me once, "The spark is neither necessary nor sufficient for long-term relationship happiness."

Stop using the spark as your first-date indicator. Stop optimizing for that exciting feeling and focus on what matters, like loyalty, kindness, and how the other person makes you feel (and return to Chapter 7 if you need a reminder).

Ditch the spark and go for the **slow burn**—someone who may not be particularly charming upon your first meeting but would make a great long-term partner. Slow burns take time to warm up, but they're worth the wait. In the next chapter, I'll help you decide how to identify a promising slow burn, why you should give that person a chance, and when to call it.

A medical student friend of mine named Katrina had minimal success on dating apps. She is shy, which comes across as aloof on early dates. While she was going on first date after first date, she started spending time with her neighbor Suzanna. She would tell Suzanna all about her dating disasters. Months into the friendship, Suzanna confessed her love to Katrina. They started dating shortly after that. Suzanna told me that she continues to fall deeper and deeper in love with Katrina. That's the power of the slow burn.

KEY TAKEAWAYS

1. **F**k the spark!** Fireworks and instant chemistry are often absent at the beginning of a relationship. **Chemistry can build over time.**

2. **Context matters.** You may not feel the spark with someone, simply because of the environment in which you meet.

3. **The spark is not always a good thing.** That feeling of chemistry may actually be anxiety because the person doesn't make it clear how they feel about you. Sometimes the presence of a spark is more an indication of how charming someone is—or how narcissistic—and less a sign of a shared connection.

4. **If you feel the spark, that doesn't necessarily mean the relationship is viable.** Even if it leads you into a long-term relationship, it's not nearly enough to keep the relationship going; nor is it a sign that you're meant to be together.

5. **Ditch the spark and go after the slow burn**—someone who may not be particularly charming but would make a great long-term partner.

CHAPTER 12

GO ON THE SECOND DATE

*How to Decide if You
Should See Someone Again*

Over time, Jonathan, my client who had been going on dates that felt like job interviews, changed his approach. He ditched the coffee shop for a tiki bar near his house with great bartenders and flattering lighting. A place just noisy enough to give him an excuse to whisper in his date's ear. And he stopped worrying about the spark.

Soon we were able to laugh at that seven a.m. coffee date. Jonathan had mastered the first date. But he struggled to decide whom to see again.

"Honestly," he told me during one session, "I'm meeting a lot of nice guys. But after the date, I find myself dwelling on their flaws: boring job, cheesy sense of humor, wearing a vest."

It wasn't Jonathan's fault that he tended to focus on the negative. Our brain evolved to do just that. (And in my opinion, wearing a vest should not disqualify anyone from a second date. As comedian Demetri Martin explains, vests have a purpose: You never know when you might encounter a "narrow cold front.")

Fortunately, we can take action to override these impulses so that we don't miss out on great matches for silly reasons. We can train our mind to look for the positive and follow the dating version of the Golden Rule: **Do not judge others the way you would not want to be judged.**

THE NEGATIVITY BIAS

In my interview with Helen Fisher, a biological anthropologist and the author of several popular books on relationships, she explained that our brains have developed a **negativity bias,** an instinct to ruminate on what's gone wrong.

If you've ever received feedback from a manager or coworker, what do you remember more clearly: the compliments or the criticism? This is the negativity bias in action. Fisher said that our brain evolved to vividly remember negative experiences so that we can avoid them in the future. This wiring helped us to perceive and avoid threats. If you almost get eaten by a saber-toothed tiger, it's helpful to remember what that animal looks like and where it lives. We have fewer flesh-eating predators around these days, but our brains still hold on to the modern equivalent: "If you have five ex-girlfriends and one of them hates you," Fisher said, "it's helpful to remember which one that is."

But this mindset that served our ancestors well, and retains some value, creates challenges today—especially for dating. It means we're likely to remember a person's bad qualities most clearly after a date. (Which is why you remember your last date as the girl whose breath smelled like scallion pancakes, not the one who raved about your outfit.)

THE FUNDAMENTAL-ATTRIBUTION ERROR

In addition to the negativity bias, we unconsciously fall prey to cognitive biases that make us bad judges of character. One such bias is the **fundamental-attribution error,** our tendency to believe someone's actions reflect who they are rather than the circumstances. When someone makes a mistake, we interpret the misstep as revealing something essential, and essentially *bad*, about that person's character. We don't look for external reasons to explain the behavior.

For example, if someone arrives late to a date, we see them as selfish instead of assuming they hit traffic. Or if they don't text back when they said they would, they must be inconsiderate rather than experiencing a busy week at work. You know as well as I do that these generalizations aren't fair. But in the moment, our brains naturally make those leaps.

LOOK FOR THE POSITIVES

It's no surprise that, thanks to the negativity bias and the fundamental-attribution error, Jonathan's first instinct was to turn down second dates. But if he wanted to find a long-term partner, he had to learn how to override these natural impulses and seek the positive. If not, he'd misjudge a lot of wonderful potential partners. If he couldn't get to the second date, how would he ever achieve his goal of walking down the aisle?

Seeing the positives in life is a muscle, a skill you can develop. It requires practice. Psychologist Shawn Achor's research on gratitude journals found that simply writing down three new things you are grateful for, every night for three weeks, will start to change the way your brain perceives the world. The exercise trains you to *notice* things you might have otherwise missed, like how wonderful it is to catch the bus right before it leaves or how good it feels to laugh with your coworker.

You can do the same thing in your dating life. Train yourself to see the positives. Look for what others might miss when they talk to the same person. As philosopher and writer Alain de Botton told me:

Rather than focusing on someone's negative traits, use your "imagination" to "search for what is desirable and good."

I once coached a guy named Grant who was incredibly negative. Almost every sentence started with "Yes, but . . ." He lived life with his arms crossed over his chest, ready to challenge even good news. Unsurprisingly, his post-date texts to me were like mini–*Mean Girls* burn books: "Too short, didn't laugh, boring job, might want to move back to Canada, mispronounced the word 'concomitant.'"

At our next meeting, I sat him down. "Grant, you are not simply a compilation of your worst qualities or habits, right? You are not your flaws. You are a whole person with good traits and bad ones, and you want to be seen and evaluated based on that whole package, not just your areas for improvement. Do not judge others the way you would not want to be judged."

After each date, he wasn't allowed to list his date's flaws to anyone, including himself. Instead, he had to send me five nice things he noticed about her. Just like Alain de Botton said, *he had to use his imagination* and see beyond the surface.

In the beginning, Grant found this exercise tough. He wrote things like "was not late" and "did not misuse any words." Over time, he got better at it. Here's one list he sent me:

1. She's kind. I love the way she treats the restaurant staff.
2. She's thoughtful. She asked me about my big meeting at work.
3. She's family-oriented. She actually seemed interested in hearing about my grandma.
4. She's super-smart.
5. GOOD KISSER!!!

Even though he hasn't found his person yet, Grant is going out on far more second dates these days. He's learned to use his imagination and, by extension, given himself the time to explore, understand, and appreciate potential partners.

EXERCISE: Look for the Positives

Look for the positives in people, whether you're evaluating them on a dating app or they're across the table from you at a restaurant. It will be easy to see their flaws—the way our brain has evolved practically guarantees it. But force yourself to look for the good. After your next date, text a friend five things you liked about your date. Heck, if it helps, you can even email them to me (5goodthings@loganury.com).

Now, that will help you spot the positives. But what happens when your date makes a mistake and the fundamental-attribution error kicks in? You can choose to override this impulse by coming up with an alternate—more compassionate—explanation for their behavior.

Situation: He's late to your first date.
Fundamental-attribution mode: He's selfish.
Compassion mode: Even though he left his house an hour before your date, his train was delayed.

Situation: He's slow to respond to initial dating messages.
Fundamental-attribution mode: He's rude.
Compassion mode: He has a lot going on at work this week but is still trying to find time to date.

Situation: She made a bad joke during dinner.
Fundamental-attribution mode: She has a cheesy sense of humor and we're not compatible.
Compassion mode: She was nervous and tried to make me laugh.

Try switching into compassion mode the next time you find yourself in one of these situations, so you don't mistakenly reject a wonderful potential match.

HARNESS THE POWER OF DEFAULTS

All of the mindset changes I'm describing are hard. It's natural to focus on someone's negative qualities and decide you don't want to go out with that person again. But there's a way to make this whole thing a lot easier: Harness the power of defaults.

Countless behavioral science experiments demonstrate how **defaults**, or preset options that require no action, impact our behavior. Imagine you're setting up a menu at a burger joint and you need to choose the go-to side, what your customer will automatically get with a burger. Will it come with fries, which people can swap out for a salad? Or will it arrive with salad, but people can request fries instead? Whatever you select will become the default option, which the majority of people will stick with.

You can see the power of defaults by looking at this graph:

ORGAN DONATION RATES ACROSS EUROPE

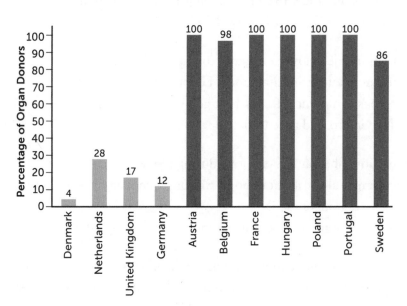

As the graph shows, in some European countries, almost everyone is signed up to donate their organs. In other countries, barely anyone has registered as a donor. While we might attribute this to differences such as religious views or a more or less communitarian approach, that's not the case. Similar countries (like Denmark and Sweden) have very different organ donation rates.

Why did this happen? It isn't because of religion or culture but, rather, defaults. People tend to stick with the default, especially around hard emotional decisions like what to do with your body when you die. In some countries, like the first four shown in the graph on the previous page in the lighter color, the form at the DMV says, "Check the box if you want to participate." Very few people check the box, and thus very few people sign up. In countries where the form says, "Check the box if you don't want to participate," again, very few people checked the box, and thus most people are automatically enrolled. This accounts for the high participation rates in the other countries in the graph. In both cases, the majority of people stuck with the default option and didn't check the box. This tiny difference—created by a person at the DMV who designed the form—had a huge impact on something as vital as organ donation.

You can use defaults to your advantage in all kinds of ways. For example, a friend of mine wanted to lose weight. He established a default for himself: no bread. When someone offers him bread, he refuses it. He doesn't waste brainpower on the decision. He follows his default rule.

Now imagine the implications for your dating life. You can design defaults to help you make better decisions. Why not set a default that you'll go on the second date? Not only will this help you avoid the brain's natural tendency to focus on the negative, it will also help you look for that slow-burn person instead of seeking the spark.

Of course, there are exceptions. But assume you'll go out with someone a second time unless something dramatic happens to dissuade you. (Like that hypothetical person who shows up two hours late, smelling of lobster, and on crystal meth.)

My client Emma was going on very few dates when we met. We worked on her profile, her opening lines, her listening skills, and more. We set a goal of at least one date a week. Being the over-achieving, metrics-driven operations manager she is, she went from having very few dates to multiple dates a week.

After a month, I realized I was rarely hearing the same name twice. "Emma, are you going on any second dates?" I asked in our next session.

She thought about it for a moment. "No, I guess not. Just first dates. But look at how many I've had!"

"That's great," I said. "But don't lose sight of our overall goal—helping you find a long-term partner. I want you to try to go on more second and third dates with people."

She agreed to make second dates her default rather than the exception. A week later, she sent me a text: "I already have second dates lined up with both of the guys I went out with yesterday!"

It might seem obvious, but this simple change—from focusing on second dates instead of first ones—made a meaningful difference to her approach. Within another month, she found herself on a second, and then a third, and then a tenth date with a great guy who was getting over a difficult breakup. "He was afraid of getting hurt, but we just kept going out. We got deeper and deeper until we'd built an intense bond." They're still dating—and considering moving to Austin together.

In the end, it was the default-second-date rule that led Jonathan to meet his now-partner. Jonathan said that before we worked together, he likely wouldn't have gone out with this guy in the first place because he is below Jonathan's previous height minimum. Or, if they'd gone out, Jonathan would've turned down a second date because they had a "just okay" first date. Luckily, he gave the guy another shot.

"My boyfriend is driven and successful, but not in the ways I originally expected. We have so much fun together. He's a phenomenal listener and communicator. We have incredible chemistry. He's also super-attentive to my needs. In the past, I thought I wanted this big CEO type, but it turns out that's not what makes me fulfilled. Letting go of that faulty list of requirements was a game changer—it enabled me to focus on our experiences together."

The stakes here are pretty low. When you're on a first date, you're not looking to fill the position of life partner, you're looking to decide whether or not you want a second date. That's it. It's better to go on a second or third date with somebody and then find out that they're not a good fit than to rule out potential matches because of an initial impression that's vulnerable to all types of cognitive biases.

EXERCISE: Make the Second Date the Default

"I, _____ , commit to going on more second dates."

Signature: _____

Date: _____

PPPS (PERMISSIBLE PET PEEVES)

The second-date default will help you give more people a chance. So will my next tip: Stop confusing pet peeves with dealbreakers. Actual dealbreakers are fundamental incompatibilities that doom a potential relationship. For example, if you and your date practice different religions, and you both want your kids to be raised solely in your faith. Anything less important is a nice-to-have but not a requirement.

A few years ago, I attended a happy-hour event. A woman in her mid-thirties approached me and said she wanted to talk about her dating life. Her name was Mariah.

"I'm really open to meeting someone," she said, "as long as he's not a mouth breather."

In our conversation, I discovered that one of the reasons Mariah had been single for many years was because she did things like divide all men into two categories: mouth breathers and non–mouth breathers.

Yeah, sure, mouth breathing is annoying. So is talking with your mouth full or interrupting people or leaving your clothes all over the house until you can't see the floor. (All things I do.) But there's absolutely no research that correlates non–mouth breathing with successful long-term relationships.

Prioritize what actually matters long term. Do not let yourself get off track because of small distractions. You may be using these distractions as a defense mechanism—a way of staying single while still giving the appearance of dating, to avoid, for whatever reason, taking the leap into a relationship.

That's what was going on with Mariah. She was guilty of mistaking a **PPP (Permissible Pet Peeve)** for a dealbreaker. Let's make sure we have our definitions straight:

Pet Peeve: a minor thing that an individual finds particularly annoying, perhaps more than other people do.

PPP (Permissible Pet Peeve): a preference that feels like a dealbreaker but is really just a pet peeve.

Dealbreaker: a genuine reason not to date someone.

Think about your big dealbreaker. Is there any way you could imagine being in a long-term relationship with someone who has this characteristic? If yes, it is not a dealbreaker. For example, suppose you are a straight woman and one of the dealbreakers for your potential partner is "he's shorter than five-ten." Now imagine you met someone gorgeous, charming, kind, a good listener with amazing friends who made you laugh—but then he stood up and you saw he was five-nine. Would you still want to date him? Almost certainly yes. Height is not a dealbreaker.

But let's say you're certain you don't want kids. And you go on a great first date that ends with your date gushing about her nieces and nephews and how she can't wait to be a parent. I don't care how gorgeous she is and how much you loved spending time with her—you two have fundamentally different plans for the future. That's a dealbreaker.

Other examples of dealbreakers include: One of you wants monogamy, the other doesn't believe in it. One of you has very old-fashioned views about gender roles in relationships, the other believes in a different balance. You smoke and aren't willing to quit, and the other person has serious asthma.

Push yourself to make two different lists: What are *critical dealbreakers* for you? And what are just preferences or nice-to-haves? This exercise really helped Jonathan. It was how he determined that height was way less important than he thought. So was being a business executive. But he knew he could never date someone who didn't have a sense of humor.

EXERCISE: Identify Genuine Dealbreakers

Using our new definitions, write out what truly matters to you.

Actual dealbreakers:

1. _____

2. _____

3. _____

Permissible Pet Peeves that I won't confuse with dealbreakers:

1. _____

2. _____

3. _____

Nice-to-haves that I won't confuse with dealbreakers:

1. _____

2. _____

3. _____

HOW MANY DATES DO I NEED TO GO ON BEFORE I CALL IT?

If you're on board with going on second dates as a default, the next question is: How long should I see this person? Should third dates be defaults?

I can't tell you that two or three dates are all it takes to know if someone could be a great long-term partner. There's no data to determine that number. Take a look at what unfolds when you two hang out: Do you enjoy spending time with this person? Do they make you happy? Do you like who you are with them? Do you want to kiss them? Is your interest in them growing, waning, or just kind of trudging along? If your date is rude or disrespectful—to you or anyone else—don't see that person again. Ditto if your date made you feel uncomfortable, anxious, or sad.

Take an honest look at yourself. How old are you? How long have you been going on dates and complaining that there's no spark? Maybe it's time to switch things up and give someone a try. Look back at the Secretary Problem that I described in Chapter 4. Realize that you've likely already met someone who would make a great long-term partner.

Look, I'm not telling you to go out and put a ring on it right away. You'll have plenty of time between the second date and that milestone to reflect on the relationship. I don't want you to get married because of a default! Instead, focus on the question at hand: Do you want to see this person again? If so, let them know!

GHOSTBUSTERS PLEDGE: DON'T YOU DARE GHOST!

You'll inevitably reach a moment when you decide you don't want to move forward with someone. What should you do? Ghost? NO! OF COURSE NOT. This whole book is about making intentional dating decisions. And that includes how you choose to end things.

Here's how I define ghosting: communication in which one party has the expectation of a response from the other person and doesn't get it. For example, if two people went on a date and neither texted the other person afterward, I call that a mutual opt-out, not ghosting. But if they went out and one person wrote back and said, "Hey, that was fun. Can I see you again?" and the other person never responded? That's ghosting.

Why do people ghost? I've interviewed dozens of people about their ghosting habits. Here's what I heard:

"I ghost because I don't know how to explain why I don't want to see them again."

"I ghost because it's uncomfortable to reject people."

"I ghost because it's less hurtful to just disappear than to straight-out reject someone."

People often ghost because they think they're avoiding an awkward situation and protecting that person's feelings.

But that's just not true. Ghosting *is* awkward. Plus, it's hurtful and leaves the other person in limbo. Besides those obvious reasons not to ghost, here's another one: Ghosting makes *"ghosters"* feel worse than if they'd been up front with their feelings.

Two cognitive biases help explain way this happens: first, our poor ability to make **affective forecasts**. In other words, we're lousy at predicting how situations will make us feel in the future, like how we'll feel after we've ghosted someone. Second, our views about ourselves change over time, depending on how we behave. According to psychologist Daryl Bem's **self-perception theory**, this happens because we don't have access to our inner thoughts and feelings. We look to our actions to tell us who we are. This helps explain why research shows that volunteering is one of the most reliable ways to boost our happiness. Volunteers consistently see higher levels of happiness and self-esteem than non-volunteers, because when they're done, they look at their actions and think, *I'm spending my time helping people. I must be pretty generous after all!*

People ghost to avoid feeling awkward. Yet, in accordance with self-perception theory, after people ghost they look at their actions and think, *I did kind of a mean thing. I might be a dick.* And then they feel worse about themselves.

I ran a small experiment to prove that ghosting makes people feel worse, not better. I recruited participants through Facebook and Reddit. These were self-described ghosters who claimed to ghost people at least once a month. In a survey, I asked them how happy they *predicted* they'd feel on a scale from one to five (not at all happy to very happy) after either A) ghosting someone or B) sending someone a more straightforward text saying they weren't interested.

Unsurprisingly, most of these ghostly respondents anticipated they'd feel "neutral" to "happy" after ghosting someone and would feel "somewhat unhappy" to "not at all happy" after sending the rejection text.

I told half the group to rank their happiness on that same one-to-five scale the next time they ghosted. I asked the other half not to ghost. If they met someone they didn't want to see again, I instructed them to send this message afterward: "Hey [insert name]. I really enjoyed talking about [insert conversation topic]. I don't think we're a romantic match, but I enjoyed meeting you." I asked these people to send me screenshots of what they sent and the responses (if any) they received.

What do you think happened? Most of the ghosters who did *not* send a message reported feeling neutral to not very happy about their behavior. In follow-up interviews, they said they felt guilty and that when the person checked in multiple times after the first date to see if they wanted to go out again, it made them want to avoid their phones altogether.

Those who sent the straightforward message indicating that they weren't interested received positive reinforcement from the other person almost two-thirds of the time. In the other cases, the person didn't write back at all. There was only one incident in which the person wrote back and requested more information about what was wrong, and that escalated into a fight.

When people ghost, they think they're taking the easy path

for themselves. But they're wrong. If we instead choose the kind, up-front, polite path, we get positive reinforcement. The person is likely to respond and say something like: "Thanks for letting me know. Good luck out there." Hear that sound? It's a sigh of relief. We feel better because the person has just affirmed that we are a good person.

Hopefully, I've convinced you *why* you shouldn't ghost. But sometimes it's difficult to compose that "Thank you, next" text. Make it easy on yourself. Go to the Notes folder on your phone or save a copy of the Mad Libs–style goodbye text I gave you above. Commit to sending it as soon as you realize you're not interested in someone.

REJECTION DOS AND DON'TS

Do:

1. Be polite.
2. Be clear. You can use some combination of "I don't think we're a romantic fit" or "I don't think we're the right match."
3. Make it short and sweet. You're writing a polite heads-up note, not a manifesto on the perils of modern dating. (That's my job, not yours!)

Don't:

1. Say you want to be friends if you don't mean it. Someone might take you up on it, and if you're not genuine about that, it will just hurt more.
2. Criticize the person or give feedback. That's unsolicited, and it's not your place to judge.

3. Get into a long back-and-forth if they want more details. It's nice to be clear, but you don't owe them a drawn-out conversation.

Let's start a *Ghostbusters* Pledge where we all commit to being up front and honest with how we're feeling. Stop ghosting. It's hurting you.

KEY TAKEAWAYS

1. The **negativity bias** is our natural tendency to ruminate on what's gone wrong. You can override it by seeking out your date's best qualities. Remember the dating version of the Golden Rule: **Do not judge others the way you would not want to be judged.**

2. **We're prone to the fundamental-attribution error**—our tendency to believe someone's actions reflect who they are rather than their circumstances. For example, if someone arrives late to a date, we may assume they're selfish. We can override this error by coming up with a more compassionate reason for their behavior. Perhaps their boss dropped by their desk for a last-minute conversation when they were trying to leave work.

3. **We are worse judges of character than we think**, and it often takes time for attraction to grow. Therefore, we should create a default: **Go on the second date.**

4. **Distinguish your Permissible Pet Peeves from your dealbreakers.** Don't write someone off because of something silly that doesn't really matter long term.

5. Don't you dare ghost!

SECTION 3

GETTING SERIOUS

CHAPTER 13

DECIDE, DON'T SLIDE

How to Consciously Navigate
Relationship Milestones

Have you ever polished off an entire tub of movie theater popcorn by yourself, not realizing how much you were eating until your hand grazed the cardboard bottom? If you're anything like me, probably. What about eating a whole package of snack-size bags in one sitting? Probably not. That's because reaching the end of a container—however big or small—creates a **decision point**: a moment that interrupts our automatic behavior and gives us an opportunity to make a conscious choice. In this case: "Do I want to keep eating popcorn?"

Research by behavioral scientists Amar Cheema and Dilip Soman demonstrated the power of decision points in a clever (and, I assume, delicious) study. They gave each participant a package of twenty cookies to snack on while completing a series of tasks. They packaged the cookies in three different ways: all twenty stacked in one column; divided up into smaller sections with white waxed paper; or divided up with pieces of colored waxed paper.

The tasks themselves didn't matter. What the researchers really cared about was whether the packaging affected how many cookies the participants ate and how quickly they ate them. They found that the participants whose cookies were separated by colored paper ate fewer cookies and took longer to consume them. That's because the colored waxed paper created more obvious decision points, chances to shift their brains from unconscious thinking (or, in this case, snacking) to deliberate decision-making. The stack of cookies offered no decision point, and the white waxed paper was easy to ignore. But the colored paper jolted the cookie eaters out of their mindless snacking and forced them to consider: "Should I keep eating these cookies?"

All areas of life present decision points, not just eating cookies or popcorn. Relationships, in particular, are full of decision points. Many of them stress us out and keep us up at night. But I see decision points as gifts—opportunities to pause, take a breath, and reflect on what we're doing. We can take inventory of our lives and strategize about our next move. This allows us to make better, more thoughtful decisions.

But relationship decision points are never as obvious as the colored pieces of paper that divided the cookies. They can be easy to miss, especially when we're being carried along by the momentum of life.

Psychologists describe two ways couples transition into the next stage of a relationship: **deciding** or **sliding**. Deciding means making intentional choices about relationship transitions, like becoming exclusive or having children. Sliding entails slipping into the next stage without giving it much thought. This distinction matters. The National Marriage Project, an annual report on American marriages conducted by researchers at the University of Virginia, found that couples who made a conscious choice to advance to the next stage of their relationship enjoyed higher-quality marriages than those who slid into the next stage. Furthermore, researchers from the University of Louisville and the University of Denver found that individuals who tend to "slide" through relationship milestones feel less dedicated to their partners and engage in more extramarital affairs.

These findings suggest sliding through decision points can put a relationship at risk. While relationships present many crucial decision points, in this chapter, I'll help you address two of them: defining the relationship and moving in together.

DEFINE THE RELATIONSHIP (DTR)

Remember my client Jing? She was the Hesitater who started dating for the first time at thirty-one. After a few short romances, she began seeing a guy named James. She loved his friends. They were kind, welcoming, and hilarious. But most of all she loved how quickly James had introduced her to them. She met his family shortly afterward, at a rowdy Sunday dinner with his mom, dad, sisters, and nephews. She felt accepted. Finally, she thought, she'd found the relationship she'd been looking for.

"Exactly four months to the day after we met, we went away for the weekend," Jing told me during our first meeting. He drove, she navigated. "When my phone died, I asked if I could pull up the directions on his phone." James hesitated. "He said something about needing to keep his phone near him in case his manager texted."

Jing could tell something wasn't right. She grabbed his phone. Even without unlocking it, she could see the notifications coming in from dating apps: *You've got a match!* Her heart sped up as she scrolled down, reading the name of each girl he'd matched and messaged with.

"What is this?" she said.

"I'm sorry," he said. "But we never said we were exclusive."

That was the last time they hung out.

Jing told me this experience left her humiliated. In her mind, meeting James's family and friends and going away together meant they were in an exclusive relationship. She'd deleted her apps and told her mom she had a boyfriend. But James had a different perspective: They were not exclusive until they'd explicitly had *the talk*. You know, the chat when you check in on what you're doing together, aka the DTR (define the relationship) or the WUWU (what's up with us?). "I just feel so pathetic," she said.

Jing wasn't alone. And she wasn't struggling with misaligned expectations just because she was relatively new to dating. All the time, I see people making different assumptions about what's going on in their love lives. They avoid bringing up the DTR because it feels awkward, or they're scared they'll ruin things.

But the DTR is an essential decision point. It's a chance to discuss where you are and where you're headed. If someone doesn't take you seriously as a potential partner, wouldn't you rather know that sooner than later? In order to gain the insight you need to make the right choice for yourself, you must DTR. It's also important from a sexual health perspective. If either of you is sleeping with someone else, the other one deserves to know.

There's no perfect time to DTR. Bring up the conversation when you feel like you're ready to stop seeing other people and would feel comfortable calling the person your boyfriend or girlfriend. This is different for everyone. If you know you're someone who rushes into things, check in with a few friends for a gut check on your timing. (Rushing to DTR is common among anxiously attached folks. Revisit Chapter 6 for a refresher.)

Make sure to talk in person. Think through how you'll open the conversation. One trick for tough talks is to start by announcing how awkward you feel. This alerts the person to the fact that you feel vulnerable, which helps elicit a more empathetic response. Try an opener like "I feel awkward bringing this up, but . . ." or "It's always hard to ask this, but . . ."

Obviously, you could just straight up ask, "Are we dating?" If that feels too direct, one technique is to say you're confused about how to refer to this person in the presence of others. For example, "My friends are asking me what we are. What should I tell them?"

or "How should I introduce you tonight when we meet my co-workers?"

Be clear with the other person about what you want to know. Are you looking for clarity on your labels? Do you want to know if you're sexually exclusive? Are you hoping to complete the ultimate modern-day romantic ritual: deleting your dating apps?

You may not get the response you want. Remember, this is a conversation, not a negotiation. Respect what the other person says. Listen. This is about learning how they feel, not persuading them to give you what you want.

Even if you don't receive the answer you hoped for, at least you have additional information. More data is always better in these situations. Now you can decide for yourself whether you want to stay or go.

That's what happened with Jing. Several months after the James debacle, she met someone new, a friend of a friend named Cal. She didn't want to repeat what had happened with James, so a few weeks after she started seeing Cal, she brought up the DTR.

Cal said he was struggling to get over his ex and didn't feel like he could commit right away. He wanted to continue seeing Jing but wasn't ready for labels or exclusivity. Jing decided that worked for her: She felt comfortable continuing to date Cal, even though they hadn't made the relationship official.

"I actually feel fine about it," she explained to me. "I realized I don't need him to commit just yet. What matters is that he's being clear with me."

Keep in mind: The way you handle the DTR will have an impact on your future relationship, whether or not you decide to make it official at that moment. If you want a relationship, and you discover the other person does, too, you'll feel happy and relieved. But what if you don't get the answer you're looking for? Make sure you thank them for sharing, even if you're disappointed with the news.

Welcome their words with compassion and curiosity to show your partner they're free to tell you what's on their mind, even if it's not what you want to hear.

EXERCISE: Prepare for the DTR

Sit down with a journal and answer the following questions to help you prepare for this conversation:

1. How do you want to open the conversation?
2. What's your goal for the conversation?
3. How will you respond if the other person shies away from the topic or isn't ready to DTR?

Check out the Critical Conversation Planning Doc in the Appendix for more information on prepping for this discussion.

MOVING IN TOGETHER

One of the most important decision points in a relationship is choosing to get married. (You know, that whole thing with the ring and the knee and the Instagram post.) But for many modern couples, the decision to move in together comes first.

While the U.S. population has grown by 80 percent since 1960, the number of unmarried couples living together before marriage has exploded by 1,500 percent (from around 450,000 in 1960 to 7.5 million today); 50 to 60 percent of couples now live together before they get married.

But many people don't take this decision point as seriously as they should. They think of moving in together as the ideal way to test their relationship. The Pew Research Center surveyed a nationally representative panel of randomly selected U.S. adults. Two thirds of respondents between the ages of eighteen to twenty-nine agreed that couples who live together before marriage are more likely to have a successful marriage. However, the research into living together before marriage tells a different story: Married couples who move in together before they get married tend to be less satisfied and more likely to divorce than those who don't. This association is known as the **cohabitation effect**.

When researchers first investigated the cohabitation effect, they figured only a certain kind of couple moved in together before marriage. These couples, the researchers assumed, were laxer about marriage and thus more open to the idea of getting divorced. However, as more and more people choose to cohabitate before marriage, it's much harder to say that only a particular type of couple is choosing this path.

Researchers have a new theory. They now blame living together *itself*.

Consider two hypothetical couples: Ethan and Jamie and Adam and Emily. Ethan and Jamie move in together because Jamie's lease is up. Adam and Emily discuss moving in together but decide they're not ready yet.

Both relationships deteriorate over time. Adam and Emily end their relationship, but Ethan and Jamie do not. That's because they now share a dog, a rubber tree plant, and a secondhand West Elm rug. The process of separating their stuff, finding new places to live, and coming up with a calendar to share the dog is expensive and annoying. Instead, they end up getting married and then divorcing a few years later. What does the tale of Ethan and Jamie teach us? First, cohabitation can lead to marriages (and subsequent divorces) that wouldn't have occurred if the couple hadn't moved in together. Second, never buy a secondhand rug.

Moving in together makes it harder to be honest with yourself about the quality of the relationship because the cost of separating goes up significantly. Yet again, we encounter the status quo bias, our tendency to leave things as they are. When you break up with someone you live with, you're not just changing your relationship status, you're also upending your housing situation and your daily routines. This makes the status quo bias even harder to overcome. If you move in together and things aren't great, you're more likely to stay in the relationship than if you each had your own space.

Since moving in together makes you more likely to get married, honor this moment as the milestone—and decision point—that it is. Forty-two percent of couples who *decided* their way into living together enjoyed a happy marriage, compared to 28 percent of those who *slid*. (If these numbers seem low, that's the sad reality of long-term marital satisfaction for most couples. But there are ways to buck this trend. I'll tell you more in the last chapter.)

The practicalities of life—like wanting to save money—are fair reasons to start the conversation about moving in together. But make sure your discussion covers more than just logistical questions, like how to split rent and who's in charge of decorating. Arguing over whose couch to keep or what neighborhood to live in does not count as planning your future together. Take this moment to be intentional. Confirm that you and your partner are aligned on where the relationship is now and where it's headed in the future. *Decide, don't slide.*

Sometimes moving in means one thing to one person and something completely different to the other one. But without this type of conversation, a couple may not discover the misalignment until it's too late and they've already signed the lease.

When Priya and Kathryn approached the conversation, it didn't turn out the way they expected. "We first discussed it after a year," Priya told me. "Kathryn found this great place near my office and wanted us to take it. She felt ready."

"We loved each other, this place was perfect, and we weren't getting any younger," Kathryn added.

During that talk, they discovered they weren't aligned. For Kathryn, moving in together was the logical next step in their relationship but wasn't a clear sign about whether they'd get married. For Priya, moving in carried the expectation that they were going to get married.

"In my mind, if I move in with you, I'm planning to marry you," he said. "Maybe I won't, but that's the intention." Priya worried that once she and Kathryn moved in together, they might stay together out of inertia. Priya saw the moving-in-together decision point as closely tied to the marriage one. "I said to Kathryn, 'I respect where you're coming from, and I just need a little bit more time before it feels like the right moment.'"

For some couples, deciding not to move in together might signal the end of the relationship. But not for Priya and Kathryn. They continued to date. A few months later, they checked in again. "This time it was completely different. We both felt like we could say, 'Yes, this is a step toward getting married,'" Priya said.

They moved in together and got engaged the next year. Their wedding was a giant family affair full of old friends, baby cousins, and rowdy aunts and uncles.

"Now we handle every decision like that," Priya told me. "What's the point of rushing if you're not headed in the same direction?"

In addition to discussing what moving in together means to you, I recommend you talk about any fears or hesitations you have about this big change. Your conversation can lead to clarity about more than just the question at hand. I worked with a client named Laura who was planning to move in with her boyfriend. He was warm and loving. He made her—a naturally anxious person—feel content and calm. It was her first long-term relationship in six years, and she feared they might ruin things by moving in together too quickly. She told me she tended to be the "CEO of the relationship." She liked being in control. But she worried that sharing a house would exacerbate this tendency and turn her into a nag. She'd seen that happen in her parents' relationship and believed it was what had pushed her dad away from her mom.

"My boyfriend works remotely, and I'm a corporate lawyer," Laura said. "He's a super-capable guy, but he doesn't always do what he says he will, or at least not in the time frame I want. I know it sounds terrible, but I'm just worried I'll end up texting him non-stop with reminders to walk the dogs and pick up groceries."

I coached her through a conversation with her boyfriend. I gave her advice on how to bring up the conversation (tactfully), split their household duties (equally), and check in on the adjustment of moving in together (frequently).

And Laura did, even though it was awkward and she risked hearing an answer she didn't want. Over burgers one night, Laura told him how it made her feel when she had to remind him about shared responsibilities. She expressed her fear that she'd turn into a constant criticizer. He listened carefully and then confessed his fear that she would feel resentful of him because he was paying only a small share of the rent. They stayed up late talking about what was really going on for them.

That weekend, they sat together and developed a system for managing household tasks. They would keep a shared Google Calendar to add reminders and appointments. That way she could put a reminder on the calendar without having to feel like she was nagging him. And she promised never to hold the rent situation over him. They're now living together peacefully. Laura tells me their dogs get plenty of walks.

EXERCISE: Get Aligned Before You Sign a Lease

Before you move in together, set aside a weekend to answer these questions:

1. Why are we moving in together?
2. What does moving in together mean to you?
3. Where do you see this relationship going in the future?
4. Is marriage something we're considering? If so, when do you see us getting married?
5. What are your fears about living together?

WHERE DO WE GO FROM HERE?

When you hit decision points such as the DTR, moving in together, or other relationship milestones, you may wonder if you should move forward with the relationship. You might wake up in the middle of the night and ask yourself, *Is this the right person for me?* If you feel plagued by this question, the next few chapters address how to determine your answer. They will help you decide if you want to end the relationship; guide you through a compassionate breakup conversation; and help you overcome heartbreak.

If you decide that you *don't* want to break up, you might find yourself facing a different serious and potentially life-changing question: *Should we get married?* In Chapter 17, I'll walk you through specific exercises to lead you to an informed choice—and explain why it's crucial to do your homework before you put a ring on it.

KEY TAKEAWAYS

1. **A decision point is a moment in which you decide whether to continue what you're doing or choose a different path.** It shifts your brain from unconscious thinking to deliberate decision-making. Relationships are full of decision points. They provide an opportunity to pause, take a breath, and reflect.

2. Psychologists describe **two ways couples transition into the next stage of a relationship: deciding or sliding**. Deciding means making intentional choices about relationship transitions. Those who slide slip into the next stage without giving it much thought. **Couples who decide tend to enjoy healthier relationships.**

3. When you start seeing someone, don't make assumptions about whether you're in a relationship. **You need to DTR (define the relationship) to ensure that you're on the same page** about where you are and where you're headed.

4. **Moving in together makes you more likely to slide into marriage**, so it's important that you take this step seriously and talk about what it means for your future.

CHAPTER 14

STOP HITCHING AND STOP DITCHING

How to Decide
if You Should Break Up

My phone rang at eleven p.m. on a Friday from a number I didn't recognize. I was brushing my teeth and getting ready for bed. "Hello?" I said hesitantly, mouth full of spearmint foam.

The person on the other end burst into tears.

I spit into the sink. "Who is this? What's wrong?"

After some sniffling and nose blowing, the voice said, "This is Sydney. I got your number from our mutual friend, Hannah. It's about my boyfriend."

I relaxed the death grip on my toothbrush. This I could handle. "What's wrong?" I repeated. I could guess where the conversation was headed. He'd just broken up with her and she needed support.

She took a deep breath, composed herself, and said, "He wants to propose to me!"

A proposal. Not at all what I'd expected. "And why is this a bad thing?"

"I think I need to break up with him."

I get calls like this all the time—okay, usually not at eleven p.m., and usually not spoken through tears—from people of all ages, genders, and sexual orientations. My work as a dating coach isn't just about getting people into relationships. It's also about helping them leave bad ones.

Every step of a relationship requires conscious decision-making, from whom to go out with, to when to move in together, to whether or not to get married. At some point, you may find yourself right where Sydney was in that moment, considering one of the most pivotal decisions of all—whether to stay together or break up.

I wish I could give you a quiz or a flowchart that would magically reveal what to do. But I can't. There's no easy answer, and every situation is unique. I don't know all of the factors at play—how you *think* you feel, how you *really* feel, what else might be causing your discontent—and you probably don't, either. However, I *do* know the cognitive forces at play that make this decision harder. Understanding them will help you decide what to do next.

People who ask me for breakup consultations usually fall into one of two categories. Some tend to stick around in relationships that aren't working. I call these people **Hitchers**. The other group consists of people who tend to leave relationships too soon, without giving them a chance to grow—**Ditchers**. Of course, you may fall somewhere in the middle on the Bad Breakup Behavior Spectrum (not an official scientific scale, but it should be). These tendencies wax and wane depending on whom we're with, what's going on in our lives, and many other factors.

DITCHING

Before I tell you what happened with Sydney, I want to introduce you to Mike. Mike is thirty-six and lives in Albuquerque. When he first contacted me, he explained that he'd been seeing his girlfriend for around three months. She made him happy. She called him on his bullshit. She helped him figure out what he wanted to do next after he'd been laid off. "She's so incredibly kind," he said, "maybe the kindest person I've ever met."

Unfortunately, for the last few weeks, he'd felt a familiar pull: He wanted to break up with her.

"This is what I always do," he explained. "I meet someone awesome, but after three months, I start to fixate on their flaws, and then boom! I end it."

"What is it about your current girlfriend that's bothering you now?" I asked.

"I know this sounds snobby, but it's the way she speaks. She misuses and mispronounces words. She says 'pitcher' instead of 'picture.' I think it's a Boston thing."

A Permissible Pet Peeve if I'd ever heard one. "Thank you for sharing those hesitations with me," I said, making sure to e-nun-ci-ate my words carefully. "What are your long-term goals?"

"I want to get married and have kids."

At this rate, it seemed unlikely that Mike would reach domestic bliss, given his proclivity for ending things at the three-month mark, but I could see that he was trying. He admitted that he usually had one foot out the door from the very beginning. He tended to leave before giving his partner a fair chance (which undoubtedly affected how he behaved in the relationship). He abandoned relationships early because he always wondered if there was someone better out there. And yes, if this sounds familiar, it's because Mike was definitely a Maximizer.

FALLING VERSUS *BEING* IN LOVE

Some Ditchers are motivated by their Maximizer tendencies. They leave relationships too quickly because they believe they can find something better.

Others ditch because of a Romanticizer tendency. They expect relationships will always offer the exciting infatuation that abounds in the early stages—the feeling of hearts fluttering, palms sweating, minds racing. They end relationships too early because of a cognitive error called the **transition rule**.

As behavioral economists Daniel Kahneman and Amos Tversky explained, when we estimate how something will feel in the future, we tend to focus on the *initial* impact. For example, you might imagine that lottery winners end up extremely happy, but it turns out that's incorrect: As I mentioned earlier in the book, a year after they win, lottery winners are about as happy (or unhappy) as non–lottery winners.

When imagining the lottery winner, we focus on that *transition*—going from being an average Joe to being *a big winner*. Now, that's a huge change. But in reality, once you're rich, you eventually adapt to your new circumstances, and sooner or later, the money doesn't seem to hold as much intrigue. You go back to how you felt before the major event. (This dynamic unfolds in challenging situations as well: Research shows that becoming a paraplegic has a smaller impact on people's long-term happiness than you might expect.)

Ditchers make the same mistake with love. Thanks to the transition rule, they confuse *falling* in love with the state of *being* in love, and they expect the whole relationship to offer that initial excitement. But people adapt. Being in love is less intense than falling into it. Which, by the way, seems like a good thing! How could we get any work done with everyone walking around acting like the classic cartoon character Pepé Le Pew—smitten and speaking broken French?

Ditchers believe the feeling of falling in love will last forever. When they experience that shift from *falling* to *being*, they interpret it as a mark of disaster for their relationship. Over and over, they panic and leave, chasing the high of new romance.

WHAT'S WRONG WITH DITCHING?

This behavior causes problems, and not just for the person who gets dumped. Ditchers underestimate the opportunity cost of leaving, never learning how to be a good long-term partner.

Let's say you go on a hundred first dates. You might develop excellent first-date skills. You discover the perfect cozy wine bar. Or you perfect the story of that time you got lost backpacking in Nepal. But what happens on dates five through seven? Or date twenty-five? Or fifty-five? You don't know, because you haven't gotten there. And if you keep dating people for three months and breaking up with them, you'll never get your reps in. You'll lack the experience of truly getting to know someone, of seeing the face of the person you love lit up by birthday candles or streaked with tears because of a parent's illness. And you'll continue to hold false expectations of how relationships feel over time. You won't learn that how you feel on day one differs from how you feel on day one thousand.

WHAT CAN DITCHERS DO INSTEAD?

On the phone that day, I asked Mike to close his eyes.

"Imagine you're at a fork in the road," I said. "There are two paths in front of you. Now imagine you're stepping out onto the first path. You'll break up with your current girlfriend, find another one, break up with her, and so on. This path is full of first dates and first kisses. It keeps going and going as you get older and older. There are nights out in Vegas and fancy restaurants, but no wife, no kids.

"The other path holds something different for you. You commit to your girlfriend. You do your best to make it work. As you walk along, you can see holiday dinners with both of your families. Look further ahead. You'll see fights, and makeup sex, and then a wedding, romantic trips, and then a baby, and then wiping poop from her forehead, and then passing out from exhaustion, and then another baby, and more forehead-poop-wiping, and then college graduation, and so on."

When I finished the exercise, Mike was quiet.

"What's on your mind?" I asked.

"I need to think about it."

Two weeks went by. During our next session, Mike spoke first: "Last time I feel like you showed me that I'm at a crossroads between Dad Mike and Sad Mike. Sad Mike keeps dating women, breaking up with them, and repeating the cycle all over again. He never learns how to be in a relationship, and he never gets the chance to have kids. When I closed my eyes, I saw him alone, living in a bachelor pad, with a pullout futon for a bed."

"So, what do you want to do about it?"

"I'm ready to take a different path."

Mike decided to give his relationship a chance. As we worked together over the next year, he shifted his behavior and committed to his girlfriend. We developed techniques to help him remind himself of her strengths. Every Sunday morning, he'd send me five things he'd appreciated about his girlfriend during the previous week. (Don't forget! I'm waiting for your email with the list of five things you liked about your date: 5goodthings@loganury.com.)

If you want to be in a long-term relationship, eventually you have to commit to someone and give it a try. When Mike gets the occasional itch for something new, I reassure him that's normal. He's chosen the path toward Dad Mike, and there's nothing *sad* about it.

HITCHERS

While Ditchers can't figure out how to stay in relationships, Hitchers struggle to leave them. Sydney, crying into the phone at eleven p.m., was a classic Hitcher.

"I'm twenty-six," Sydney said. She had been with her boyfriend, Mateo, for ten years. "We're from very small towns in Ohio, and we started dating at sixteen."

Sydney felt she'd outgrown the relationship: "We both care for each other deeply, but he's no longer the person I want to share the details of my day with. We don't have anything to talk about. He brings out my most impatient, bratty side."

"How long have you been feeling this way?" I asked.

"About three years, and it's only gotten worse," she said. "I know that in a long relationship, you go through periods of ups and downs. But now that it's been a few years, this feels like a major shift that needs to be addressed."

She wondered aloud: "Should I listen to this voice telling me to break up with him? Am I about to lose something good? I almost wish something dramatic would happen, like my work would transfer me to a different country where he couldn't join me, so we'd be forced to reevaluate."

I knew it was time for the **Wardrobe Test**.

It's a technique I developed while conducting research on breakups. Of all the probing questions I ask, it's the one that seems to help most.

I'm going to tell you the question, but first I want you to promise that, if you're considering a breakup, you'll take a moment and answer this question for yourself as honestly (and quickly) as possible. We're going for a gut reaction here.

EXERCISE: Take the Wardrobe Test

If your partner were a piece of clothing that you own—something in your closet—what piece of clothing would they be?

The question is abstract and absurd enough that it allows people to reveal their true feelings. Some people say their partner is a warm coat or a snuggly sweater. To me, this suggests that they find their partner very supportive. One woman said her boyfriend was her little black dress—something she felt sexy and confident in. One man said his girlfriend was like his favorite pair of loud pants he wears to music festivals, which she'd given him as a gift. They're an item he loves but never would have chosen for himself.

Other people reveal how much frustration they feel about their relationship. One guy said his boyfriend was a wool sweater, something that keeps you warm but then gets itchy when you wear it too long.

I asked Sydney the question.

"Mateo is like that kind of scrubby old sweatshirt that you have that you love but maybe wouldn't wear to an important meeting," she said. "When you put it on, you're like, 'Ahhhh, yes. I'm in my element.' But at the same time, 'I'm not going to go anywhere looking like this.'"

Yikes. A scrubby old sweatshirt? A revealing answer if I'd ever heard one. It suggested to me that she'd outgrown the relationship. That it was no longer something she was proud of or invested in. It was no longer the right relationship for her—or Mateo.

It was time to take off that sweatshirt and exit the relationship.

WHY HITCHERS STICK AROUND

There are several cognitive biases that help explain why Hitchers stay in relationships too long.

Imagine this situation: You buy a ticket to an amateur improv show for twenty-two dollars. You sit down, and within ten minutes, you can tell it's not for you. The improv is *really* amateur: I'm talking "Yes, and . . . no, thank you" bad.

You might say to yourself, *I should stay. I paid twenty-two dollars.* In that scenario, you'd sit through the show and spend ninety minutes doing something you don't enjoy. Or you could leave. You might choose to go for a walk or meet up with a friend who lives near the theater.

In both situations, you've spent twenty-two dollars on the tickets. The money is gone. But if you leave, at least you get your time back. Behavioral economist Amos Tversky used to go to the movies, and if he didn't enjoy the first five minutes of the film, he'd leave. "They've already taken my money," he explained. "Should I give them my time, too?"

Tversky understood—and therefore tried to avoid—the **sunk-cost fallacy**. It's the feeling that once you invest in something, you should see it through. It explains why most people force themselves to sit through a bad improv show.

Or a bad relationship. The sunk-cost fallacy keeps Hitchers in relationships. Once, a man called me and said, "I've spent three years with my girlfriend. The first six months were great, the last two and a half years have been terrible." When I asked why he was still with her when he was clearly unhappy, he responded, "I've invested all this time with her. It would be dumb to quit now."

I explained the sunk-cost fallacy in terms I thought he'd appreciate: "The first six months of your relationship were like season one of *True Detective*—wonderful. Seasons two and three of the show were lackluster. Will you stick around and wait to see how season four turns out? Or is it time to start a new show?" No matter what, he'd already dated her for three years. He needed to decide: Did he want to date her for another three, or was he ready to find a new show?

Hitchers are also impacted by **loss aversion**. Behavioral economists Amos Tversky and Daniel Kahneman identified this phenomenon in a seminal paper. They explained that "losses loom larger than gains."

Let's say you walk into a store to buy a new phone that costs $500. The salesperson hands you a coupon for $100 off your purchase. You'd be pretty pumped, right? Now imagine a different scenario, where you walk into the store and the salesperson says they *were* running a $100 off promotion, but it just ended the day before. You'd feel some pain at that loss.

In one situation, you're gaining $100, because the phone now costs $400 instead of $500. In the other situation, you're *losing* $100, because you know you just missed out on that coupon. Both involved $100, so you might expect to experience equal amounts of pleasure and pain. But that's not the case. Remember, losses loom larger than gains. Because of loss aversion, we experience twice as much psychological *pain* from losing that $100 as we experience *pleasure* from gaining $100. In other words, to feel the intensity of losing $100, you'd have to gain $200.

We've learned to adapt our behavior to this cognitive bias: We do what we can to avoid losses. For our clothes, that means holding on to old T-shirts that we'd never buy if we encountered them in a store today. In dating, that means holding on to a bad relationship. We're more terrified of the potential *loss* of our partner than intrigued by the potential *gain* of the person we could date instead.

THE PROBLEM WITH HITCHING

Breaking up is a major decision, with major consequences, a decision you might be tempted to delay. But what you don't realize is that by staying in the relationship, *you are already making a decision.*

A breakup isn't an exit ramp—it's a T-shaped junction. To the left, Breakup Point. To the right, Stay Together Mountain. No matter which direction, you're making a choice.

Like Ditchers, Hitchers underestimate opportunity cost. But Hitchers miss out on finding a new relationship. To extend my highway metaphor, the longer you sit idling at the intersection, the longer it takes to get to your destination. (You're also wasting gas, which is just so inappropriate. Climate change is real, people!)

But here's the worst thing: You're not alone in the car. Your partner is with you. If you're planning on ending the relationship, every day you wait, you're wasting *their* time, too. You should be especially sensitive if you're dating a woman who is hoping to give birth to her own kids. You're underestimating *her* opportunity cost of being with you. The longer you put off breaking up with her, the less time she has to find a new partner and build a family. The kindest thing is to give her a clear answer so she can move on and find someone else.

SHOULD I STAY OR SHOULD I GO?

Hopefully, you now have a good sense of whether you're more of a Ditcher or a Hitcher. But you might still be struggling to decide what to do next when it comes to your relationship. Below is a series of questions that will help you decide whether to end it or mend it. Carve out some time, make yourself some tea, and sit down with a journal to answer these questions.

1. *Take the Wardrobe Test: If your partner were a piece of clothing that you own—something in your closet—what piece of clothing would they be?*

How to interpret your answer: Use this answer to understand how you view your partner and the relationship. As I mentioned, the abstract nature of this question helps reveal some underlying truths about our partnerships. Interpreting your answer will require you to analyze your own psyche. In general, it bodes well for your relationship if the answer is a piece of outerwear, like a sweater or jacket that keeps you warm, or a favorite shirt, pair of pants, or shoes. It's worrisome if your item involves something that's worn out, itchy, or uncomfortable, or something you don't want to be seen wearing in public, like a tattered banana hammock.

2. *Are there extenuating circumstances going on in your part-*
   ner's life right now—like a new job or a sick parent—that
   make it hard for them to show up for you the way you want
   them to? Is it possible that things will go back to normal
   when this situation is resolved?

How to interpret your answer: Let's say there's an external
situation—like a demanding assignment at work—that's causing
your partner to be distracted, less present, less patient, or less giving.
Yes, it's useful to know how they respond to stress, but that doesn't
mean you should interpret their behavior as a sign of who they are
or how they'll act throughout the relationship. Their behavior might
be temporary. Remember who they were before this happened. Can
you ride it out a little longer to see if they return to their normal
behavior once the situation is resolved?

3. *Have you tried to fix things and given feedback?*

How to interpret your answer: Imagine if you were fired before you
were told your job was on the line. That would suck, wouldn't it?
That's why a lot of companies have routine performance reviews.
Regular check-ins give people an opportunity to improve. While
your ex can't sue you for breaking up without a heads-up, I don't
recommend this behavior. Give the person a chance to address whatever is going on. Instead of bailing, face the challenge of talking
to your partner and explain the changes you'd like to see in the
relationship. (More in the next chapter on how to navigate tough
conversations like this one.)

4. *What are your expectations of a long-term relationship? Are*
   they realistic?

How to interpret your answer: First, understand that no one is perfect, including you, so stop being so freakin' picky about tiny char-

acter flaws! Those are pet peeves and not dealbreakers. Don't be like the character Jerry on *Seinfeld*, the perpetual bachelor who breaks up with women because they have "man hands," "shush" him, eat their peas one at a time, or enjoy a khakis commercial he dislikes.

If you're a Romanticizer (look back to Chapter 3 if you need a refresher), check in on those expectations. Romanticizers tend to expect a happily ever after and then struggle when issues inevitably arise. They think, *If this person were really my soul mate, it wouldn't be so hard.* But all relationships go through periods of highs and lows, and you're better prepared to handle the low points if you know they're coming.

You may encounter a low when that initial infatuation fades. Our brain is on this drug of love for the first few years of a relationship. The next phase is more familiar, less intense. More "What can I pick you up from the grocery store?" and less "Let's do it on the kitchen floor." That change can feel disappointing; some people try to recapture the rapture by starting over with someone else. However, if your goal is to be in a long-term relationship with a committed partner, understand that the shift is more or less inevitable. You can keep chasing the new-relationship high, but the dynamic always changes eventually.

5. *Finally, it's time to look at who you've been in the relationship. You are half of the dynamic. Are you bringing your best self to the partnership? Are you doing everything you can on your end to make it work? Can you work on being a more generous, present partner?*

How to interpret your answer: Don't just focus on your partner's flaws. Look at yourself, too. If there's more you can do to make the relationship work, perhaps by being kinder, try that before you pull the plug. If it turns out that you've been bringing your best self to others (work and friends and family) and leaving your partner with the scraps, see what your relationship feels like when you invest in it first. Check out Chapter 18 for tips on how to make a long-term relationship work.

ASK A TRUSTED FRIEND OR FAMILY MEMBER

If you're still struggling to decide whether you should stay in a relationship, it may be time to phone a friend. You'll likely need to ask for feedback outright. Etiquette dictates that we keep our mouths shut about other people's relationships, even when we notice red flags, so most people won't offer this kind of feedback without being called on first. As my dad says, "I'm part of the welcoming committee, not the hiring committee." But our friends and family can see things that we're blind to. That's because we're infatuated with our partners during the first two to three years we're together, which turns us into poor judges of our own relationships.

A friend of mine called off her wedding a few weeks before the big day. At that point, several people confessed they'd had doubts about her ex-fiancé but didn't want to offer unsolicited advice.

Don't let that happen to you. Ask a trusted friend or family member what they really think about your relationship. Choose your adviser wisely. This should be someone who knows you and your partner well, has your best interests at heart, and is good at helping you think through decisions. Avoid people who might project their own issues onto your situation (read: have trust issues after being cheated on), who might want you to be single or in a relationship because of how it affects their lives (read: want you to go on double dates with them or serve as their wingperson), or who are in love with you and therefore can't give impartial feedback!

Tell them that you feel bad putting them in an awkward situation, but you really need an honest opinion. A woman I know named Meredith has a contract with her best friend that if either of them is dating someone the other thinks is not a good match, they will call it out, no matter how hard it is to have that conversation.

Honor your commitment not to hold the advice against your friend or family member, even if you decide not to follow it. Please don't punish someone for giving honest, *solicited* feedback! And if they resist having the conversation, don't force it.

In the end, the decision is still yours. But what did you learn from discussing it with a trusted confidant? Did they confirm your fears? Did they advise you to stick it out? Often it's as useful to pay attention to your *reaction* to the advice as it is to receive the advice itself. How did you *feel* when they shared their thoughts? Relieved? Panicked? Use this experience to tune in to your own feelings about what to do next.

WHAT TO DO NEXT

If you're a Ditcher who has given this relationship a chance and it just isn't working: Leave the relationship. Maybe this just isn't the person for you, and that's okay.

But you're not off the hook yet. It's important that you keep your Ditcher tendency in mind. The next time you're in a relationship and you feel that familiar urge to leave, I want you to revisit the questions above and make sure you're bidding adieu for the right reasons.

If you're a Ditcher or a Hitcher who hasn't given the relationship a real chance (for example, you haven't brought your best self to it): Stay in the relationship and see what happens when you're patient and invested. Relationships go through natural ups and downs over time. The longer the relationship, the more likely it is that there will be periods—perhaps even several years—when relationship satisfaction dips. It's important to recognize that often a low point isn't a breaking (or breakup) point.

In his book, *The All-or-Nothing Marriage*, Northwestern professor Eli Finkel suggests that couples learn to **recalibrate** their expectations during a relationship's downturn. Downturns can happen for a number of reasons—perhaps because of demands from young children, aging parents, or a stressful job. While some marriage experts might tell you that when things are rough in your relationship, you need to invest *more* time and energy to make it work, that's often unrealistic. When you're depleted, there's not much left to give. Instead, ask less from your relationship—temporarily—while you sort out other parts of your life.

Focus on yourself first. We're most able to love when *we* feel complete. The more confident and comfortable we feel about ourselves, the easier it is to give and share with others. If you can work on making yourself happy first, instead of expecting it to come from someone else, your relationships will be easier.

While the idea of couples therapy might seem scary, you may want to consider it, even if you're not married. There's a misconception that if a relationship needs therapy, it's too late to save it. No! Give it a chance. According to relationship scientist John Gottman, despite there being almost a million divorces in the United States every year, fewer than 10 percent of these couples ever talk to a professional. Couples therapy has been studied and validated over the past few decades. Who knows how many of those couples may have been able to save their relationship if they'd received professional support?

I feel comfortable giving you this advice because of my own experience choosing to stay.

A few years ago, I sat with Scott at a fancy restaurant in New York. A waiter appeared at our table, offering a basket full of bread rolls just pulled from the oven. I picked one out and carved out a heap of cultured butter, flecked with sea salt.

"What have you been up to at work?" I asked Scott.

At the time, we'd been dating for three years and living together in San Francisco for one. I'd moved to New York temporarily to participate in the four-month TED Residency. He'd surprised me with this dinner to celebrate the end of the program. It was a grand gesture, and one I appreciated, because we were not doing well.

Our relationship had been shaky since January, turned upside down by several big changes in my life. After almost a decade in the corporate world, I'd quit my job to pursue my passion. I'd gone from earning a tech salary to earning no salary, and from working in an office with thousands of people to working alone from a different city.

We'd had several long, difficult conversations. I stated my values that I felt weren't being met (community, friends, travel) and asked him to put more effort into those areas of our lives. We even went to a terrible couples therapist who quoted his own lame Facebook posts and suggested that we, neurotic Jews, should start doing extreme sports together to reconnect. Ironically, we bonded over our mutual dislike of him.

During one of those challenging conversations, Scott mentioned that I never seemed to listen to him when he talked about work. "You think what I do is boring," he said. "It's not. We're trying to help save women's lives by improving breast cancer screening."

He was right. I'd never really understood what he did. Though I worked in tech, I'm not a particularly technical person; I can barely work my DSLR camera. When people asked me about Scott's job in artificial intelligence at Google, I usually replied with a word salad of "machine learning," "computer vision," and "medical imaging" until they nodded sympathetically and the conversation moved on.

Finally, the four months of long distance were over. Scott had flown across the country to see my TED Talk, which focused on romantic relationships. The irony wasn't lost on me that I was trying to help others create lasting love while my own relationship faltered.

He'd taken me to that fancy restaurant to celebrate. In that moment, I finally decided to learn what he did for a living.

He provided the basics of his job—what he did and how it had the potential to advance the practice of radiology. I sat there, listening to him explain the intricacies of his role on the mammography team, and I felt proud of him. I wondered why I'd never cared to ask him about his work before.

Prior to that dinner, I'd spent many hours alone and with friends, wondering if we should break up. I'd gone through all of the exercises and anguish I described above.

But that night, when I really reflected on my behavior, I realized how much I'd asked him to change for our relationship without being willing to put in the work myself.

The work: paying attention, asking questions, listening. Prior to that dinner, I was guilty of the critique in that old saying: "The shoemaker's children go barefoot." In my quest to help others with their relationships, I'd forsaken my own.

During dinner, I made an impassioned effort to connect with Scott about his job. I opened the door, and he walked through it. What followed was one of the best conversations of our relationship.

I see that dinner as the turning point in our partnership, the moment when I realized I'd been taking him for granted and prioritizing my work, emails, and dating coaching clients over him.

While things weren't easy, they got better. I put in more effort and paid more attention to Scott. And Scott committed to getting to know more of my friends, investing more in our community, and being more proactive about travel. We made our relationship a bigger priority in our lives. We tended to it. We fixed it instead of giving up on it.

If you're a Hitcher who has given this relationship a chance and it just isn't working: Leave the relationship. It's going to be painful for both of you, but it's time to move on.

Why spend more weeks or months or even years of your life in a relationship that isn't working? I believe there's a fulfilling partnership waiting for you out there, but you have to say goodbye to this relationship so you can say hello to that one.

Ultimately, that's what Sydney decided she needed to do. A few months after our call, I asked her if we could meet up in San Francisco.

We decided to meet up for vegan Mexican food. I arrived at the restaurant early, excited to finally meet her in person. Soon a blond woman in a bright yellow raincoat approached me. As I stuck out my hand, she pulled me into a big hug. "Thank you," she whispered.

Later, as we dug into our chips and salsa, she caught me up on her love life. "The day after you and I spoke, I just couldn't stop thinking about how I'd called Mateo a scrubby old sweatshirt," she said. "I knew I had to break up with him." A few weeks later, she did. "Getting out of the relationship felt like taking off a heavy coat—or I guess a scrubby old sweatshirt—that had been weighing me down."

I nodded. I was proud to hear that she'd made a decision and stuck to it.

Several months later, Sydney met another guy while in New York. He was the opposite of Mateo. Ambitious, worldly—and constantly challenging her. He soon moved to San Francisco to be with her. Later that year, she emailed me with an update: "I am in a beautiful and healthy relationship with someone I adore. And you helped me find the courage to make that happen."

The decision to stay or leave, end it or mend it, is challenging. But if you're confident you want to break up, it's vital you take the other person's feelings into consideration when you do it. Read the next chapter for tips on how to close the relationship with compassion.

KEY TAKEAWAYS

1. When people are deciding whether they should end it or mend it, they often fall into two categories: **Ditchers** or **Hitchers**.

2. **Ditchers leave relationships too quickly, without giving them a chance to develop.** They confuse *falling* in love with *being* in love, and expect the whole relationship to offer that initial excitement. They underestimate the **opportunity cost** of learning how to make relationships work.

3. **Hitchers stay in relationships too long.** Hitchers are affected by cognitive biases like the **sunk-cost fallacy** (continuing to invest in something because you've already dedicated a lot of resources to it) and **loss aversion** (our tendency to try and avoid losses because we experience them as particularly painful). Hitchers forgo the opportunity to find a more satisfying partnership.

4. To figure out whether to stay or go, **consider your historical tendencies and determine if you've given the relationship a fair chance.** Get input from someone you trust to help you make your decision. Ask yourself **the Wardrobe Test** question: If my partner were a piece of clothing in my closet, what would they be?

CHAPTER 15

MAKE A BREAKUP PLAN

How to Break Up with Someone

When I set out to help people find love and build lasting relationships, I never imagined that work would include "breakup consulting." I know the idea of working with someone to plan a breakup sounds odd, but I've come to see it as one of the most important parts of my job. In order to create the partnership of their dreams, people may first need to exit a middling or bad relationship. And I help them do that.

Often, even though people have decided they want to end things, they struggle to do it. They're afraid of the difficult conversation, of hurting their partner, and of being alone. Their goal is to break up, but they spend months or even years hesitating. Researchers have dedicated a lot of time exploring the best techniques to help people accomplish their goals. That's why—as awkward as it may seem—it's useful to apply goal-setting research here.

When people don't execute on their goals, it's usually because they're missing a plan. For example, economist Annamaria Lusardi and her team researched how a company could get more employees to set up and maintain an employer-sponsored savings plan. They provided a planning aid for new hires. This written aid suggested the new employees set aside a specific time to enroll in the savings plan, laid out the exact steps to enroll, provided estimates of how long each step would take, and offered advice on what to do if you got stuck. This aid raised enrollment rates in the plan by 12 percentage points to 21.

Consider this your breakup-planning aid. I'll explain the steps to take as well as the research backing them up. Note: This plan is for people who are in a relationship but aren't married and don't have kids together. For people in that situation, your breakup entails far more logistics, such as how to manage divorce or custody agreements. This plan doesn't address all of those complexities. And if you've been out on only a few dates, the steps outlined below will be overkill. Instead, send a short text to thank the other person but let them know you're not interested, or call the other person to break the news. (Check out the anti-ghosting sidebar in Chapter 12 for tips on what to say.)

Step 1: Record your reasons for wanting the breakup.

Motivation isn't constant. We experience what behavioral scientist and Stanford professor BJ Fogg calls "motivation waves"—our motivation ebbs and flows. During moments of peak motivation, we're able to do really hard things we couldn't have accomplished otherwise. The trick is to take action at this time. For example, if there's a hurricane scare in your town, it may give you the motivation you need to get storm shutters for your home.

If you're feeling ready to break up with someone, you're likely experiencing peak motivation. It's going to get you through the first bit—actually breaking up—but your motivation will likely decline later, when you might wonder if you've made a huge mistake. With that in mind, I want you to capture your feelings during this peak so you can steel yourself later on, when motivation drops.

Write yourself a letter about why you've chosen to end things. In a few weeks, when you're horny or lonely (or, in extreme cases, "hornly") or want someone to feed your rabbit during a trip, you'll remember exactly why you made this difficult decision.

Here's a letter written by one of my clients:

When I lie in bed at night next to him I feel like I'm lying to myself. He's not nice to me. I treat him like a priority and he treats me like an option. He lets me down, and he doesn't care about my friends. I'm attracted to him and we have fun together but that's not enough. I can't keep pretending that I am okay being #5 on his priority list after his job, going to the gym, swimming, and riding his bike. I want a relationship that feels like we're both giving. I'll miss him and I'll miss the great sex but I am doing this because I really believe I deserve something more than what he can give me right now.

Now it's your turn.

EXERCISE: Record Your Reasons for the Breakup

In a notebook, write yourself a letter explaining why you're making the decision.

Step 2: Make a plan.

Research from psychology professor Gail Matthews showed that participants who wrote down their goals, defined their action plan, and provided weekly progress updates to a friend were 33 percent more likely to achieve their goals than those who did not take those actions.

You've already written out the reasons you want to go through with the breakup, painful and scary as it might be. It's time to pull off the Band-Aid. Once you've decided to do it, stop delaying it. Throughout this book, I've discussed the power of deadlines, especially short ones. This advice holds true for breakups. Set a deadline for yourself so you actually get it done. I recommend clients set a deadline that's within the next two weeks. It's enough time to prepare, and to ride that motivation wave, but not enough time to chicken out.

EXERCISE: Set a Clear Deadline

I commit to having this conversation by: _____

Once you've set your deadline, it's time to make a more specific plan for when and where you'll have the breakup conversation. Research from David W. Nickerson of the University of Notre Dame and Todd Rogers of Ideas42, a nonprofit dedicated to social science research, demonstrates the power of making a plan for when and where we'll act. They asked people in single-voter households specific questions about their plan for voting. For example: "Around what time do you expect to head to the polls on Tuesday?" "Where do you expect you will be coming from when you head to the polls on Tuesday?" and "What do you think you will be doing before you head out to the polls?" It turned out that the people in single-voter households who were asked those questions were 9 percent more likely to show up to vote than those who hadn't been asked those questions. Merely being prompted to make a plan made a difference!

Not only does having a specific plan make you more likely to *follow through* on the breakup conversation, it's also a way to make sure you're being as compassionate as possible to your partner during this difficult moment.

Choose a quiet location, preferably your home or your partner's. Don't break up with someone in public. I see that as a weaselly attempt to ensure the other person doesn't make a scene. You know what? Maybe they will! It's your right to break up with them, and it's *their* right to have a strong emotional response to that action.

Consider your timing. You're about to detonate a bomb in someone else's life. You know this is coming; they don't. Don't break up with someone the day before they have to take a big exam, or give a presentation, or interview for a new job. One of my clients planned to break up with his girlfriend on a Saturday night at six p.m. They had committed to attending her niece's recital at seven p.m. that night. That's not fair. Understand that the breakup will likely derail the night, their weekend, and beyond, so choose your timing carefully.

Another client realized her girlfriend had a big presentation the following Monday, so she decided *not* to break up with her that weekend. They had the conversation the following Friday night, after she'd given the presentation. This gave her the full weekend to start the recovery process. (Flip ahead to the next chapter for tips on getting over a breakup—this can help you keep your soon-to-be ex's needs reasonably in mind.)

Delay within reason. Don't push back the conversation for months if your partner has a super-stressful job with nonstop important meetings, but don't be a dick.

EXERCISE: Commit to a Specific and Thoughtful Time for the Conversation

I'm going to do it on _____ because

_____ .

(For example: I'm going to do it Friday night after his big presentation next week, because that gives him the weekend to recover.)

Once you've decided when and where you'll initiate the breakup, you'll want to make a plan for what you're going to say. How do you want to start? I suggest you emphasize that you've given this decision deep consideration and you want to end the relationship. Be compassionate but direct.

You could say something like: "I really care about you, and I don't want to hurt you, but I think we need to break up. We both know this relationship hasn't been working for a while. We tried to make it better, but at this point, I don't think we can make the changes we need to. I want us to both find love and be happy, but I don't think this relationship is going to give us that."

Another example of an opener: "I need to talk to you. I love you, and I love so many aspects of our relationship, but I'm not happy, and I don't know that you are, either. This is insanely hard to say, because I don't want to hurt you. I'm so grateful for the time we've had together, but after giving it a lot of thought, I don't think we should be together."

Obviously your partner will be hurt. That's unavoidable. Do your best to make them feel better. But if they say, "What's wrong with me?" don't answer. Here's why: They're the wrong person *for you*, but there's nothing inherently "wrong" with them, and even if there is, you're not in a position to say that. You're a very biased source at this point. You've just convinced yourself to dump this person. You can share reasons why you don't want to stay together—for example, you bring out an anxious side of each other, fight all the time, or repeatedly asked the other person to work on certain issues in the relationship and they refused—but you're not the ultimate authority on what's "good" and "bad" about them. The same advice holds if they ask what they did wrong. This is a *breakup*, not a *feedback session*. As I mentioned in the previous chapter, it's your responsibility to bring up any issues and try to address them *before* you decide to end things.

This helps protect the person from unnecessary pain during the recovery period. Know that whatever you say is likely what they'll fixate on after the breakup because of something called the **narrative fallacy**. Our brain tries to create a cause-and-effect story to explain the events we witness and experience, even when that story is false. Any breakup is likely a response to a whole number of situations and dynamics, but when you end things with someone and give a specific reason for doing it, they'll obsess over that reason. Don't plant that unhelpful seed in their mind.

I had a client whose boyfriend broke up with her because he "didn't like her smell." Yes, pheromones are real, and yes, scientists have shown that people often prefer the pheromones of someone who's the most genetically different from them, which is evolutionarily beneficial since it gives future offspring the most genetically diverse immune system and a greater chance at survival. But when the woman heard this critique of how she smelled, she *was not* thinking about her offspring—heck, they'd been dating only six months. Instead, she freaked out that she smelled bad! She changed her deodorant. And her body lotion. And got a pap smear. She even had her gut bacteria tested! I tried to tell her that she didn't smell bad. But once she'd gotten it in her head that her smell was why he'd broken up with her, she couldn't stop focusing on it as *the* reason.

If you find yourself put on the spot, say something about the fact that you respect them, and you don't think this will work long term, so you don't want to waste their time.

It's tempting to want to stay and offer the other person support. Or you may feel like it's your responsibility to answer every single question. However, marathon discussions detailing everything you both felt went wrong in the relationship are not useful. You don't want this meeting to cause you to say something hurtful. Therefore, I want you to set a time limit on the first conversation. Talk for an hour, maybe ninety minutes, and then end the conversation. Now, I don't recommend telling your soon-to-be ex, "We have an hour to talk, and that's it." And you certainly don't want to use a stopwatch to time yourself. But don't let the conversation drag on forever. Tell them you can talk again the next day if needed. If you've been dating for a long time or there are complicated logistics to work out, these conversations may unfold over a series of days.

To help you express yourself as clearly and compassionately as possible, plan out the conversation with my Critical Conversation Planning Doc. Below, you'll see how my clients have us1ed it before a breakup. I've included a blank one in the Appendix. It's useful for preparing for all types of tough conversations, not just breakups.

EXERCISE: Critical Conversation Planning Doc

1. What's your goal for this conversation? (In other words, what does success look like?)

We both get to express how we're feeling, she feels heard, and it's clear we're broken up.

2. What's the core message you want to communicate?

I've given this a lot of thought, and I really care about you as a person, but I don't think this is the right relationship for me.

3. What tone do you want to use? What tone do you want to avoid?

Calm, compassionate, caring. I want to avoid sounding defensive or callous.

4. How do you want to open the conversation?

"I trust this won't come as a surprise to you, because in the past few months, we've both shared that we aren't feeling happy. I've given it a lot of thought, and even though I care deeply about you, I don't think this is the right relationship for me, and I think we should break up."

5. What needs to be said?

- *"Thank you for supporting me during my job transition, for being so kind to my family, and for teaching me so much about the world."*
- *"I've been feeling unsure about this for a while. I did a lot of soul-searching, and I don't think this is the right relationship for me."*
- *"We've been fighting a lot lately, and I don't like the side of myself that the relationship brings out."*
- *"We've done the work to see if we can save this relationship, and I believe it's best for both of us if we end it."*

6. What are your concerns about how the other person will react?

She will ask me exactly what she did wrong or she will say mean things to me.

7. What will you do if that happens?

- *If she asks what she did wrong: "This isn't about anything you did or about who you are. It's about what we create when we're together. I don't feel like this relationship brings out the best side of me. You didn't do anything wrong, and I don't want you to blame yourself."*
- *If she says mean things to me: "I understand that you're mad and I've hurt you, so now you want to hurt me. You have every right to be upset, but I don't want this to be more painful for us than it has to be. Please don't attack me."*

8. How do you want to close the conversation?

I'll repeat some of my points, thank her for the time we had together, and offer to text her brother to ask him to come check on her when I leave. No sex!

You can also ask a friend to help you practice what you're going to say. (I always role-play breakups with my clients, even though they find it awkward to "reject" me.) This gives you a chance to hone your message. It also helps ensure that you're being as kind and empathetic as possible. Practice might not make perfect, but this pre-work will help you select the right words in the moment.

Step 3: Create a social accountability system with a friend.

You've got a specific deadline in mind, and now you know what you're going to say, and when and where you're going to say it. How do you make sure you go through with it? Increase your chances of following through by setting up a **social accountability system**. With this technique, you ask others to hold you responsible to the goal you've set for yourself.

Accountability works so well because many of us are what best-selling author Gretchen Rubin calls "obligers." We easily meet expectations set by others but struggle to uphold our own. That's why you may often miss goals you set for yourself (like exercising more) but don't miss appointments for someone else (like picking up a friend's child from school). If you involve a friend, you make this goal about committing to them, not just to yourself.

Find a trusted friend (someone who doesn't like your current partner may be especially enthusiastic about helping you). Make a commitment to contact them after your breakup conversation. If you want to take your accountability system to the next level, incorporate incentives. Behavioral scientists love to use positive incentives or negative incentives to change how people act. For example, one of my clients wrote a check for $10,000 to the presidential campaign of a candidate he strongly opposed. He gave his friend permission to mail it in if he missed the deadline to break up with his girlfriend.

He broke up with her later that day.

EXERCISE: Design Your Accountability System

My accountability partner is: _____

I promise to _____

_____ if I don't meet my deadline.

(For example: My accountability partner is Seth. I promise to publicly post my last three porn searches if I don't meet my deadline.)

Step 4: Have the conversation, but don't have sex!

We've arrived at the hardest part: breaking up. Remember all the things you did to prepare and plan, and don't forget to limit the conversation on day one and continue it later if needed.

Throughout the conversation, check in with both yourself and the other person to avoid **flooding**. This is a physical and mental state when your cortisol—stress hormone—rises and your body enters fight-or-flight mode. It helped our ancestors when they were at risk of being killed by a tiger, but it's definitely not the right mental setting for a crucial conversation. When we flood, we're not able to really listen or take in new information. If either of you feels like you're starting to flood, take a twenty-minute time-out to calm down. Return to the conversation with your original objective in mind. Be kind but firm. Your goal is that by the end of the conversation, it's clear you've broken up.

After the breakup, please, please, please don't have sex!!! Maybe you don't think I need to say this. But trust me, I've heard about enough breakups to know otherwise. Breakup sex is fun, but it's not worth it. It introduces a lot of confusing feelings. That's especially true if you haven't had sex in a while, and the intense emotions of the breakup propel you into bed. Plus, sleeping with someone makes it harder to stick to your resolution to break up, so you may end up taking back what you said. That only complicates the process.

To avoid making this mistake, set up a **Ulysses Contract** or a **pre-commitment device**. In Homer's epic tale *The Odyssey*, Captain Ulysses knows his crew will be sailing past the enchanting Sirens. He's heard about their captivating song, which causes sailors to redirect their ships and crash into their shores. Rather than depend on his own willpower, he makes a plan. He directs his crew to tie him to the mast of his ship so he can't change course. He tells his sailors to put wax in their ears so they won't be able to hear the song. He protects himself from temptation by making a plan in advance.

Behavioral scientists design Ulysses Contracts, too, as a way to help people avoid temptation. Economist Nava Ashraf and her team tested this approach in a study at a local bank in the Philippines. Some clients *voluntarily* opted into a program that restricted their ability to withdraw from their savings account until a certain date or until they'd reached a certain savings goal. They set the dates and goals on their own. Other clients were not offered this program and could withdraw their money at any time. After twelve months, those who had pre-committed had bank balances that were 81 percent higher.

After the breakup, you're vulnerable to temptation. The metaphorical Sirens may be calling you to bed with your ex-partner. Set up a Ulysses Contract by making plans for immediately after the breakup conversation, and create an accountability system to hold you to it. One of my clients worried he would sleep with his soon-to-be ex-girlfriend. He made sure he didn't by promising to pick up a friend from the airport shortly after the conversation. This was something he absolutely could not miss, and he didn't.

Step 5: Make an immediate post-breakup plan for yourself.

Even if you're not tempted to sleep with your ex, you'll likely experience some pretty intense feelings after your breakup. You might feel relieved. And sad. In any case, it's helpful to make a post-breakup plan to keep you from making decisions that you'll end up regretting.

Figure out in advance what you're going to do after the breakup, including where you're going. Don't commit to any demanding plans. Perhaps you can go to a friend's house, order in your favorite food, and rewatch *The Sopranos* from the beginning. Ideally, this is a friend who will either distract you or help you process your feelings. I don't recommend being alone those first few nights. Feeling lonely and uncertain makes you more likely to slide back into the relationship.

Note: If you and your now ex lived together, this post-breakup plan is especially important. Ask a friend if you can stay with them for at least a few days.

EXERCISE: Make a Plan for the First Few Days

Directly after the breakup, I'm going to head to:

_____

During the first few days, I'm going to do these activities:

_____

(For example: Directly after the breakup, I'm going to head to: my sister's house. During the first few days, I'm going to do these activities: watch the British version of The Office, *go to restorative yoga, make a lot of smoothies.)*

Step 6: Create a Breakup Contract with your ex.

After your initial breakup conversation, your ex may want to talk again. Agree to speak, but remember Steps 1 through 3.

It's important to have a plan for yourself. But you also need to make a plan with your ex. Research shows if someone *actively chooses* to do something, they feel more involved in the process and more invested in the outcome. Social scientists Delia Cioffi and Randy Garner demonstrated this effect by asking college student volunteers to help out with an AIDS education project at nearby schools. Half the students were told that if they wanted to volunteer, they should fill out a form stating their interest. The other half were given a form and told to leave it blank if they wanted to volunteer. They were instructed to fill it out only if they were *not* interested in volunteering. Both groups signed up to volunteer at roughly the same rate. But the researchers saw a meaningful difference in who actually showed up. Those in the passive condition, who signed up by not filling out the form? Only 17 percent showed up. Of those in the active condition, who had to fill out the form, 49 percent upheld their commitment: almost three times as many as the other group. When you actively agree to do something, you feel like the decision is yours, and you see it as a reflection of your own preferences and ideals. This doesn't happen when you passively commit. That's why making a plan with your ex will help you both feel a little better about an otherwise painful process. I've created a Breakup Contract to help.

Whoa—did she just say "contract"?

Yes, I did. I know it seems a little out there, but a few years ago I was struck by Cioffi and Garner's research, and the power of active commitment. I wrote the contract to help friends navigate a tricky breakup. Since then, several thousand couples around the world have accessed the online version of my contract, and I've received dozens of emails from people about how it helped them manage the end of their relationship. (As I mentioned at the beginning of this chapter, breakups are much more complicated if you're married and/or have kids together. This Breakup Contract is designed for pre-marriage, no-kids relationships.)

Introduce the idea by saying something like: "I know this sounds ridiculous, but I think it might be helpful if we get on the same page about what we both want moving forward. Are you willing to take a look at this with me?"

You don't have to agree on every point, and you likely won't. But the contract is a great way to get a tough conversation going while figuring out what would help both of you move on. You can find a blank Breakup Contract on my website—loganury.com.

Step 7: Change your habits to avoid backsliding.

Your breakup will likely leave a number of holes in your life. Let's work on filling them. Was the background on your phone a picture of the two of you at the park with his dog? Replace it with one of you with your best friends—that glamorous shot from last year's New Year's where you look tan and happy. Was she the person with whom you watched your favorite TV show? Recruit a friend to either join you on your couch or watch it with you over the phone. Was he your go-to running partner or dim sum collaborator? See if your mom is up for some jogging . . . to a restaurant with pork siu mai.

Perhaps one of the most challenging aspects of modern break-ups is not being able to text your partner when something exciting happens at work or when you need to vent about your family. Research from *The Power of Habit* author Charles Duhigg shows that a powerful strategy to break a habit is to replace it with a new activity.

To help my clients break their texting habit and avoid backsliding, I ask them to list specific moments that might be difficult for them, then write down the people they'll contact instead of their ex. I call it Text Support.

Fill out your own Text Support worksheet. I've provided some suggestions, but feel free to add your own below.

MY BREAKUP TEXT SUPPORT LIST

Situation	Whom I'll contact
Want to share good news about work	
Want to share bad news about work	
Want to make plans on a weekday night	
Want to make plans on a weekend	
Want to discuss politics	
Want to share a funny story	

Want to watch "our show" (the TV program I used to share with my ex)	

Step 8: Don't be the "Nice Breakup Person."

The aftermath of a breakup, even if it's one you wanted, isn't easy. You might have some moments of doubt, fear, or uncertainty. Just because you initiated the breakup doesn't mean you're not in pain. I'll cover more about how to get over heartbreak in the next chapter, but here's some advice that's written specifically for the person who asked for the breakup.

For a while, you may experience a roller coaster of emotions, from extreme relief to extreme regret. "Why did I do this?" or "Am I going to die alone?" If that happens, return to the external accountability system you created at the beginning of the process. Revisit the letter you wrote about why you did it. Ask the friend who helped you role-play the conversation to remind you why you did it.

You might also be feeling guilty for hurting someone you care about. Even if that happens, resist the urge to check in on your ex too much, especially in the first few weeks after a breakup. When I spoke to author and philosopher Alain de Botton, he gave the same advice: "There's a terrible phenomenon of the **Nice Breakup Person.** We hear a lot about the horrible breakup person, but we don't hear so much about the nice person who stays around, who keeps calling you on your birthday, etc."

Don't be the Nice Breakup Person. You're not actually being nice. In many cases, your behavior is more about helping yourself than helping the other person. "Have the courage to assume responsibility for the damage you've done in their life, without trying to make it all better immediately," de Botton said. "They may see you as the devil for a while. Just live with that. I see a lot of people wanting always to be the nice person, even while doing something that's going to be really difficult for the person."

Don't be "nice" just to make yourself feel better. Give them space to move on.

KEY TAKEAWAYS

1. **When you've decided you want to break up with someone, it's time to make a plan.** Think through what you're going to say and when and where you're going to say it. Be kind but firm.

2. Use an **accountability system** and **incentives** to ensure that you follow through with your plan.

3. **Make a post-breakup plan with your partner** to take their needs into consideration. And don't have breakup sex!

4. **Make a post-breakup plan for *yourself*,** including whom you'll reach out to when you're tempted to text your ex.

5. After the breakup, give the other person space. **Don't try to be the Nice Breakup Person.** It makes you feel better but makes it harder for them to move on.

CHAPTER 16

REFRAME YOUR BREAKUP AS A GAIN, NOT A LOSS

How to Overcome Heartbreak

Imagine you're a cancer doctor. You have a patient with lung cancer, and you have to decide how to treat them. Surgery or radiation? Surgery gives your patient a better chance at living long term, but is also riskier in the short term—they could die while under the knife.

You consult your research and see short-term survival rates: 90 percent for surgery and 100 percent for radiation. What would you pick? What about if, instead, you read about short-term mortality rates—10 percent for surgery and 0 percent for radiation?

In a now-famous study, health care researcher Barbara McNeil asked physicians to make that exact hypothetical choice. And she asked one group of doctors to choose based on survival rates and the other group on death rates.

Perhaps alarmingly, the exact same information, presented in two different ways, resulted in vastly different decisions. When she described the surgical option in terms of the chance of survival, 84 percent of physicians chose this option. When she discussed surgery in terms of the chance of dying, only half of them opted for this treatment.

Why did this happen? The doctors responded to how the outlooks were **framed**. The framing effect is our tendency to evaluate things differently based on how they're presented—whether that's a surgeon assessing risk, or a heartbroken person deciding how to move on after the end of a relationship.

Framing, I believe, is the key to getting over breakups. In fact, you can speed up your recovery process by changing your frame. For example, you can focus on all of the activities that you used to love but paused because your partner wasn't a fan. More on that later in the chapter. The point is that, rather than viewing the experience as a devastating loss, you can see it as a gain, something empowering that will improve your life in the long run.

So turn off that *Bridget Jones* TV marathon, put on some rose-colored glasses, and let's turn this pity party into a joy fest. In this chapter, I'll give you four different reframes for your breakup and help you see that overcoming heartbreak is all about perspective.

WHAT'S HAPPENING IN YOUR BRAIN AND BODY

Before we jump into those reframes, I want to share what's happening in your brain and your body when you experience a breakup. Relationship scientists like Claudia Brumbaugh and R. Chris Fraley identify a breakup (or what they call a "relationship dissolution") as "often one of the most distressing events that an individual can experience in life."

As I've mentioned, biological anthropologist Helen Fisher studies the brain in love. One of her favorite research techniques is using fMRI (functional magnetic resonance imaging) brain scans to peek into our heads. She pops people into the brain scanner at different stages in relationships: couples newly in love, people who claim to still be deeply in love after decades, and those who are going through a breakup.

Fisher and her team found that a region of the brain called the nucleus accumbens lights up when we see a picture of a person we're in love with. It's the same part of the brain that's activated when a drug addict thinks about getting a hit. It's also the region of the brain affected during a breakup. Our brain undergoes the same experience during a breakup and a drug withdrawal. It's no wonder we want to keep getting high on our ex's supply. Might as well face it: You're addicted to love.

Breakups wreak havoc on our body, our feelings, and our behavior. Add to that a dash of loneliness and a teaspoon of distress, and you've got the deadly breakup cocktail. According to Fisher, breakups have been found to increase our cortisol (stress hormone) levels, which then suppress our immune system and weaken our coping mechanisms. People may experience insomnia, intrusive thoughts, depression, anger, and debilitating anxiety. What's surprising is that they also score lower on IQ tests and perform worse on complex tasks that require reasoning or logic skills. Heck, people going through breakups have been found to use drugs and commit crimes at higher rates. This holds true even if the person in question was the one who asked for the breakup (whom researchers refer to as "the initiator").

I've guided many clients through breakups. One of the reasons breakups are so painful is because our brain is hypersensitive to loss. And breakups are a dramatic loss. They are the death of your imagined future with your partner. You're grieving the loss of what was, what no longer is, and what will never be. No wonder, thanks to loss aversion, we do so much to steer clear of them.

Here's the good news: Psychologists Eli Finkel and Paul Eastwick found that "a breakup is not nearly as bad as people imagine," and that no matter how happy a couple was in their relationship, when they break up, the pain is rarely as intense as they expected it would be.

According to Gary Lewandowski, a professor and former chair in the department of psychology at Monmouth University, we're more resilient than we think. He studied a group that you might anticipate would be the saddest in the wake of a breakup: people who had been in a long-term relationship for at least a few years, had been broken up within the last few months, *and* hadn't found a new partner. Instinctually, we'd expect the majority of them to view the breakup as a terrible experience. Yet, when Lewandowski and his colleagues talked to this group, they learned that only a third of them saw the breakup as negative. Around 25 percent saw it as neutral, and 41 percent saw it as positive.

So allow me this cliché: This too shall pass. What you're feeling now is temporary. Your weird bodily reactions (goodbye, immune system and sleep!) will end, the pain will fade, and you will overcome this terrible stage.

Reframe #1: Focus on the positives of the breakup.

While you can't *wish* away your pain, you can *write* your way to a less painful story. Remember, your brain is your friend, and it's really quite good at helping you rationalize and get over things. It's time to feed the beast! You can speed up the healing process by giving your brain what it's craving: reasons why the breakup was actually for the best.

Lewandowski conducted an experiment in which he asked participants to write about either the positive aspects of the breakup (why it's good you broke up), the negative aspects of the breakup (why it's bad you broke up), or something superficial and unrelated to breakups. They completed this writing assignment for fifteen to thirty minutes a day for three consecutive days. The people who wrote about the *positive* aspects of the breakup reported feeling happier, wiser, more grateful, confident, comfortable, empowered, energized, optimistic, relieved, and satisfied than when the study began.

When my clients go through breakups, I ask them to complete this same assignment. Here's one list that Jing, my client who started dating for the first time at age thirty-one, emailed me after her breakup:

The pros of my breakup:

1. Don't have to worry about relocating to be near my ex's family in Montana
2. No more fighting about stealing the covers
3. More time with my friends who my ex never prioritized
4. Shorter commute since I won't be staying at my ex's apartment anymore
5. No more going to work with dog hair on my clothes
6. Don't have to go to that expensive wedding over Labor Day weekend
7. More time to spend working on music
8. Don't have to justify spending time with my brother, who my ex hated
9. Don't have to pretend to care about *The Bachelor*
10. Chance to find a happy/healthy relationship

EXERCISE: Write About the Positives of the Breakup

Channel your angst into a manifesto. It will be just like those emo songs you wrote as a teenager, except you won't force eighty people to listen to them at the local Battle of the Bands.

Go to a café or sit on a park bench. Take a blank notebook (but don't watch *The Notebook*). Set a timer on your phone for thirty minutes. Without stopping, and without looking at your phone, write about all the positive aspects of the breakup. If you're feeling a bit of writer's block and are having trouble getting started, try making a list.

Ten Positive Aspects of My Breakup:

1. _____

2. _____

3. _____

4. _____

5. _____

6. _____

7. _____

8. _____

9. _____

10. _____

Reframe #2: Focus on the negatives of the relationship.

Okay, okay. So maybe you're not ready to "think positively" just yet. There's another way forward. In a study similar to the one I described above, clinical psychologists Sandra Langeslag and Michelle Sanchez asked participants experiencing a breakup to do one of three things: Think negatively about the relationship that ended; read statements about how it's normal to experience strong feelings after a breakup; or do something entirely different—like eating. They found that those who were asked to think about the negative elements of the relationship ultimately felt less infatuated with their ex than people in the other two groups.

EXERCISE: Write About the Negatives of the Relationship

Focus on the dark to find the light. Journal about the negative aspects of the relationship. That time she embarrassed you in front of your friends because you thought "soup du jour" was a specific type of soup. Or the moment he let you down and left you stranded without a ride to the airport. From that sinking feeling you had at the dinner table when you'd tried repeatedly to get him to ask about your call with your sister but he never took the bait, to the time she got way too drunk, vomited, and said her ex was more fun than you. Wow, I'm getting exhausted just remembering all of these, and they're *your* experiences.

Spend three consecutive nights writing for thirty minutes about the negative elements of this relationship. What your partner did that annoyed you, the ways in which you were dysfunctional as a couple, or what side of yourself you had to give up for the relationship.

Reframe #3: Rediscover Yourself.

Additional breakup research from Finkel and his colleagues found that breakups can cause a bit of an identity crisis, because so much of who we are is tied up in that relationship. Perhaps you're dwelling on who you were—one half of a dynamic duo, the perfect wedding date. That perspective, while completely understandable, is *loss*-oriented. Instead, let's focus on what you can *gain* from the breakup—who you can be again now that you're single.

Relationship researchers have found this reframe particularly effective. In one experiment, Lewandowski divided people going through breakups into two groups. He instructed one group to go out into the world and spend two weeks doing **routine activities**—things the participants already liked doing, such as going to the movies or the gym or seeing friends. The other group was told to do **"rediscover yourself" activities**—things they had given up on because their ex wasn't into them—like going to spin classes or jazz bars.

Lewandowski found that both interventions worked. Routine activities helped prevent people from staying home and binge-swiping through pictures of their ex or drowning themselves in barrels of macaroni and cheese (my medication of choice). But those who participated in rediscovery activities saw even better results. Those participants regained a part of their identity that had been lost in the relationship. Lewandoskwi explained that "for those people, it was like the dawn of a new day." They felt happier, less lonely, and more self-accepting.

EXERCISE: Rediscover Yourself

Think back: What are the activities you gave up because your ex wasn't interested in them? Did she hate the beach and frown whenever you mentioned live music? (Who is this monster?) Well, now you can go do those things on your own as rediscovery activities.

Get out there! Dig out those boxing gloves, buy some new watercolors, call up that old college friend your ex thought was annoying. Go explore who you were and who you might become again. If you're okay with a little spirituality talk, I recommend the book *The Artist's Way* by Julia Cameron, even if you don't think of yourself as an artist. It's full of inspiration and ideas for you to reconnect with yourself (and your inner creative spirit).

List three rediscover yourself activities you'll explore this month:

1. _____

2. _____

3. _____

KEEP FISHING

Sometimes people wink at me and say, "So, is it true? The best way to get over someone is by getting under someone else?" First, don't wink at me. Second, it depends.

Not everyone who leaves a relationship needs months to heal. Especially if you were the one who initiated the breakup. Sociologist and Columbia University professor Diane Vaughan conducted extensive research on breakups in her book *Uncoupling* and found that we grieve a relationship over a certain timeline. People who initiate a breakup may have experienced negative feelings about the relationship while still in it, perhaps for a year or more. So, when the breakup actually happens, they don't need as much time. If you don't feel as upset as you expected after a relationship ends, don't be alarmed. You're not a heartless demon. You did the grieving while still dating, and now you're ready to move on.

If you were broken up with, your timeline likely started after the relationship ended, so it makes sense that you'll take longer to heal.

What about rebounds? Psychologists Claudia Brumbaugh and R. Chris Fraley found that "people who rapidly begin a new rebound relationship are not necessarily any worse off than those who wait longer to get reinvolved. In fact, in some areas, they appear to be better functioning." The authors explain that people who wait longer to get into a relationship often suffer from decreased self-esteem, while people who enter a new relationship quickly tend to be spared that self-confidence hit. Moving from one relationship to the next means they spend less time alone, questioning their value.

How do you know when you're ready to start dating? The only way to know whether you're ready to start dating is to go on an actual date. If you come home from that date and cry, you probably need a bit longer. But if you find yourself having fun, even just a little, take that as a sign that you can keep going, one step at a time.

Reframe #4: See this as a chance to learn from the past and make better decisions in the future.

As challenging as it sounds, try to see the breakup as a learning opportunity. Psychologists Ty Tashiro and Patricia Frazier found that people often don't take advantage of the potential for personal growth following a breakup. Many individuals "Tarzan" (swing from one relationship to the next) without considering what they've learned from their last partner and how that should inform whom they choose to date next. Don't make that mistake.

This is particularly important if you're trapped in a pattern of choosing partners who don't work out for the same reason. I've had several clients who date the same type of person over and over.

For example, I worked with one client who always pursued younger guys. Nice, fun, attractive men who ultimately refused to commit. She was searching for a Prom Date, not a Life Partner. Her last breakup happened to occur during the COVID-19 pandemic. This gave her the time she needed to pause and reflect on her habits. Through our weekly remote sessions, she learned to recognize her pattern. She came to the conclusion that her actions were preventing her from finding love. Though she'd met plenty of potentially great partners over the years, she'd self-sabotaged, going after the emotionally unavailable younger guys to prevent herself from getting into a real relationship and possibly getting hurt. She committed to making changes to break that habit. She started dating with different priorities and opened her eyes to Prom Date red flags. She gave guys her own age and older a chance. She video-chatted with a number of eligible suitors. Then she went for a walking date with the guy she liked most. After some more socially distanced hangs, they decided to give quarantining together a chance. Moving in with someone she barely knew was completely outside her comfort zone. But the world felt so upside down that she decided to try something new. They're still happily cohabitating and are planning a road trip to visit each other's families.

EXERCISE: Consider What You Want to Do Differently in Future Relationships

A key part of moving on is getting clear about the choices you made in your last relationship and changes you'll make in your next one. In a journal or with a friend, take some time to answer the following questions:

1. Who were you in your last relationship? (For example, the pace-setter, pulling your partner along with you? Or the caboose, being pulled? The mentor or the mentee? The one who committed easily or the person who struggled to put down roots?)
2. Whom do you want to be in your next one?
3. What have you learned about what truly matters in a long-term relationship?
4. Moving forward, what will you look for in a partner that you didn't prioritize this time?

The key to this reframe is recognizing that there's gain even in loss. Psychologists refer to "meaning-making," the process through which people come to understand a life event, a relationship, or themselves. In his landmark book *Man's Search for Meaning*, Viktor Frankl, an Austrian neurologist and psychiatrist who survived the Holocaust, explained that meaning-making allows us to move from suffering to growth: "In some way, suffering ceases to be suffering at the moment it finds a meaning."

Try to not see the breakup as a failure but, rather, as a chance to make better decisions in the future. Update your thinking from "Time heals all wounds" to "Meaning heals all wounds."

EXERCISE: Explore the Deeper Meaning

Take some time to answer the following questions:

1. What did you learn from this relationship?
2. What did you learn from the breakup?
3. How are you different from the person you were before this relationship?
4. What changes will you make in your life as a result of this experience?

Instead of breaking down, break open. Perhaps you'll even wind up a stronger, more beautiful person. In his TEDx Talk, Gary Lewandowski explained the concept of Kintsugi. It refers to a Japanese art form in which broken pottery is put back together using precious metals like gold and silver; the repaired pottery is often more beautiful than it was before it was damaged.

Lewandowski encourages us to see heartbreak as art break: "It's also a philosophy which treats damage and its repair as an opportunity—something to take advantage of, not to conceal, right? This is exactly what can happen in your relationship. Sure, your relationship might leave you with a few cracks, but those cracks, those imperfections, those are sources of strength and beauty, because breakups don't have to leave you broken, because you're stronger than you know."

You may not have gotten to choose what happened to your relationship, but you do get to choose (in part) how it makes you feel—and what you do next.

KEY TAKEAWAYS

1. **We're affected by framing—our tendency to evaluate things differently based on how they're presented.** You can speed up your recovery process after a breakup by reframing this experience from a loss to an opportunity for growth and learning.

2. Breakups wreak havoc on your physical and emotional health. But **we're more resilient than we think**. What you feel during a breakup is only temporary.

3. **Journaling helps.** Write about the positive aspects of the breakup, and the negative aspects of the relationship, to help yourself move forward.

4. **You can regain your sense of identity**, which is often disrupted by a breakup, **by participating in "rediscover yourself" activities**—things that you enjoyed doing previously but gave up during your relationship.

5. You can grow from the experience by focusing on what you learned and what you'll do differently in the future. **Go from "Time heals all wounds" to "Meaning heals all wounds."**

CHAPTER 17

BEFORE YOU TIE THE KNOT, DO THIS

How to Decide if You Should Get Married

"Please complete these three worksheets before Wednesday," I said.

And no, I wasn't talking to a client.

I handed Scott several pieces of paper full of probing questions about his life, his family, and our relationship. He groaned. I didn't blame him.

Welcome to life as my boyfriend. We'd been dating for four years, so he was used to serving as my guinea pig, piloting my relationship activities before I made recommendations to my clients.

This particular homework assignment was designed to help us discuss getting married, something we'd been considering for a while. We'd gone through major relationship decision points: *Are we dating? Should we move in together? Should we break up?* But now we faced a new set of intimidating questions: *Do we want to spend our lives together? What would that life look like?* I was in love with him, but I also knew enough about relationship science to understand the challenges we faced. So many marriages don't last.

This felt like the biggest decision of our lives so far. And it turned out we were right to make the choice carefully. Marriage matters, in more ways than you may realize. In their book *The Case for Marriage*, journalist Maggie Gallagher and sociologist Linda J. Waite found that the happiness and satisfaction of marriage has a tremendous impact on the happiness, physical and mental health, life expectancy, wealth, and well-being of children.

I thought Scott and I needed a pre-marriage boot camp, so I created one. It's called **"It's About Time: Past, Present, and Future."** (Note: The runner-up title was "It's About Time: F**king Put a Ring on It.") It's designed to help you think about where you've been, where you are, and where you're going. Luckily, Scott was game to participate. This process helped us, so I've since shared it with my clients and friends. And now I'm sharing it with you.

You may be thinking, *I don't care about marriage. It's a dumb institution. I don't need the government and the church telling me how to live.* That's fine. But I assume that if you're reading this book, you're hoping to find a long-term partner. In this chapter, I refer to "marriage," but if you don't plan to get married and would rather substitute the phrase "long-term committed relationship" (or replace the tradition of rings with mutual tattoos of the other person's face on your face), that's also a great way to read this chapter.

WE'RE IN LOVE: ISN'T THAT ENOUGH?

Remember, love is a drug. Here's how writer George Bernard Shaw put it in his play *Getting Married*: "When two people are under the influence of the most violent, most insane, most delusive, and most transient of passions, they are required to swear that they will remain in that excited, abnormal, and exhausting condition continuously until death do them part." During the first few years of a relationship, when our brain experiences the effects of this drug, it's almost impossible to rationally evaluate that partnership.

Couples who date longer before getting married have better odds of staying together, in part because that honeymoon-period high is already wearing off when they tie the knot. Their eyes are more open when they say "I do." Couples who wait one to two years before getting engaged are 20 percent less likely to get divorced than those who wait under a year before putting a ring on it. Couples who wait at least three years before engagement are 39 percent less likely to get divorced than those who get engaged before a year.

It's not just about waiting until you've been with the person for a longer period of time. It also might pay to get married when you're a bit older. Researchers like sociologist Philip Cohen attribute the declining divorce rate since the 1980s partially to couples getting married later. Perhaps you should follow my quirky aunt Nancy's rule with her kids: "No marriage until thirty!"

Even if you wait a few years, love can still obscure your priorities. When I interviewed a series of divorce lawyers (a bit of an awkward hobby to explain to Scott), several said that couples often make the same big mistake when considering marriage. They're so fond of each other that they assume the other person wants the same things in life; therefore, they don't set aside the time to talk explicitly about major decisions like where to live or if they want children.

In fact, journalist Naomi Schaefer Riley, author of 'Til Faith Do Us Part: How Interfaith Marriage Is Transforming America, found: "Remarkably, less than half of the interfaith couples in my survey said they'd discussed, before marrying, what faith they planned to raise their kids in." By the time couples discover their incompatibility on fundamental values, they're already married. Enter the divorce lawyer.

This optimistic assumption that you and your partner want the same thing makes sense, by the way. We're led astray by the **false-consensus effect**—a tendency to assume that the majority of others agree with our own values, beliefs, and behaviors. For example, imagine someone who cares about the environment and tries to limit her own meat eating, fossil-fuel usage, and plastic consumption. If a local referendum asked voters to rule on a plastic-bag ban, that person might expect the rule to pass easily, because she would assume that others see the world through the same green-tinted glasses. In a relationship, we take it for granted that our partner sees the world the same way we do—and therefore wants the same things, whether it's how many kids to have or where to live or how to spend or save money. The drug of infatuation, combined with the false-consensus effect, leads a lot of couples to skip crucial pre-marital conversations. So, no, being in love is not enough. It's time to think critically about whether you should get married.

PART 1: ALL ABOUT ME

EXERCISE: Answer the All About Me Questions

Before you think about yourself as part of a couple, consider your individual wants and needs. Schedule some time alone. I recommend blocking off a weekend morning, going solo to a coffee shop with a notebook, and answering these questions.

1. Is my partner more of a Prom Date or a Life Partner? In other words, is this someone who will be by my side for the long term, or someone who's just fun now?
2. The Wardrobe Test: If my partner were a piece of clothing in my closet, what would they be?
3. Is this someone I can grow with?
4. Do I admire this person?
5. What side of me does this person bring out?
6. Is this the person I want to share my good news with?
7. When I have a hard day at work, do I want to talk about it with my partner?
8. Do I value my partner's advice?

9. Am I looking forward to building a future with this person? Can I envision reaching key life milestones together, such as buying a house or having a family?
10. Is this someone I can make tough decisions with? If I imagine worst-case scenarios, like losing a job or losing a child, is this the person I'd want by my side to think through questions like "Should we relocate?" or "How can we manage our grief while taking care of our other children?"
11. Do we communicate well and fight productively?

Read through your responses. But instead of reviewing them as yourself, pretend you're reading what your best friend wrote about *her* relationship. The goal here is to be as honest with yourself as possible. Giving yourself some distance—by imagining you're helping a friend—should provide some perspective.

If this were your close friend, for whom you care deeply and want only the best, how would you advise this person? Are you in favor of the marriage? Do you harbor some concerns? What unanswered questions should they address before moving forward?

Sit with the feelings that come up as you review your answers. This is your moment to decide whether you hit the gas or the brakes. Move to Part 2 only if you decide this is the *right* relationship for you *right now*. If you're unsure, you may want to revisit Chapter 14, to see if it's time to end it or mend it. And if you don't feel ready to get married, that does not spell disaster. You may simply need to spend more time investing in the relationship before you're ready for the next stage. There's no point in rushing such a momentous decision. Remember, couples who wait at least three years are 39 percent less likely to get divorced than those who get engaged after less than a year.

PART 2: ALL ABOUT US

If Part 1 goes well, and you decide to continue, it's time to talk to your partner. These are heavy conversations. Set aside three nights over a month. Don't cram them all into one evening!

Your goal, throughout these conversations, is to stay curious. Discover what your partner wants and understand if this aligns with what you want. Remember, you're trying to avoid the false-consensus effect.

EXERCISE: Answer the All About Us Questions

Set aside one night per conversation. I recommend doing an activity together first to help you feel connected. Psychotherapist Esther Perel notes that one of the moments when we feel most attracted to our partners is when we admire their individual talents. Invest in that attraction by teaching each other a new skill. If one of you is a great cook, why not teach the other a new recipe?

You also want to make the experience feel romantic. I mean, you're talking about possibly getting married—what could be more romantic than that? Set the scene. Dress up. (Read: Don't wear those hideous red sweatpants you got at someone's bat mitzvah ten years ago and refuse to throw away even though your fiancé hates them.) Pull out the bottle of wine you've been saving, cue the Sam Cooke playlist, and snuggle up to answer these questions.

Conversation #1: The Past

- What are three moments about your past that you feel define you?

- How do you think your childhood affects who you are today?

- Did your parents fight? What are your fears around relationship conflict?

- What traditions from your family do you want to carry on in our family?

- How did your family talk (or not talk) about sex when you were growing up?

- What did money represent in your family?

- What baggage from your family do you want to leave in the past?

Conversation #2: The Present

- Do you feel comfortable talking to me as things come up?

- Is there anything about our communication style that you want to work on?

- Do you feel like you can be yourself in the relationship? Why or why not?

- What changes would you like to make to our relationship?

- How well do you think we handle conflict?

- What's your favorite ritual that we do together?

- What's something you wish we did more of together?

- How well do you feel like I know your friends and family? Is there anyone in your life (family, friend, coworker) whom you'd like me to get to know better?

- How often would you like to be having sex? How could our sex life be better? What can I do to improve it? What's something you've always wanted to try but have been afraid to ask for?

- How often do you think about money?

- Let's talk openly about our finances. Do you have student loans? Credit card debt? Is my debt your debt?

- What's the most you'd spend on a car? A couch? A pair of shoes?

Conversation #3: The Future

- Where do you want to live in the future?

- Do you want to have kids? If yes, how many? When? If

we can't conceive on our own, what other options would
we consider? Adoption? Surrogacy?

- What are your expectations around splitting child care
  and housework duties?

- How often do you want to see your family?

- What role do you want religion or spirituality play in our lives?

- Do you want to discuss a prenup? What fears does that
  bring up for you?

- How do you expect to split finances in the future?

- Do you expect you'll always want to work? What happens
  if one of us wants to take time off?

- If I were considering a big purchase, at what point would
  you want me to call you? (For example, what's the cutoff for
  how much I can spend without checking in with you first?)

- What are your long-term financial goals?

- What are you most looking forward to in the future?

- What is a dream of yours for the future? How can I help
  you achieve it?

You may worry that these conversations will be awkward or
forced. Scott and I expected that, too. But as we made our way
through them, we shared long-forgotten stories from our childhoods.

Like the time I had a middle-school meltdown because I was jealous that my neighbor received ten shimmery MAC eye shadows—the sixth-grade equivalent of a Rolex—from her parents for Valentine's Day. (What kind of parents even *give* their kids presents on Valentine's Day?) Scott told me a hilarious story about how his mom refused to buy him a pricey pair of JNCO jeans—the pinnacle of fashion for middle-schoolers in the late '90s. (After looking at pictures of these hideous jeans on the Internet, I think his mother made the right call.)

During one of these conversations, we discovered that Scott wants only one child, and I would like two. He's an only child and I have a sister, and apparently, we both want to re-create the dynamic we had growing up. Our date suddenly turned combative as we argued the merits of our respective childhoods. Scott expressed his belief that it's morally questionable to add more than one child to an overpopulated planet, while I argued that having a sibling automatically enrolls you in ten thousand hours of training in emotional intelligence. Even though we didn't see eye to eye on this point, I was happy we identified our differing views. We decided it wasn't a dealbreaker, because while our preferences weren't aligned, we were both willing to compromise. We plan to have one kid and see how we feel after that.

These conversations convinced me that not only was this the right relationship for right now, it was also the right partnership moving forward. I admire Scott's discipline—the way he works out every day, cooks healthy vegan meals, stays up late finding bugs in his software. I love our silly voices and inside jokes. And I believe in us as a team. We know how to compromise and take turns getting our way. When I asked myself the **Wardrobe Test** question, I imagined him as my favorite pair of red-checkered onesie pajamas, which make me feel safe, warm, and supported. Like I'm wearing a hug.

About six months after we completed this process, Scott invited me to our friend David's magic show. David is a talented mentalist magician who can divine the names of childhood pets and obscure vacation destinations of total strangers. He has a regular Wednesday-night show at a theater nestled in the back of a bar called PianoFight.

That night, as David finished, the crowd rose in a standing ovation. After the applause, David said, "I have one more trick." At the beginning of the show, audience members had written their name and a single word on blank playing cards. David asked a volunteer to select a card. I heard him call my name, and I made my way to the stage.

Then David told me to pull another card at random. Magically, the one I chose had Scott's name on it. Scott walked down the stairs to sit next to me onstage.

We sat there, the lights blinding us to the fifty-person audience. David took a volunteer's phone, opened the calculator app, and started multiplying numbers supplied by members of the crowd. The final tally emerged: 452015. David asked if this number meant anything to us. I didn't recognize it.

Then he drew two slashes between the digits, transforming the number into 4/5/2015. He asked, "Is this your birthday? Scott's?" No—it was our anniversary.

Then David took the deck of cards with names and words on it and asked me to split it into five piles. He asked Scott to turn over the top cards one at a time, and instructed me to transcribe the message on a large easel.

"Will . . . ," I wrote on the board as Scott read the first card.

"You . . . be . . . my . . ."

I covered my face with my hands as I waited for the final card.

"Wife."

Scott stood up from his chair and pulled a ring from his pocket. He got down on one knee. I nodded, grabbed the ring, and pulled him into a hug. After the crowd erupted, David whisked us out of the theater. We emerged into the bar, where a group of thirty friends greeted us. They had formed a "love tunnel," standing two by two with their arms extended overhead. We ran triumphantly through the tunnel.

Although the proposal was a huge surprise, the fact that we wanted to marry each other wasn't. We'd done the work. We'd had the hard conversations. We'd chosen to decide, not slide.

KEY TAKEAWAYS

1. Love is a drug that intoxicates us.

2. **The false-consensus effect is our tendency to think other people see things the same way we do.** When love and the false-consensus effect combine early in relationships, **couples often fail to discuss important aspects of their future before they decide to get married.** They assume they both want the same things without ever confirming that, which can lead to unhappy endings.

3. Before you decide to tie the knot, you can **override the false-consensus effect by completing a series of self-reflection and partner activities called "It's About Time: Past, Present, and Future."** You should have conversations about the past (where you've been), the present (where you are now), and the future (where you're going). And it's crucial to make time to discuss topics like money, sex, religion, and children.

CHAPTER 18

INTENTIONAL LOVE

*How to Build
Relationships That Last*

Remember the Happily-Ever-After Fallacy? It's the mistaken belief that the hard work of love is finding someone. But that's only the first act of your love story. The next part is hard, too—making the relationship last for the long haul. That's what this chapter is designed to help you do.

I'm not going to sugarcoat it. This is what the long haul looks like for many couples:

The first graph on the next page shows the average reported marital satisfaction over time. It turns out the longer you're married, the less happy you are. Happily ever after, my ass.

Another important graph follows it. It shows the percentage of couples who rated their relationships as "very happy" from 1972 to 2014.

As you can see, over the last forty years, fewer and fewer of us are finding long-term relationship satisfaction.

But there's hope. You are not destined to have a disappointing relationship. Great relationships are created, not discovered. You can form a lasting bond by putting in the work. The opportunity is yours to build the relationship of your dreams.

REPORTED MARITAL HAPPINESS OVER TIME

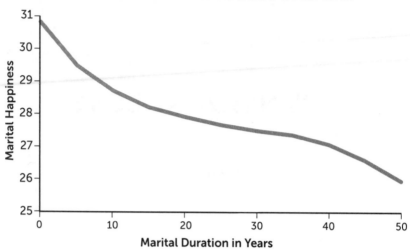

DECLINE OF THE HAPPY MARRIAGE

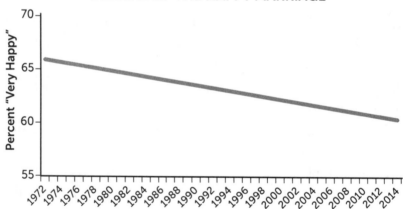

CREATING A RELATIONSHIP
THAT CHANGES WITH THE PEOPLE IN IT

When people ask me what makes a relationship work long term, I often refer to this quote about Charles Darwin's findings on natural selection: "It is not the strongest of the species which survives, nor the most intelligent, but the one most responsive to change." Even if you have a strong relationship today, your relationship may fail if you don't adapt. Your life or your partner's life might take an unpredictable course. Creating a relationship that can evolve is the key to making it last.

Perhaps you don't think you'll change much in the future. You've already become the person you're going to be long term.

EXERCISE: Answer These Two Questions

1. How much do you think you've changed over the last ten years?

_____

2. How much do you think you'll change in the next ten?

_____

Harvard psychologist Daniel Gilbert and his team posed these same questions to a large group of participants. They asked some people to predict how much they'd change in the coming decade. Others answered questions on how much they'd changed over the previous decade. Most people believed they'd changed significantly in the previous decade, but they didn't expect to change much in the next ten years. They're wrong. Gilbert calls this the **end-of-history illusion**.

Gilbert pointed out that we fully expect to physically age—our hair will go gray and our body will change—but we each think that "by and large the core of me, my identity, my values, my personality, my deepest preferences, are not going to change from here on out." The truth is, we never stop growing and changing.

And just as we, as individuals, will continue to change over the course of our lives, so will our relationships. Sometimes one partner will struggle and the other will keep the family afloat. Sometimes you'll feel deeply in love and sometimes you won't be able to stand each other. Sometimes you'll find it easy to talk and sometimes it will feel like a wall has cropped up between you.

Because of the ever-changing nature of relationships, we should act as if they are living, breathing things. But too often we treat our relationship like a toaster. We take it out of the box, plug it in, and hope it stays the same. A toaster works best on the day you buy it, and it slowly gets worse over time. No one assumes their toaster will adapt or improve. In marriage, we commit to the institution on our wedding day and expect it to stay the same—till death do us part.

Well, how's that toaster working out for us? If you look at divorce and separation rates, 50 percent of people are returning their toasters. Our relationships are failing in part because they're not designed to be, in Darwinian terms, "responsive to change."

Let's ditch the toaster and bring romance into the twenty-first century by adopting the philosophy of Intentional Love. This book is about being intentional in how you enter a relationship. That way of thinking guides the next part of your story, too.

To get there, I've designed a set of tools, informed by behavioral science, that will help create the kind of lasting relationship we all say we want but very few of us know how to maintain. For the past few years, thousands of couples around the world have accessed these tools in hopes of creating a relationship that is adaptable, durable, and most important, built to last.

THE RELATIONSHIP CONTRACT

For many of us, the only time we articulate the specifics of the marital commitment is during the wedding ceremony itself. But as we live longer, there might be over half a century between when we say our vows and when that whole "till death do us part" clause kicks in. We need a modernized system that helps us adapt our partnerships as the people in them grow and change. Enter the Relationship Contract.

In Chapter 15, I explained the power of creating a written plan for a breakup, and how *actively* signing up to participate in something makes you far more likely to do it than if you passively agree to it. That's the same logic behind this living, breathing Relationship Contract, a document that's designed to change and grow over time.

This works for couples who are either married or in a long-term committed relationship. Let's start with a disclaimer: The word "contract" might sound scary, but this is by no means a prenup. We're talking about a non–legally binding, mutually agreed-upon document that helps couples create a shared vision for their relationship. Scribble it down on a napkin, draft it in a Google doc, or spell it out in fridge magnets.

These agreements catalyze conversations that couples should have periodically to figure out what they want out of their relationship. They should address questions like: *How often do we want to see our extended families? How do we split our bills? Is sex important to us? Are we monogamous? And how do we define monogamy?*

Psychologists Jesse Owen, Galena Rhoades, and Scott Stanley observed that couples who take the time to talk through big decisions are happier than those who don't. I've led workshops around the country to help hundreds of couples do just that by creating a Relationship Contract.

When you fill out this Relationship Contract, you should be honest, vulnerable, and willing to compromise. This is absolutely not a time to dwell on your partner's shortcomings; nor is it the moment to make demands. The focus should not be transactional—"I'll do the laundry if you'll do the dishes"—but, rather, value-based—"We commit to supporting each other's dreams and making the sacrifices necessary to enable those dreams."

Without fail, I'm surprised by the diversity of clauses in these contracts. Some are serious, like those from the couple who outlined how they'd pay off their student debts. And some are silly, like the ones composed by the pair who pledged to stop buying IKEA furniture.

On the first page of the contract, the couple sets a specific date in the future when they'll revisit the agreement. On that date, they give each other feedback on how they're doing. Some couples re-evaluate their contract annually. Others do it after five or seven years. This conversation forces a decision point when the couple can ask: *What does our relationship need now?* Then they're able to amend the contract to reflect how they've changed as individuals. It also allows for consistent relationship tune-ups, well before there's a breakdown. As John F. Kennedy said, "The time to repair the roof is when the sun is shining." He wasn't talking about his marriage, but you get the idea.

Choose to decide, not slide. In the Appendix, I've included a two-part exercise for writing your own Relationship Contract. These materials have been created in partnership with my friend and collaborator Hannah Hughes. First you'll see the Self-Reflection Worksheet, which you should fill out on your own. It asks questions about how much alone time you need, what your love languages are, what rituals you value in the relationship, and more. Then you'll see a blank copy of the Relationship Contract, which you should collaborate on with your partner afterward.

EXERCISE: The Relationship Contract

Find a weekend when you and your partner are both free. If you can go on a weekend getaway, great! If not, plan a romantic staycation. First and foremost, turn off your phones. Throughout the weekend, in between delicious meals and constant canoodling, find time to work on your Relationship Contract. Make this discussion about love and connection. Think: *Love Actually*, not *love contractually*.

THE CHECK-IN RITUAL

I love this quotation from psychotherapist Esther Perel: "The quality of your relationships determines the quality of your life. Relationships are your story, write well, and edit often."

How often does she mean? I'm a fan of the weekly **Check-In Ritual**, a short conversation in which you and your partner discuss what's on your mind. The Relationship Contract helps you set the direction for your partnership—and the Check-In Ritual ensures that you keep it on track. Many couples are afraid to speak honestly about what they want, whether it's about having kids, opening their relationship, or even ending it. All relationships have issues, and almost all of us feel awkward about bringing them up. The Relationship Contract and the Check-In Ritual are tools expressly designed to make it less awkward.

Every Sunday night, Scott and I sit down on our big white couch to talk. He always sits near the door (which I choose not to read too much into), and I sprawl out on the ottoman. He's usually eating popcorn, and I'm still feeling stuffed from dinner.

We ask each other these three questions: *How was your last week? Did you feel supported by me? How can I support you in the coming week?* Sometimes this Check-In flies by in under five minutes. But when we're having an off week, the Check-In turns into a long, intimate conversation. Sure, these discussions can be difficult, but they're frequently important and illuminating. We try to deal with problems as they arise. It's how we stay connected and discover new things about ourselves and our relationship. Creating this ritual lets us address what's going on before too much time passes and too much resentment has built up.

Just as important as the Check-In conversation is the ritual itself. Making this a consistent, recurring event takes advantage of a super-simple principle behavioral scientists often employ: If we put something on our calendar, and make it the **default**, we're way more likely to actually do it. And because these Check-Ins are recurring events on our calendar, neither of us has to nag the other into finding the time to talk about what matters. The calendar does the nudging for us. Many couples I've worked with who've adopted the Check-In Ritual report feeling happier, more passionate, and more resilient.

Ask yourself this question: What would my life look like if I sat down with my partner on a regular basis and expressed what's really going on for me? I promise you, it's worth it. Choose Intentional Love.

EXERCISE: Design Your Own Check-In Ritual

Sit with your partner and answer these questions together:

1. When do you want to have this weekly ritual?
2. Where do you want your Check-In to take place? Think of a spot where you're both comfortable. The couch? A favorite bench at a nearby park?
3. What questions do you want to ask each other each week?
4. How can you make this ritual special? For example, could you eat your favorite dessert while answering the questions, or give each other a foot massage?
5. What will you do to check in if you're not physically together?

WHAT'S NEXT: A WORLD OF INTENTIONAL LOVE

Strong partnerships don't appear by accident. They need attention and choice. They require Intentional Love. In this world of Intentional Love—really, in a world of intentional living—the hope is that when you reflect back on your life, you'll see a series of decisions that you made thoughtfully, deliberately. Maybe you loved one person better, maybe you had three important relationships, or maybe you were single and had a life full of excitement. Either way, it was an adventure, not an accident. You designed your life, you held yourself accountable, you were honest with yourself about who you were and what you wanted, and most important, you course-corrected when you had to. You didn't live someone else's idea of life, you lived yours.

In researching this book, I had the honor of meeting many people who inspire me: people who embody the ideals of Intentional Love.

For instance, there's the man who goes on dates and tells the truth about what he wants—nothing serious—and more often than not, his words are met with appreciation and relief.

Then there's the trans woman who finally found a partner who can make her orgasm in her new body. They just bought a house together, using their veteran benefits.

There's the man who learned to ask his wife for what he wanted from their house—a space he could decorate that feels like his own.

There's the couple who embraces non-monogamy and bought a home for their secondary and tertiary partners to all raise a family together.

Some of these couples shouldn't work at all on paper, yet because they are intentional, their lives are filled with pleasure and joy. Some of these couples have lived through tragedies like rare cancers and multiple miscarriages. But they work through it by putting tremendous energy into their relationship every day. They are determined to beat the odds, to be part of that too-small percentage of couples who are happy and thriving.

You have a chance. It's not a secret how to do it. I hope this book has shown you how. Now go out there and live *intentionally* ever after.

KEY TAKEAWAYS

1. Over the last forty years, **fewer and fewer of us are finding long-term relationship happiness.** The good news is that great relationships are created, not discovered. **You can build the relationship of your dreams.**

2. **Creating a relationship that can evolve is the key to making it last.** We underestimate how much we'll grow and change in the future, and should seek out relationships where we can learn and grow together with our partner.

3. Writing a **Relationship Contract** allows you to set the direction for your partnership and revise that vision over time. A weekly **Check-In Ritual** helps you deal with problems as they arise.

4. In a world of **Intentional Love**, you design your life, you hold yourself accountable, you are honest with yourself about who you are and what you want, and most important, you course-correct when you need to. You don't live someone else's idea of life, you live yours. **Now go out there and live *intentionally* ever after.**

ACKNOWLEDGMENTS

Writing a book is something you do alone. Unless, like me, you're lucky enough to have a community of trusted friends and advisers who take on your project as their own.

Scott Mayer Mckinney, you spent countless hours editing the manuscript, stewarding my mental health, and reminding me that I have much to learn in the field of relationship science. You are my forever coauthor.

Molly Glauberman, my beloved product manager, you created the structure and support I needed to give birth to this book. It's only fair you'd get Ben in return. Ellen Huet, my grammarian and trusted advisor, your generous feedback at all hours strengthened my ideas, writing, and jokes. Making friends in adulthood is challenging. It took me eight years to find you two, but I am grateful every day that I never stopped looking.

Connor Diemand-Yauman, I feel so lucky that you chose to pour yourself into this project. Each chapter is funnier and deeper because of your input.

Liz Fosslien, I admire your creativity, wit, and brilliance. Thank you for your candid feedback throughout the book process. I am always myself with you and that is a rare gift.

Kimberly Baudhuin, we make a great team. Thanks for saving the day, often.

Britt Nelson and Hannah Hughes, thank you for lending me your excellent taste. Your design skills offered strength during a challenging time.

Rose Bern, thanks for your invaluable contributions to the proposal and the book's foundational research.

Toby Stein, my partner in mischief. You are the paragon of friendship, and your hands-on support throughout the book process proved invaluable.

Emily Graff, my indefatigable editor at Simon & Schuster. You saw this book in me so early on, and have been my advocate at every step along the way. Together we brought this project to life.

To my lifelong friends, you define me. Our relationships are my greatest accomplishment. I live for our conversations and time together. I am here—having achieved this long-standing goal—because you were there with me this whole time.

Dani Helitzer, our friendship has spanned three decades—and outlasted so many ex-boyfriends. You are forever my family.

Lana Schlesigner, how did we manage to find each other at fourteen? Everything that's mine is ours; you are more than a friend, you are a part of me.

Alison Congdon, Tori Simeoni, and Michela DeSantis, I am so proud of what we've achieved with one another's support and guidance. How lucky we were to live in the fourth dimension together.

Tessa Lyons-Laing, my sister. You've plotted with me since the beginning, and I love going through life by your side.

Martabel Wasserman, I appreciate your fierceness, originality, and intelligence. I love seeing myself through your eyes.

Kristen Berman, you're the captain of our Bay Area superhero league. You always say yes, and all of those yesses over the last decade have led to so many good things, including this book.

Erik Torenberg, my first self-proclaimed "fan." Your investment and faith in my work have made so many things possible. Our friendship is a joy in my life.

Misha Safyan, you're a true mensch.

Sara Sodine, throughout this process you generously read so many outlines, drafts, and late-night texts. You are a trusted adviser and friend.

Tara Kousha, your wisdom and guidance in our coaching sessions gave me the courage to pursue my passion. It's an honor to call you my friend.

Meikaela Zwieryznski, your generous hospitality in New York has unlocked so many opportunities for me. There is nowhere I'd rather be than on your couch, talking with you past our bedtime.

This book would not exist without the generosity and wisdom of my mentors, giants in the fields of behavioral and relationship science.

Dan Ariely, learning by your side was the best behavioral science education I could imagine. You've shown me so much about how to live a full and experimental life.

Esther Perel, your visionary work paved the way for this book. From our first conversation about my parents, to our chat about having children, you've added depth, complexity, and wisdom to my life. You inspire me.

To John and Julie Gottman, the original "relationship masters," thank you for both your mentorship and your contributions to the field. My bond with Scott is stronger because we attended your workshop so early on in our relationship.

To Eli Finkel, thank you for your rigorous research that defines how I think about love and relationships. Thanks for your kindness and generosity and for taking a chance on working with me. To Alison Finkel, I see you. Thanks for welcoming me into your home and heart.

Dan Jones, Steven Levitt, Helen Fisher, Alain de Botton, Alexandra Solomon, Barry Schwartz, Sheena Iyengar, Ty Tashiro, and the dozens of people I interviewed about their love lives, thank you for sharing your wisdom with me. Our conversations shaped this book.

To my early readers—Lana, Tori, Tessa, Toby, Kristen, Molly, Ellen, Connor, Martabel, Liz, Etosha Cave, Alexis Konevich, Regina Escamilla, Michael Fulwiler, Laura Thompson, Faryl Ury, Cindy Mayer, Craig Minoff, and Fiona Romeri—thank you for your careful eyes, creative suggestions, and constructive feedback. You saved future readers from awkward jokes and opaque advice.

Thank you to Mike Wang, Jessica Cole, Rui Bao, Tyler Bosmeny, Ryan Dick, Brenna Hull, Tessa, Sam Steyer, Stephanie Sher, MayC Huang, Josh Horowitz, Natalie Tulsiani, and Marina Agapakis for generously hosting accountability dinners. The ideas and feedback shared around your tables shaped this book.

David Halberstein, thank you for generously lending me your brilliant legal mind, even during your first week of paternity leave.

Allison Hunter, my agent, you believed in this book from the beginning. I couldn't have asked for a better advocate.

To my clients, thank you for trusting me with your love lives. Your vulnerability, dedication, and passion motivated me to write this book.

To my family, so much of what was required to write this book came from you and how you raised me: tenacity, a love of language, and an outsized confidence in my own abilities. Faryl Ury and Ben Sacks, we are so lucky to have your love and loyalty just across the bridge. Aunt Nancy, your marriage set the bar high, and your *kavanah* (intention) in this realm inspired many of the ideas in this book. Bonnie and John Ury, you instilled in me a love of reading. It was my greatest wish to write a book that my parents would read, and here we are.

APPENDIX

CRITICAL CONVERSATION
PLANNING DOC

1. What's your goal for this conversation? (In other words, what does success look like?)

_____

_____

_____

_____

2. What's the core message you want to communicate?

_____

_____

_____

_____

3. What tone do you want to use? What tone do you want to avoid?

_____

_____

_____

_____

4. How do you want to open the conversation?

_____

_____

_____

_____

5. What needs to be said?

_____

_____

_____

_____

6. What are your concerns about how the other person will react?

_____

_____

_____

_____

7. What will you do if that happens?

_____

_____

_____

_____

8. How do you want to close the conversation?

_____

_____

_____

_____

RELATIONSHIP CONTRACT:
SELF-REFLECTION WORKSHEET

INSTRUCTIONS

Fill this out on your own. Be honest and open with yourself about
your needs.

TIME

AVAILABILITY

I can spend time with my partner during the following times
(Choose all that apply):

- ☐ Weekday mornings _____
- ☐ Weekday afternoons _____
- ☐ Weekday evenings _____
- ☐ Weekend mornings _____
- ☐ Weekend afternoons _____
- ☐ Weekend evenings _____

Ideally, I'd spend one-on-one time with my partner on _____
occasion(s) per week.

RITUALS

Three of my favorite rituals in my current or former relation-ship are:

(For example, Saturday grocery shopping, movie dates, Sunday breakfast in bed, etc.)

1. _____

2. _____

3. _____

One new ritual I'd like to create in the future is:

_____

_____

_____

SPECIAL ACTIVITIES

Three special activities I enjoy doing with my partner are:

(For example, traveling, fancy restaurants, taking a class together, etc.)

1. _____

2. _____

3. _____

SOLO TIME

When it comes to alone time, I need:

- ☐ A lot (multiple hours per day)
- ☐ Some (at least one night a week)
- ☐ Not much (I get it when I can)

Two activities I enjoy doing alone are:
(For example, yoga, grocery shopping, etc.)

1. _____

2. _____

SOCIAL LIFE

FRIENDS

An activity or tradition I do with my friends that I want to always maintain is:

_____

_____

_____

The friends of mine I care most about my partner getting to know are:

1. _____

2. _____

3. _____

How involved do I want my partner to be in my social life?

- ☐ Totally integrated (we have all the same friends and activities)
- ☐ Partially integrated (we have common friends and activities but separate groups and hobbies as well)
- ☐ Separate (I prefer to have a separate social life and hobbies from my partner)

FAMILY

I would like us to see my family:

- ☐ At least once a week
- ☐ At least once a month
- ☐ A few times a year
- ☐ Once a year
- ☐ Rarely

I want us to spend the following holidays or occasions with my family:

1. _____

2. _____

3. _____

EMOTIONAL NEEDS

AFFECTION

People prefer to receive love in different ways. The five love languages are words of affirmation, quality time, gifts, acts of service, and physical touch.

My love language is:

- ☐ Words of affirmation
- ☐ Quality time
- ☐ Receiving gifts
- ☐ Acts of service
- ☐ Physical touch

STRESS MANAGEMENT

When I get stressed, I help myself unwind by doing the following:
(for example, taking a bath, spending time alone, talking things out, going for a walk, calling a friend)

_____

_____

When I get stressed, I want my partner to support me in the following ways
(Choose all that apply):

- ☐ Listening to me vent
- ☐ Distracting me

- ☐ Giving me time alone
- ☐ Offering solutions
- ☐ Other: _____

FIGHTING

When you and your partner disagree, what are your preferred forms of communication?
(Choose all that apply):

- ☐ Face-to-face conversation
- ☐ Email
- ☐ Text
- ☐ Other: _____

SEX

To me, sex is:

- ☐ Very important
- ☐ Somewhat important
- ☐ Not important

Ideally, I'd like to have sex with my partner _____ times a week/month.

In terms of exclusivity, I want our relationship to be:

- ☐ Monogamous
- ☐ "Monogamish" (somewhat open)
- ☐ Completely open
- ☐ Other: _____

RELATIONSHIP CONTRACT

INSTRUCTIONS

Find time to complete this contract with your partner, ideally in a setting where you feel relaxed and romantic. First fill out the Self-Reflection Worksheet. Then share your answers and practice active-listening techniques to make your partner feel heard, including echoing their thoughts back to them. Take a break when you need it. Seal it with your signatures—and a kiss!

THE CONTRACT

We recognize that relationships take effort. We choose to continue to invest in each other and our mutual love, satisfaction, and growth. We understand that it's easier to deepen and strengthen a relationship during periods of love and happiness rather than trying to improve it during a rough patch.

This commitment is drafted for the mutual benefit of all parties in this relationship.

This agreement is entered into by and between:

Partner 1: _____

Partner 2: _____

(hereafter referred to as **Partner 1** and **Partner 2**)

The term of this agreement shall begin on _____ .

We agree to revisit this agreement on _____ .

BIDS FOR CONNECTION

Relationship researchers John and Julie Gottman tell us that a "bid" is the "fundamental unit of emotional communication." Bids can be small or big, verbal or nonverbal. At their core, they're simply requests to connect. And they might take the form of an expression, question, or physical outreach. Or they can be funny, serious, or even sexual in nature. Every time your partner makes a bid, you have a choice. You can "turn toward" the bid, acknowledging your partner's needs; or "turn away," ignoring the request for connection. People in successful relationships turn toward each other 86 percent of the time. Those in struggling relationships turn toward each other only 33 percent of the time. Couples that turn toward each other's bids enjoy a relationship that's full of trust, passion, and satisfying sex.

We commit to bidding often and turning toward our partner's bids as often as we can:

Partner 1

Initial here: _____

Partner 2

Initial here: _____

TIME

RITUALS

Each week, we want to spend the following one-on-one time together:

(Mark the number of times per week you'll see each other during this time slot)

- ☐ Weekday mornings _____
- ☐ Weekday afternoons _____
- ☐ Weekday evenings _____
- ☐ Weekend mornings _____
- ☐ Weekend afternoons _____
- ☐ Weekend evenings _____

We'll spend one-on-one time together _____ occasion(s) per week.

We'll spend _____ days/nights together without using our phones each week.

Some of our favorite shared rituals are:
(For example, grocery shopping, movie dates, breakfast in bed, etc.)

_____

_____

_____

We commit to doing these as often as we can.

If we miss _____ number of opportunities for quality time per month, we will make it up by:
(For example, going away for a weekend, cooking dinner at home together, etc.)

_____

_____

_____

We also want to try new rituals.

Between now and our next check-in, we will adopt the new ritual of:
(For example, cooking Sunday brunch, saying what we're grateful for before bed, etc.)

_____

_____

_____

SPECIAL ACTIVITIES

Three special activities that really matter to us are:
(For example, traveling, fancy restaurants, taking a class together, etc.)

1. _____

2. _____

3. _____

We commit to making time for these activities with the following frequency:
(For example, cooking together—once a week, etc.)

1. _____

2. _____

3. _____

SOLO TIME

We recognize people need different amounts of alone time to re-charge.

Partner 1

I require the following amount of alone time:

- ☐ A lot (multiple hours per day)
- ☐ Some (at least one night a week)
- ☐ Not much (I get it when I can)

A treasured solo activity for me is:

_____

Partner 2

I require the following amount of alone time:

- ☐ A lot (multiple hours per day)
- ☐ Some (at least one night a week)
- ☐ Not much (I get it when I can)

A treasured solo activity for me is:

_____

We both acknowledge the other's needs in terms of time apart.

FRIENDS

We prefer our friend group to be:

- ☐ Completely shared
- ☐ Somewhat overlapping
- ☐ Completely separate

Partner 1

I commit to getting to know the following three people in Partner 2's social circle:

1. _____

2. _____

3. _____

Partner 2

I commit to getting to know the following three people in Partner 1's social circle:

1. _____

2. _____

3. _____

One goal for our social lives between now and our next check-in is: (for example, attend more parties together, join a sports team, host monthly dinners)

_____

_____

_____

FAMILY

We'll see Partner 1's family with the following frequency:

☐ Weekly
☐ Monthly
☐ Yearly
☐ Other: _____

We'll see Partner 2's family with the following frequency:

☐ Weekly
☐ Monthly
☐ Yearly
☐ Other: _____

HOLIDAYS AND SPECIAL OCCASIONS

The following holidays/special occasions are prioritized as follows:
(for example, at a certain family's house, through a certain faith, etc).

Occasion 1: _____

How we'd like to spend it: _____

Occasion 2: _____

How we'd like to spend it: _____

Occasion 3: _____

How we'd like to spend it: _____

EMOTIONAL NEEDS

LOVE LANGUAGES

We understand that people prefer to receive love in different ways. The five love languages are words of affirmation, quality time, gifts, acts of service, and physical touch.

We like to receive affection in the following ways:

Partner 1
My love language is:

_____

Partner 2
My love language is:

_____

STRESS MANAGEMENT

We understand that everyone handles stress differently.

Partner 1

I handle stress by:

_____

I feel supported during stressful times by:

_____

Partner 2

I handle stress by:

_____

I feel supported during stressful times by:

_____

FIGHTING

We understand that some behaviors in relationships are damaging. John and Julie Gottman tell us that couples who engage in **criticism, contempt, defensiveness**, or **stonewalling** are more likely to break up or stay together unhappily. For this reason, these behaviors are collectively known as "The Four Horsemen of the Apocalypse."

Avoiding the Four Horsemen

Criticism: Instead of verbally attacking my partner's character or personality, I will talk about how I'm feeling and make a specific request for different behavior in the future (for example, "I feel lonely when you don't spend time with me. I want us to spend one night a week together" rather than "You don't care about me!").

Contempt: Instead of attacking my partner, I'll build a culture of appreciation and remind myself of my partner's strengths.

Defensiveness: Instead of trying to reverse blame or victimize myself, I'll accept my partner's feedback and perspective and apologize.

Stonewalling: Instead of withdrawing from conflict when I feel flooded, I'll take a break to calm myself down. I'll revisit the conversation when I feel like I can talk productively again.

Partner 1

Initial here: _____

Partner 2

Initial here: _____

When we fight, we prefer the following communication methods: (For example, in person, through written communication, etc.)

Partner 1

I prefer:

_____

_____

_____

Partner 2

I prefer:

_____

_____

_____

People may experience emotional flooding when their emotions go into overdrive. When we're flooded, we'll request a time-out using the following word: _____

SEX

For us, sex is:

☐ Very important
☐ Somewhat important
☐ Not important

We commit to having sex a minimum of _____ times a _____ .

In terms of exclusivity, we are:

☐ Monogamous
☐ "Monogamish" (somewhat open)
☐ Completely open
☐ Other: _____

We agree to follow the principles of Dan Savage's **GGG policy**: When it comes to our sex life, we will be **good, giving,** and **game**.

Partner 1

Initial here: _____

Partner 2

Initial here: _____

CLOSING

We understand that strong relationships require ongoing effort. We acknowledge that our priorities, interests, and feelings may—and likely will—shift over time. We commit to uphold the aforementioned commitments until our next contract review or until the relationship ends.

Partner 1

Print name: _____

Signature: _____

Partner 2

Print name: _____

Signature: _____

Date: _____

NOTES

Introduction

3   "*a thousand songs in your pocket*": Steve Jobs, quoted by Tony Long, "Oct. 23, 2001: Now Hear This . . . The iPod Arrives," *Wired*, October 23, 2008, https://www.wired.com/2008/10/dayintech-1023/.

Chapter 1: Why Dating Is Harder Now Than Ever Before

9   *Religion, community, and social class:* "Belonging" (Oxford: Social Issues Research Centre, July 2007), 4.

10 *When it came to finding a partner:* David Graeber, *Debt: The First 5,000 Years* (New York: Melville House, 2011), 131.

10 *Today all these decisions:* Esther Perel, "The Future of Love, Lust, and Listening," SXSW, March 9, 2018, Austin, Texas, 55:12.

10 *Dating itself only:* Moira Weigel, *Labor of Love: The Invention of Dating* (New York: Farrar, Straus and Giroux, 2016), 13.

10 *Online dating started:* Jeff Kauflin, "How Match.Com Was Founded by Gary Kremen," *Business Insider*, July 14, 2015, https://www.businessinsider.com/how-matchcom-was-founded-by-gary-kremen-2015-7.

10 *Psychologists, including Barry Schwartz:* Barry Schwartz, *The Paradox of Choice: Why More Is Less* (New York: Ecco/HarperCollins, 2016).

12 *They witnessed other couples:* Perel, "The Future of Love, Lust, and Listening."

12 *"the children of":* Esther Perel, *The Tim Ferriss Show*, Ep. 241: "The Relationship Episode: Sex, Love, Polyamory, Marriage, and More," interview by Tim Ferriss, June 1, 2018, https://tim.blog/2018/06/01/the-tim-ferriss-show-transcripts-esther-perel/.

12 *Around 50 percent of marriages:* Paul R. Amato, "Research on Divorce: Continuing Trends and New Developments," *Journal of Marriage and Family* 72, no. 3 (June 18, 2010): 651.

12 *about 4 percent of:* Tom Smith, Jaesok Son, and Benjamin Schapiro, "Trends in Psychological Well-Being, 1972–2014," NORC at the University of Chicago, April 2015, 8.

12 *a majority of:* Amato, "Research on Divorce: Continuing Trends and New Developments."

12 *or are enduring:* Smith, Son, and Schapiro, "Trends in Psychological Well-Being, 1972–2014."

13 *In fact, they're:* Alex Bell et al., "Who Becomes an Inventor in America? The Importance of Exposure to Innovation," *Quarterly Journal of Economics* 134, no. 2 (May 1, 2019): 699–700.

14 *"I truly believe that":* Sheryl Sandberg, *Lean In: Women, Work, and the Will to Lead* (New York: Alfred A. Knopf, 2013), 110.

Chapter 3: Disney Lied to Us

24 *When it comes to romantic:* Renae Franiuk, Dov Cohen, and Eva M. Pomerantz, "Implicit Theories of Relationships: Implications for Relationship Satisfaction and Longevity," *Personal Relationships* 9, no. 4 (2002): 345–67.

26 *"Until the late eighteenth century":* Stephanie Coontz, *Marriage, a History: How Love Conquered Marriage* (New York: Penguin Books, 2006), 5.

26 *In the four-thousand-year-old:* Michael R. Burch, trans., "Sumerian Love-Song," in James B. Pritchard, *Ancient Near Eastern Texts Relating to the Old Testament*, 3rd ed. (Princeton, NJ: Princeton University Press, 2016), 496.

26 *for most of human history:* Esther Perel, *Mating in Captivity: Unlocking Erotic Intelligence* (New York: Harper Paperbacks, 2017), 7.

26 *he explained how:* Alain de Botton, interview by Logan Ury, Los Angeles, February 21, 2019.

27 *It wasn't until:* Alain de Botton, "How Romanticism Ruined Love," School of Life, *The Book of Life*, April 28, 2016, https://www.theschooloflife.com/thebookoflife/how-romanticism-ruined-love/.

27 *this model's adoption by mainstream society:* Coontz, *Marriage, a History.*

27 *Take a look at:* de Botton, "How Romanticism Ruined Love."

Chapter 4: Don't Let Perfect Be the Enemy of Great

38 *American economist, political scientist:* H. A. Simon, "Rational Choice and the Structure of the Environment," *Psychological Review* 63, no. 2 (1956): 129–38.

42 *"Maximizers make good":* Barry Schwartz, quoted by Elizabeth Bernstein, "How You Make Decisions Says a Lot About How Happy You Are," *Wall Street Journal*, Health and Wellness, October 7, 2014.

42　*Once we commit:* Johanna M. Jarcho, Elliot T. Berkman, and Matthew D. Lieberman, "The Neural Basis of Rationalization: Cognitive Dissonance Reduction During Decision-Making," *Social Cognitive and Affective Neuroscience* 6, no. 4 (September 1, 2011): 460–67.

44　*In the book:* Brian Christian and Tom Griffiths, *Algorithms to Live By: The Computer Science of Human Decisions* (New York: Henry Holt, 2016), 15.

46　*Robert De Niro:* Sara Hammel and Julie Jordan, "Robert De Niro Baby Girl Born Via Surrogate," People.com, accessed April 4, 2020, https://people.com/parents/robert-de-niro-baby-girl-born-via-surrogate/.

Chapter 5: Don't Wait, Date

51　*Economists often refer to:* Britannica Online Academic Edition, "Opportunity Cost," accessed April 4, 2020, https://www.britannica.com/topic/opportunity-cost.

54　*Before her breakout Netflix comedy:* Ali Wong, *Dear Girls: Intimate Tales, Untold Secrets & Advice for Living Your Best Life* (New York: Random House, 2019), 50.

54　*Behavioral science warns us:* Feng-Yang Kuo and Mei-Lien Young, "A Study of the Intention-Action Gap in Knowledge Sharing Practices," *Journal of the American Society for Information Science and Technology* 59, no. 8 (2008): 1,224–37.

55　*Researchers have studied:* Dan Ariely and Klaus Wertenbroch, "Procrastination, Deadlines, and Performance: Self-Control by Precommitment," *Psychological Science* 13, no. 3 (May 2002): 219–24.

55　*Suzanne Shu and Ayelet Gneezy:* Suzanne B. Shu and Ayelet Gneezy, "Procrastination of Enjoyable Experiences," *Journal of Marketing Research* 47, no. 5 (October 2010): 933–44.

56　*A team of researchers:* Kevin D. McCaul, Verlin B. Hinsz, and Harriette S. McCaul, "The Effects of Commitment to Performance Goals on Effort," *Journal of Applied Social Psychology* 17, no. 5 (May 1987): 437–52.

57　*A group of Stanford:* David W. Nickerson and Todd Rogers, "Do You Have a Voting Plan?: Implementation Intentions, Voter Turnout, and Organic Plan Making," *Psychological Science* 21, no. 2 (February 2010): 194–99.

59　*Psychologists Edwin Locke:* Edwin A. Locke and Gary P. Latham, "New Directions in Goal-Setting Theory," *Current Directions in Psychological Science* 15, no. 5 (October 2006): 265–68.

61　*Daniel Gilbert and Jane Ebert:* Daniel T. Gilbert and Jane E. J. Ebert, "Decisions and Revisions: The Affective Forecasting of Changeable Outcomes," *Journal of Personality and Social Psychology* 82, no. 4 (April 2002): 503–14.

62　*once you commit to something:* Johanna M. Jarcho, Elliot T. Berkman, and Matthew D. Lieberman, "The Neural Basis of Rationalization: Cognitive

Dissonance Reduction During Decision-Making," *Social Cognitive and Affective Neuroscience* 6, no. 4 (September 1, 2011): 460–67.

63 *In one research paper:* Tara C. Marshall, "Facebook Surveillance of Former Romantic Partners: Associations with Post-Breakup Recovery and Personal Growth," *Cyberpsychology, Behavior, and Social Networking* 15, no. 10 (October 2012): 521–26.

63 *Mason found that:* Ashley E. Mason et al., "Staying Connected When Coming Apart: The Psychological Correlates of Contact and Sex with an Ex-Partner," *Journal of Social and Clinical Psychology* 31, no. 5 (May 2012): 488–507.

Chapter 6: Learn Your Attachment Style

66 *It's a popular framework:* Amir Levine and Rachel Heller, *Attached: The New Science of Adult Attachment and How It Can Help You Find—and Keep—Love* (New York: TarcherPerigee, 2012); Sue Johnson, *Hold Me Tight: Seven Conversations for a Lifetime of Love* (New York: Little, Brown Spark, 2008).

67 *developmental psychologist John Bowlby:* Inge Bretherton, "The Origins of Attachment Theory: John Bowlby and Mary Ainsworth," *Developmental Psychology* 28, no. 5 (September 1992): 759–75.

Chapter 7: Look for a Life Partner, Not a Prom Date

76 *the present bias:* Anujit Chakraborty, "Present Bias," *SSRN Electronic Journal*, 2019.

77 What would a love story: Esther Perel, interview by Logan Ury, New York City, March 27, 2019.

77 *There isn't one answer:* Dan Ariely, interview by Logan Ury, San Francisco, February 28, 2019.

79 *John Gottman:* John Gottman, "History of the Love Lab," The Gottman Institute, February 4, 2018, https://www.gottman.com/love-lab/.

79 *the focusing illusion:* David A. Schkade and Daniel Kahneman, "Does Living in California Make People Happy?: A Focusing Illusion in Judgments of Life Satisfaction," *Psychological Science* 9, no. 5 (September 1998): 340–46.

81 *Texas Tech University:* John Dakin and Richard Wampler, "Money Doesn't Buy Happiness, but It Helps: Marital Satisfaction, Psychological Distress, and Demographic Differences Between Low- and Middle-Income Clinic Couples," *American Journal of Family Therapy* 36, no. 4 (July 2, 2008): 300–311.

81 *financial woes cause:* Frances C. Lawrence, Reneé H. Thomasson, Patricia J. Wozniak, and Aimee D. Prawitz, "Factors Relating to Spousal Financial Arguments," *Financial Counseling and Planning*, no. 4 (1993): 85–93.

81 *research from Harvard Business School:* A. V. Whillans, Jessie Pow, and

Michael I. Norton, "Buying Time Promotes Relationship Satisfaction," Harvard Business School working paper, January 29, 2018.

81 *While it's difficult to determine:* Daniel Kahneman and Angus Deaton, "High Income Improves Evaluation of Life but Not Emotional Well-Being," *Proceedings of the National Academy of Sciences* 107, no. 38 (September 21, 2010): 16, 489–93.

81 *In fact, additional research:* Glenn Firebaugh and Matthew B. Schroeder, "Does Your Neighbor's Income Affect Your Happiness?," *American Journal of Sociology* 115, no. 3 (November 2009): 805–31.

82 *a 1978 study:* Philip Brickman, Dan Coates, and Ronnie Janoff-Bulman, "Lottery Winners and Accident Victims: Is Happiness Relative?," *Journal of Personality and Social Psychology* 36, no. 8 (1978): 917–27.

82 *Attractive people tend:* Daniel S. Hamermesh and Jeff E. Biddle, "Beauty and the Labor Market," *American Economic Review* 84, no. 5 (1994): 1174.

82 *beat their less attractive:* Rodrigo Praino and Daniel Stockemer, "What Are Good-Looking Candidates, and Can They Sway Election Results?: Good-Looking Candidates and Electoral Results," *Social Science Quarterly* 100, no. 3 (May 2019): 531–43.

82 *In multiple studies:* Leslie A. Zebrowitz and Joann M. Montepare, "Social Psychological Face Perception: Why Appearance Matters," *Social and Personality Psychology Compass* 2, no. 3 (May 2008): 1497–1517.

82 *Physically attractive traits:* Nancy L. Etcoff, *Survival of the Prettiest: The Science of Beauty* (New York: Anchor Books, 2000).

83 *In his book:* Ty Tashiro, *The Science of Happily Ever After: What Really Matters in the Quest for Enduring Love* (Harlequin, 2014), 17.

83 *a fourteen-year longitudinal study:* Ted L. Huston et al., "The Connubial Crucible: Newlywed Years as Predictors of Marital Delight, Distress, and Divorce," *Journal of Personality and Social Psychology* 80, no. 2 (February 2001): 237–52.

83 *Biological anthropologist Helen Fisher:* Helen Fisher et al., "Defining the Brain Systems of Lust, Romantic Attraction, and Attachment," *Archives of Sexual Behavior* 31, no. 5 (October 2002): 413–19.

84 *An episode of the TV show:* Tricia Brock, "The Bubble," *30 Rock* (NBC, March 19, 2009).

84 *Lust Fades!:* Cynthia A. Graham et al., "What Factors Are Associated with Reporting Lacking Interest in Sex and How Do These Vary by Gender? Findings from the Third British National Survey of Sexual Attitudes and Lifestyles," *BMJ Open* 7, no. 9 (September 13, 2017): e016942.

85 *In my interview with:* Eli Finkel, interview by Logan Ury, Chicago, June 25, 2019.

86 *Yet when Michigan:* William J. Chopik and Richard E. Lucas, "Actor, Partner, and Similarity Effects of Personality on Global and Experienced

Well-Being," *Journal of Research in Personality* 78 (February 2019): 249–61.

86 *There's a theory:* Raphaëlle Chaix, Chen Cao, and Peter Donnelly, "Is Mate Choice in Humans MHC-Dependent?," ed. Molly Przeworski, *PLoS Genetics* 4, no. 9 (September 12, 2008): e1000184.

86 *Claus Wedekind:* Claus Wedekind, Thomas Seebeck, Florence Bettens, and Alexander J. Paepke, "MHC-Dependent Mate Preferences in Humans," *Proceedings of the Royal Society of London: Series B: Biological Sciences* 260, no. 1359 (June 22, 1995): 245–49.

87 *Coincidentally, the effect reverses:* Ibid.

88 *One technique for managing:* Eli Finkel, "How to Build a Marriage That Truly Meets Your Needs," ideas.ted.com, October 3, 2017, https://ideas.ted .com/how-to-build-a-marriage-that-truly-meets-your-needs/.

89 *Research from social psychologists:* Elaine O. Cheung, Wendi L. Gardner, and Jason F. Anderson, "Emotionships: Examining People's Emotion-Regulation Relationships and Their Consequences for Well-Being," *Social Psychological and Personality Science* 6, no. 4 (May 1, 2015): 407–14.

90 *psychologist Ty Tashiro:* Tashiro, *The Science of Happily Ever*, 8.

90 *emotional stability and kindness:* Zahra Barnes, "Should You Have A Dating Checklist?," *Self*, accessed April 4, 2020, https://www.self.com/story /should-you-have-a-dating-checklist.

90 *"Kind partners are awesome":* Ty Tashiro, "An Algorithm for Happily Ever After," TEDSalon, New York, July 2014.

91 *It's from an article:* Robin Schoenthaler, "Will He Hold Your Purse?," *Boston Globe Magazine*, October 4, 2009.

92 *Carol Dweck has:* Carol S. Dweck, *Mindset: The New Psychology of Success* (New York: Ballantine Books, 2007).

95 *69 percent of all relationship conflicts:* John Mordechai Gottman, *The Seven Principles for Making Marriage Work* (New York: Three Rivers Press, 1999), 73.

95 *As the late couples therapist:* Daniel B. Wile, *After the Honeymoon: How Conflict Can Improve Your Relationship* (Oakland, CA: Collaborative Couple Therapy Books, 2008).

97 *"the canoe test":* Dan Ariely, "On Dating & Relationships," Talks at Google, 58:00, November 11, 2015, https://www.youtube.com/watch ?v=RS8R2TKrYi0.

Chapter 8: You Think You Know What You Want, but You're Wrong

106 *According to research:* Michael J. Rosenfeld, Reuben J. Thomas, and Sonia Hausen, "Disintermediating Your Friends: How Online Dating in the United States Displaces Other Ways of Meeting," *Proceedings of the National Academy of Sciences* 116, no. 36 (September 3, 2019): 17753–58.

106 *In the last twenty years:* Ibid.

106 *"an M&M problem":* Cecilia Kang, "Google Crunches Data on Munching in Office," *Washington Post*, Technology, September 1, 2013.

107 *in so-called thin markets:* Justin Wolfers, *Freakonomics*, Ep. 154: "What You Don't Know About Online Dating," interview by Stephen Dubner, February 6, 2014, https://freakonomics.com/podcast/what-you-dont-know -about-online-dating-a-new-freakonomics-radio-podcast/.

109 *"You are what you measure":* Dan Ariely, "You Are What You Measure," *Harvard Business Review*, June 1, 2010.

109 *Chris Hsee writes:* Christopher K. Hsee, "The Evaluability Hypothesis: An Explanation for Preference Reversals Between Joint and Separate Evaluations of Alternatives," *Organizational Behavior and Human Decision Processes* 67, no. 3 (September 1, 1996): 247–57.

110 *thanks to research from Dan Ariely:* Dan Ariely, "A Conversation with Dan Ariely, James B. Duke Professor of Psychology and Behavioral Economics at Duke University," interview by Big Think, July 1, 2010, https://bigthink .com/videos/big-think-interview-with-dan-ariely-3.

113 *called the status quo bias:* William Samuelson and Richard Zeckhauser, "Status Quo Bias in Decision Making," *Journal of Risk and Uncertainty* 1, no. 1 (March 1988): 7–59.

114 *they now speak of a new:* Rebecca D. Heino, Nicole B. Ellison, and Jennifer L. Gibbs, "Relationshopping: Investigating the Market Metaphor in Online Dating," *Journal of Social and Personal Relationships* 27, no. 4 (June 1, 2010): 427–47.

114 *A team of behavioral economists:* Jeana H. Frost et al., "People Are Experience Goods: Improving Online Dating with Virtual Dates," *Journal of Interactive Marketing* 22, no. 1 (2008): 51–61.

115 *paradox of choice:* Barry Schwartz, *The Paradox of Choice: Why More Is Less* (New York: Ecco/HarperCollins, 2016).

115 *Columbia professor Sheena Iyengar:* Sheena S. Iyengar and Mark R. Lepper, "When Choice Is Demotivating: Can One Desire Too Much of a Good Thing?," *Journal of Personality and Social Psychology* 79, no. 6 (2000): 995–1006.

117 *When companies search:* "Dan Ariely: On Dating & Relationships," Talks at Google, 58:00, November 11, 2015, https://www.youtube.com /watch?v=RS8R2TKrYi0.

117 *CEOs are often:* Xiao Bi, "In With the New—Compensation of Newly Hired Chief Executive Officers," Equilar, February 7, 2015, https://www .equilar.com/reports/15-in-with-the-new.html.

117 *but perform worse:* Ken Favaro, Per-Ola Karlsson, Jon Katzenbach, and Gary Neilson, "Lessons from the Trenches for New CEOs: Separating Myths from Game Changers," Booz & Company, 2010.

121 *Tinder was intentionally:* Eric Johnson, "Swiping on Tinder Is Addictive.

That's Partly Because It Was Inspired by an Experiment That 'Turned Pigeons into Gamblers,'" *Vox*, September 19, 2018.

121 *famed behaviorist B. F. Skinner:* B. F. Skinner, "'Superstition' in the Pigeon," *Journal of Experimental Psychology* 38, no. 2 (1948): 168–72.

123 *Hinge researchers studied:* "Hinge Report: Profile Pictures That Get the Most Likes," Medium, April 20, 2017, https://medium.com/@Hinge/hinge -the-relationship-app-28f1000d5e76.

125 *"Qualities I'm looking for":* Eddie Hernandez, "Best Hinge Prompts, Answers to Use on Your Dating Profile," Eddie Hernandez Photography, November 20, 2019, https://eddie-hernandez.com/best-hinge-questions/.

126 *Or if someone's profile mentions:* "New Leads," *The Office*. Directed by Brent Forrester, Written by Greg Daniels, National Broadcasting Company, March 18, 2010.

Chapter 9: Meet People IRL (In Real Life)

131 *He reported that Black:* Natasha Singer, "OkCupid's Unblushing Analyst of Attraction," *New York Times,* September 6, 2014.

131 *when Black women:* Christian Rudder, "How Your Race Affects the Messages You Get," OKTrends, October 5, 2009, https://www.gwern.net /docs/psychology/okcupid/howyourraceaffectsthemessagesyouget.html.

131 *Rudder found that white:* Christian Rudder, *Dataclysm: Love, Sex, Race, and Identity—What Our Online Lives Tell Us About Our Offline Selves* (New York: Broadway Books, 2014).

135 **publicly committing to a goal:** Gail Matthews, "Goal Research Summary," paper presented at the 9th Annual International Conference of the Psychology Research Unit of Athens Institute for Education and Research (ATINER), Athens, Greece, 2015.

136 *gave Alicia a **deadline**:* Phyllis Korkki, "Need Motivation? Declare a Deadline," *New York Times*, Job Market, April 20, 2013.

145 *Behavioral scientists:* Nicholas Epley and Juliana Schroeder, "Mistakenly Seeking Solitude," *Journal of Experimental Psychology: General* 143, no. 5 (2014): 1980.

Chapter 10: This Is a Date, Not a Job Interview

150 *those Google employees:* Cecilia Kang, "Google Crunches Data on Munching in Office," *Washington Post*, Technology, September 1, 2013.

152 *Esther Perel characterizes:* Esther Perel, interview by Logan Ury, New York City, March 27, 2019.

153 *Richard Wiseman:* Richard Wiseman, *The Luck Factor* (New York: Miramax, 2003), 50.

153 *Wiseman gathered these people together:* Richard Wiseman, "Be Lucky—It's an Easy Skill to Learn," *Telegraph*, January 9, 2003.

154 *"Whether you believe you can":* Quote Investigator, "Whether You Believe

You Can Do a Thing or Not, You Are Right," accessed April 5, 2020, https://quoteinvestigator.com/2015/02/03/you-can/.

154 *Wiseman created a program:* Wiseman, *The Luck Factor*, 172.

156 *Psychologists Shogo Kajimura:* Shogo Kajimura and Michio Nomura, "When We Cannot Speak: Eye Contact Disrupts Resources Available to Cognitive Control Processes During Verb Generation," *Cognition* 157 (December 1, 2016): 352–57.

157 *Dan Ariely and a team:* Jeana H. Frost et al., "People Are Experience Goods: Improving Online Dating with Virtual Dates," *Journal of Interactive Marketing* 22, no. 1 (2008): 5, 161.

160 *Research from Harvard Business School professors:* Ryan W. Buell and Michael I. Norton, "The Labor Illusion: How Operational Transparency Increases Perceived Value," *Management Science* 57, no. 9 (2011): 1564–79.

162 *In an article:* Perri Klass, "Taking Playtime Seriously," *New York Times*, Well, January 29, 2018.

162 *Play is intrinsically:* Edward L. Deci and Richard M. Ryan, "Intrinsic Motivation," in *The Corsini Encyclopedia of Psychology*, ed. Irving B. Weiner and W. Edward Craighead (Hoboken, NJ: John Wiley, 2010).

162 *When we laugh:* Sandra Manninen et al., "Social Laughter Triggers Endogenous Opioid Release in Humans," *Journal of Neuroscience* 37, no. 25 (June 21, 2017): 6125–31.

162 *Laughing releases oxytocin:* Joel Stein, "Humor Is Serious Business," Stanford Graduate School of Business, July 11, 2017, https://www.gsb .stanford.edu/insights/humor-serious-business.

162 *the same bonding hormone:* National Center for Biotechnology Information et al., *The Physiological Basis of Breastfeeding, Infant and Young Child Feeding: Model Chapter for Textbooks for Medical Students and Allied Health Professionals* (World Health Organization, 2009), 19.

162 *and makes us trust:* Stein, "Humor Is Serious Business."

162 *Laughter lowers levels:* Lee S. Berk et al., "Neuroendocrine and Stress Hormone Changes During Mirthful Laughter," *American Journal of the Medical Sciences* 298, no. 6 (December 1989): 390–96.

162 *Laughter also creates:* "Humor, Laughter, and Those Aha Moments," Scribd, 2010, https://www.scribd.com/document/372724309/Humor-Laughter-And-Those-Aha-Moments.

163 *forming close bonds:* Susan Sprecher and Susan S. Hendrick, "Self-Disclosure in Intimate Relationships: Associations with Individual and Relationship Characteristics Over Time," *Journal of Social and Clinical Psychology* 23, no. 6 (2004): 857–77.

163 *research from psychologist Karen Huang:* Karen Huang et al., "It Doesn't Hurt to Ask: Question-Asking Increases Liking," *Journal of Personality and Social Psychology* 113, no. 3 (September 2017): 430–52.

163 *In the viral* New York Times: Mandy Len Catron, "To Fall in Love with Anyone, Do This," *New York Times*, Style, January 9, 2015.

163 *They were designed by psychologist Arthur Aron:* Arthur Aron et al., "The Experimental Generation of Interpersonal Closeness: A Procedure and Some Preliminary Findings," *Personality and Social Psychology Bulletin* 23, no. 4 (1997): 363–77.

165 *give **support responses**:* Charles Derber, *The Pursuit of Attention: Power and Individualism in Everyday Life* (New York: Oxford University Press, 1983).

167 *Research from MIT:* Sherry Turkle, "Stop Googling. Let's Talk," *New York Times*, Opinion, September 26, 2015.

167 *Despite all the:* Ibid.

167 *Some patients endured:* Donald A. Redelmeier, Joel Katz, and Daniel Kahneman, "Memories of Colonoscopy: A Randomized Trial," *Pain* 104, no. 1 (July 2003): 187–94.

168 ***peak-end rule:*** "What Is Peak-End Theory? A Psychologist Explains How Our Memory Fools Us," PositivePsychology.com, March 3, 2019, https://positivepsychology.com/what-is-peak-end-theory/.

Chapter 11: F**k the Spark

172 *When psychologist Ayala Malach Pines:* Ayala Malach Pines, *Falling in Love: Why We Choose the Lovers We Choose* (Taylor & Francis, 2005), 25.

172 *the **mere exposure effect**:* Robert B. Zajonc, "Attitudinal Effects of Mere Exposure," *Journal of Personality and Social Psychology* 9, no. 2 (1968): 1–27.

172 *psychologists Paul Eastwick and Lucy Hunt:* Paul W. Eastwick and Lucy L. Hunt, "Relational Mate Value: Consensus and Uniqueness in Romantic Evaluations," *Journal of Personality and Social Psychology* 106, no. 5 (2014): 728–51.

Chapter 12: Go on the Second Date

179 *As comedian:* Demetri Martin, *These Are Jokes*, Comedy Central Records, 2006.

180 *If you've ever:* Tiffany A. Ito et al., "Negative Information Weighs More Heavily on the Brain: The Negativity Bias in Evaluative Categorizations," *Journal of Personality and Social Psychology* 75, no. 4 (October 1998): 887–900.

180 *One such bias:* "Fundamental Attribution Error—Biases & Heuristics," The Decision Lab, accessed April 5, 2020, https://thedecisionlab.com/biases/fundamental-attribution-error/.

181 *When someone makes a mistake:* Lee Ross, "The Intuitive Psychologist and His Shortcomings: Distortions in the Attribution Process," *Advances in Experimental Social Psychology* 10 (1977): 173–220.

181 *Look for the Positives:* Shawn Achor, "The Happiness Advantage: Linking Positive Brains to Performance," TEDx Talks, 12:29, June 30, 2011, https://www.youtube.com/watch?v=GXy__kBVq1M&t=512s.

181 *what others might miss:* Alain de Botton, interview by Logan Ury, Los Angeles, February 21, 2019.

184 *demonstrate how defaults:* Eric J. Johnson and Daniel G. Goldstein, "Do Defaults Save Lives?," SSRN Scholarly Paper (Rochester, NY: Social Science Research Network, November 21, 2003), https://papers.ssrn.com/abstract=1324774.

185 *brain's natural tendency:* Helen Fisher, interview by Logan Ury, New York City, April 2, 2019.

191 *Look back at:* Thomas S. Ferguson, "Who Solved the Secretary Problem?," *Statistical Science* 4, no. 3 (1989): 282–89.

192 *psychologist Daryl Bem's:* Daryl J. Bem, "Self-Perception Theory," *Advances in Experimental Social Psychology*, ed. Leonard Berkowitz, vol. 6 (Academic Press, 1972), 1–62.

192 *research shows that volunteering:* Caroline E. Jenkinson et al., "Is Volunteering a Public Health Intervention? A Systematic Review and Meta-Analysis of the Health and Survival of Volunteers," *BMC Public Health* 13, no. 1 (August 23, 2013): 773.

Chapter 13: Decide, Don't Slide

199 *reaching the end:* Amar Cheema and Dilip Soman, "The Effect of Partitions on Controlling Consumption," *Journal of Marketing Research* 45, no. 6 (December 2008): 665–75.

200 *Psychologists describe two ways:* Jesse Owen, Galena K. Rhoades, and Scott M. Stanley, "Sliding Versus Deciding in Relationships: Associations with Relationship Quality, Commitment, and Infidelity," *Journal of Couple & Relationship Therapy* 12, no. 2 (April 2013): 135–49.

200 *The National Marriage Project:* Galena K. Rhoades and Scott M. Stanley, "What Do Premarital Experiences Have to Do with Marital Quality Among Today's Young Adults?," *National Marriage Project* (2014): 5.

200 *Furthermore, researchers from:* Owen, Rhoades, and Stanley, "Sliding Versus Deciding in Relationships: Associations with Relationship Quality, Commitment, and Infidelity."

204 *While the U.S. population:* Meg Jay, "The Downside of Cohabiting Before Marriage," *New York Times*, Opinion, April 14, 2012.

205 *surveyed a nationally:* "Views on Marriage and Cohabitation in the U.S.," Pew Research Center's Social & Demographic Trends Project, November 6, 2019, https://www.pewsocialtrends.org/2019/11/06/marriage-and-cohabitation-in-the-u-s/.

205 *tells a different story:* Galena K. Rhoades, Scott M. Stanley, and Howard J. Markman, "The Pre-Engagement Cohabitation Effect: A Replication and

Extension of Previous Findings," *Journal of Family Psychology* 23, no. 1 (2009): 107–11.

205 *When researchers first:* David Popenoe and Barbara Dafoe Whitehead, "What Do Premarital Experiences Have to Do with Marital Quality Among Today's Young Adults?," *The National Marriage Project* (2): 2002.

206 *the status quo bias:* William Samuelson and Richard Zeckhauser, "Status Quo Bias in Decision Making," *Journal of Risk and Uncertainty* 1, no. 1 (March 1988): 7–59.

206 *Forty-two percent:* Emily Esfahani Smith and Galena Rhoades, "In Relationships, Be Deliberate," *The Atlantic*, August 19, 2014, https://www.theatlantic.com/health/archive/2014/08/in-relationships-be-deliberate/378713/.

Chapter 14: Stop Hitching and Stop Ditching

213 *the transition rule:* Daniel Kahneman and Amos Tversky, eds., *Choices, Values, and Frames* (UK: Cambridge University Press, 2000), 704.

214 *a year after they win:* Philip Brickman, Dan Coates, and Ronnie Janoff-Bulman, "Lottery Winners and Accident Victims: Is Happiness Relative?," *Journal of Personality and Social Psychology* 36, no. 8 (1978): 917–27.

219 *the sunk-cost fallacy:* Hal R. Arkes and Catherine Blumer, "The Psychology of Sunk Cost," *Organizational Behavior and Human Decision Processes* 35, no. 1 (February 1, 1985): 124–40.

219 *Behavioral economists Amos Tversky:* Daniel Kahneman and Amos Tversky, "Prospect Theory: An Analysis of Decision Under Risk," *Econometrica; Menasha, Wis.* 47, no. 2 (March 1, 1979): 263.

223 *"man hands":* Andy Ackerman, "The Bizarro Jerry," *Seinfeld* (Shapiro/West Productions, Castle Rock Entertainment, October 3, 1996).

223 *"shush" him, eat their peas one at a time:* Andy Ackerman, "The Engagement," *Seinfeld* (Shapiro/West Productions, Castle Rock Entertainment, September 21, 1995).

223 *enjoy a khakis commercial he dislikes:* Tom Cherones, "The Phone Message" (Shapiro/West Productions, Castle Rock Entertainment, February 13, 1991).

224 *we're infatuated with:* Helen Fisher, "The Nature of Romantic Love," *Journal of NIH Research* 6, no. 4 (1994): 59–64.

225 *recalibrate their expectations:* Eli J. Finkel, *The All-or-Nothing Marriage: How the Best Marriages Work* (New York: Dutton, 2017), 231.

226 *According to relationship scientist John Gottman:* John Gottman, "Debunking 12 Myths About Relationships," Gottman Institute, May 13, 2016, https://www.gottman.com/blog/debunking-12-myths-about-relationships/.

Chapter 15: Make a Breakup Plan

231 *economist Annamaria Lusardi:* Annamaria Lusardi, ed., *Overcoming the Saving Slump: How to Increase the Effectiveness of Financial Education and Saving Programs* (Chicago: University of Chicago Press, 2008).

232 *behavioral scientist and Stanford professor:* BJ Fogg, "Motivation," Fogg Behavior Model, accessed April 5, 2020, https://www.behaviormodel.org /motivation.

233 *Research from psychology professor:* Gail Matthews, "Goal Research Summary," paper presented at the 9th Annual International Conference of the Psychology Research Unit of Athens Institute for Education and Research (ATINER), Athens, Greece, 2015.

233 *the power of deadlines:* Dan Ariely and Klaus Wertenbroch, "Procrastination, Deadlines, and Performance: Self-Control by Precommitment," *Psychological Science* 13, no. 3 (May 2002): 219–24.

233 *especially short ones:* Suzanne B. Shu and Ayelet Gneezy, "Procrastination of Enjoyable Experiences," *Journal of Marketing Research* 47, no. 5 (October 2010): 933–44.

234 *make a more specific plan:* David W. Nickerson and Todd Rogers, "Do You Have a Voting Plan?: Implementation Intentions, Voter Turnout, and Organic Plan Making," *Psychological Science* 21, no. 2 (February 2010): 194–99.

236 *the narrative fallacy:* Doron Menashe and Mutal E. Shamash, "The Narrative Fallacy," *International Commentary on Evidence* 3, no. 1 (January 16, 2006).

240 *social accountability system:* Kevin D. McCaul, Verlin B. Hinsz, and Harriette S. McCaul, "The Effects of Commitment to Performance Goals on Effort," *Journal of Applied Social Psychology* 17, no. 5 (May 1987): 437–52.

240 *Accountability works so well:* Gretchen Rubin, *Better Than Before: Mastering the Habits of Our Everyday Lives* (New York: Crown Publishers, 2015).

241 *physical and mental state:* Stephanie Manes, "Making Sure Emotional Flooding Doesn't Capsize Your Relationship," Gottman Institute, August 4, 2013, https://www.gottman.com/blog/making-sure-emotional-flooding -doesnt-capsize-your-relationship/.

242 *In Homer's epic:* Homer and Robert Fagles, *The Odyssey* (London: Penguin, 1997).

242 *Economist Nava Ashraf:* Nava Ashraf, Dean Karlan, and Wesley Yin, "Tying Odysseus to the Mast: Evidence from a Commitment Savings Product in the Philippines," *Quarterly Journal of Economics* 121, no. 2 (2006): 635–72.

244 *someone actively chooses:* Delia Cioffi and Randy Garner, "On Doing the Decision: Effects of Active Versus Passive Choice on Commitment and Self-Perception," *Personality and Social Psychology Bulletin* 22, no. 2 (February 1996): 133–47.

246 *Research from* The Power of Habit: Charles Duhigg, *The Power of Habit: Why We Do What We Do in Life and Business* (New York: Random House Trade Paperbacks, 2014).

247 *"There's a terrible"*: Alain de Botton, interview by Logan Ury, Los Angeles, February 21, 2019.

Chapter 16: Reframe Your Breakup as a Gain, Not a Loss

251 *health care researcher Barbara McNeil*: Barbara J. McNeil et al., "On the Elicitation of Preferences for Alternative Therapies," *New England Journal of Medicine* 306, no. 21 (May 1982): 1259–62.

252 *responded to framing*: Scott Plous, *The Psychology of Judgment and Decision Making* (New York: McGraw-Hill, 1993).

252 *Relationship scientists like Claudia*: Claudia C. Brumbaugh and R. Chris Fraley, "Too Fast, Too Soon? An Empirical Investigation into Rebound Relationships," *Journal of Social and Personal Relationships* 32, no. 1 (February 2015): 99–118.

253 *Fisher and her team found*: Helen E. Fisher et al., "Reward, Addiction, and Emotion Regulation Systems Associated with Rejection in Love," *Journal of Neurophysiology* 104, no. 1 (July 2010): 51–60.

253 *addicted to love*: Arthur Aron et al., "Reward, Motivation, and Emotion Systems Associated with Early-Stage Intense Romantic Love," *Journal of Neurophysiology* 94, no. 1 (July 1, 2005): 327–37.

253 *According to Fisher, breakups*: Helen Fisher, "Lost Love: The Nature of Romantic Rejection," in *Cut Loose: (Mostly) Older Women Talk About the End of (Mostly) Long-Term Relationships*, ed. Nan Bauer-Maglin (New Brunswick, NJ: Rutgers University Press, 2006), 182–95.

253 *People may experience*: Tiffany Field, "Romantic Breakups, Heartbreak and Bereavement," *Psychology* 2, no. 4 (July 2011): 382–87.

253 *they also score lower*: Roy Baumeister, Jean Twenge, and Christopher Nuss, "Effects of Social Exclusion on Cognitive Processes: Anticipated Aloneness Reduces Intelligent Thought," *Journal of Personality and Social Psychology* 83 (November 1, 2002): 817–27.

253 *Heck, people going through breakups*: Matthew Larson, Gary Sweeten, and Alex R. Piquero, "With or Without You? Contextualizing the Impact of Romantic Relationship Breakup on Crime among Serious Adolescent Offenders," *Journal of Youth and Adolescence* 45, no. 1 (January 2016): 54–72.

253 *This holds true even if*: Stephen B. Kincaid and Robert A. Caldwell, "Initiator Status, Family Support, and Adjustment to Marital Separation: A Test of an Interaction Hypothesis," *Journal of Community Psychology* 19, no. 1 (1991): 79–88.

253 *hypersensitive to loss*: Daniel Kahneman and Amos Tversky, "Prospect Theory: An Analysis of Decision Under Risk," *Econometrica; Menasha, Wis.* 47, no. 2 (March 1, 1979): 263.

254 *"a breakup is not nearly as bad"*: Pat Vaughan Tremmel, "Breaking Up May Not Be as Hard as the Song Says," *Northwestern University News,*

August 21, 2007, https://www.northwestern.edu/newscenter/stories/2007/08/breakup.html.

254 *no matter how happy:* Paul W. Eastwick et al., "Mispredicting Distress Following Romantic Breakup: Revealing the Time Course of the Affective Forecasting Error," *Journal of Experimental Social Psychology* 44, no. 3 (2008): 800–807.

254 *Gary Lewandowski, a professor:* Gary Lewandowski Jr., and Nicole Bizzoco, "Addition Through Subtraction: Growth Following the Dissolution of a Low Quality Relationship," *Journal of Positive Psychology* 2 (January 1, 2007): 40–54.

254 *Lewandowski conducted an experiment:* Gary W. Lewandowski, "Promoting Positive Emotions Following Relationship Dissolution Through Writing," *Journal of Positive Psychology* 4, no. 1 (2009): 21–31.

257 *In a study similar to the one:* Sandra J. E. Langeslag and Michelle E. Sanchez, "Down-Regulation of Love Feelings after a Romantic Break-up: Self-Report and Electrophysiological Data," *Journal of Experimental Psychology: General* 147, no. 5 (2018): 720–33.

258 *Additional breakup research from Finkel:* Erica B. Slotter, Wendi L. Gardner, and Eli J. Finkel, "Who Am I Without You? The Influence of Romantic Breakup on the Self-Concept," *Personality & Social Psychology Bulletin* 36, no. 2 (December 2009): 147–60.

258 *Lewandowski divided people:* Gary Lewandowski, "Break-Ups Don't Have to Leave You Broken," TEDxNavesink, New Jersey, 11:30, April 11, 2015.

260 *Sociologist and Columbia University professor:* Diane Vaughan, *Uncoupling: Turning Points in Intimate Relationships* (New York: Vintage, 1990).

260 *"people who rapidly":* Claudia C. Brumbaugh and R. Chris Fraley, "Too Fast, Too Soon? An Empirical Investigation into Rebound Relationships," *Journal of Social and Personal Relationships* 32, no. 1 (February 1, 2015): 99–118.

261 *breakup as a learning opportunity:* Ty Tashiro and Patricia Frazier, "'I'll Never Be in a Relationship Like That Again': Personal Growth Following Romantic Relationship Breakups," *Personal Relationships* 10, no. 1 (2003): 113–28.

263 *"In some way, suffering ceases":* Viktor E. Frankl, *Man's Search for Meaning: An Introduction to Logotherapy* (Boston: Beacon Press, 1963), 117.

263 *In his TEDx Talk, Gary Lewandowski explained:* Lewandowski, "Break-Ups Don't Have to Leave You Broken."

Chapter 17: Before You Tie the Knot, Do This

267 *Marriage matters:* Maggie Gallagher, "Why Marriage Is Good for You," *City Journal*, Autumn 2000, https://www.city-journal.org/html/why-marriage-good-you-12002.html.

268 *"When two people are under the influence":* George Bernard Shaw, *Getting Married* (New York: Brentano's, 1920), 25.

268 *when our brain experiences the effects:* H. E. Fisher, "Lust, Attraction, and Attachment in Mammalian Reproduction," *Human Nature* (Hawthorne, NY) 9, no. 1 (March 1998): 23–52.

269 *Couples who wait one to two years:* Andrew Francis-Tan and Hugo M. Mialon, "'A Diamond Is Forever' and Other Fairy Tales: The Relationship Between Wedding Expenses and Marriage Duration," SSRN Scholarly Paper (Rochester, NY: Social Science Research Network, September 15, 2014).

269 *Couples who wait at least three years:* Ibid.

269 *Researchers like sociologist Philip Cohen:* Philip N. Cohen, "The Coming Divorce Decline," *Socius* 5, vol. 5 (January 1, 2019), https://doi .org/10.1177/2378023119873497.

269 *Naomi Schaefer Riley:* Naomi Schaefer Riley, "Interfaith Marriages: A Mixed Blessing," *New York Times,* April 5, 2013.

269 *We're led astray:* Lee Ross, David Greene, and Pamela House, "The 'False Consensus Effect': An Egocentric Bias in Social Perception and Attribution Processes," *Journal of Experimental Social Psychology* 13, no. 3 (May 1977): 279–301.

272 *Psychotherapist Esther Perel:* Esther Perel, "The Secret to Desire in a Long-Term Relationship," TEDSalon, New York, 19:02, February 2013.

278 *couples often fail:* Jesse Owen, Galena K. Rhoades, and Scott M. Stanley, "Sliding Versus Deciding in Relationships: Associations with Relationship Quality, Commitment, and Infidelity," *Journal of Couple & Relationship Therapy* 12, no. 2 (April 2013): 135–49.

Chapter 18: Intentional Love

279 *average reported marital satisfaction:* Eli J. Finkel, *The All-or-Nothing Marriage: How the Best Marriages Work* (New York: Dutton, 2017), 174.

279 *percentage of couples:* Ibid.

280 *Reported Marital Happiness:* Jody VanLaningham, David R. Johnson, and Paul Amato, "Marital Happiness, Marital Duration, and the U-Shaped Curve: Evidence from a Five-Wave Panel Study," *Social Forces* vol. 79, no. 4 (June 2001): 1313–1341.

280 *Decline of the Happy Marriage:* Tom W. Smith, Jaesok Son, and Benjamin Schapiro, "General Social Survey Final Report: Trends in Psychological Well-Being, 1972-2014," NORC at the University of Chicago, Chicago (April 2015).

280 *Charles Darwin's findings:* Leon C. Meggison, "Lessons from Europe for American Business," *Southwestern Social Science Quarterly* 44, no. 1 (1963): 3–13.

281 *Harvard psychologist Daniel Gilbert:* Jordi Quoidbach, Daniel T. Gilbert,

and Timothy D. Wilson, "The End of History Illusion," *Science* 339, no. 6115 (January 4, 2013): 96–98.

281 *Gilbert calls this:* Ibid.

282 *50 percent of people:* Paul R. Amato, "Research on Divorce: Continuing Trends and New Developments," *Journal of Marriage and Family* 72, no. 3 (June 18, 2010): 651.

283 *Psychologists Jesse Owen:* Jesse Owen, Galena K. Rhoades, and Scott M. Stanley, "Sliding Versus Deciding in Relationships: Associations with Relationship Quality, Commitment, and Infidelity," *Journal of Couple & Relationship Therapy* 12, no. 2 (April 2013): 135–49.

284 *As John F. Kennedy:* John F. Kennedy, State of the Union Address, January 11, 1962, Miller Center, accessed April 5, 2020, https://miller center.org/the-presidency/presidential-speeches/january-11-1962-state -union-address.

285 *"The quality of your relationship":* Esther Perel, "The Future of Love, Lust, and Listening," SXSW, March 9, 2018, Austin, Texas, 55:12.

Appendix

304 *"Monogamish":* Mark Oppenheimer, "Married, With Infidelities," *New York Times*, June 30, 2011.

306 *Bids for Connection:* Ellie Lisitsa, "An Introduction to Emotional Bids and Trust," The Gottman Institute, August 31, 2012, https://www.gottman.com /blog/an-introduction-to-emotional-bids-and-trust/.

313 *Love Languages:* Gary D. Chapman, *The Five Love Languages: How to Express Heartfelt Commitment to Your Mate* (Chicago: Northfield Publishing, 2004).

314 *"The Four Horsemen of the Apocalypse":* Ellie Lisitsa, "The Four Horsemen: Criticism, Contempt, Defensiveness, and Stonewalling," The Gottman Institute, April 23, 2013, https://www.gottman.com/blog/the -four-horsemen-recognizing-criticism-contempt-defensiveness-and-stone walling/.

316 *emotional flooding:* Stephanie Manes, LCSW, "Making Sure Emotional https://www.gottman.com/blog/making-sure-emotional-flooding-doesnt -capsize-your-relationship/ Flooding Doesn't Capsize Your Relationship," The Gottman Institute, August 3, 2013, https://www.gottman.com/blog /making-sure-emotional-flooding-doesnt-capsize-your-relationship/.

317 *GGG policy:* Dan Savage, "Savage Love," *The Stranger*, January 8, 2004, https://www.thestranger.com/seattle/SavageLove?oid=16799.

ABOUT THE AUTHOR

Behavioral scientist turned dating coach **Logan Ury** is an internationally recognized expert on modern love. As the Director of Relationship Science at the dating app Hinge, Logan leads a research team dedicated to helping people find love. After studying psychology at Harvard, she ran Google's behavioral science team—the Irrational Lab—and created the popular interview series Talks at Google: Modern Romance. She is also a TED Resident. Logan lives in the Bay Area with her husband, Scott. She credits her relationship success to the techniques outlined in *How to Not Die Alone*. Learn more about her at loganury.com or follow her @loganury.